The Ontario Harvest Cookbook

An Exploration of Feasts and Flavours

Julia Aitken
and Anita Stewart

Macmillan Canada
Toronto

Canadian Cataloguing in Publication Data

Aitken, Julia, date.
　　　The Ontario harvest cookbook : an exploration of feasts and flavours

Includes index.
ISBN 0–7715–7379–0

1. Cookery, Canadian – Ontario style. 2 Cookery, Ontario. I. Stewart, Anita. II. Title.

TX715.6.A57 1996　　　641.59713　　　C96–930065–4

1 2 3 4 5 TG 00 99 98 97 96

Cover and interior design by PageActive
Composition: IBEX Graphic Communications Inc.
Map: Jane Whitney
Front cover photo: Ottmar Bierwagen/Canada In Stock

Inset front cover photo and photos on chapter opening pages courtesy of The St. Lawrence Market, Toronto, Ontario
Inset back cover photo: Sean O'Neill/Canada In Stock

Macmillan Canada wishes to thank the Canada Council, the Ontario Ministry of Culture and Communications and the Ontario Arts Council for supporting its publishing program.

Macmillan Canada
A Division of Canada Publishing Corporation
Toronto, Ontario, Canada

Printed in Canada

For Mum, with love. J. A.

For our growers, a toast to the future—may you who are closest to the land enjoy the success you so rightfully deserve! A. S.

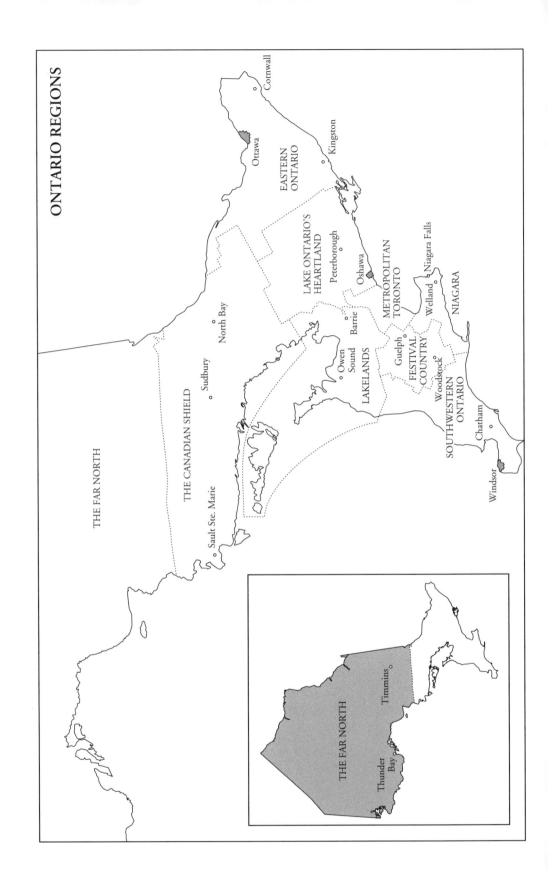

ONTARIO REGIONS

THE FAR NORTH

THE CANADIAN SHIELD

Sault Ste. Marie

Sudbury

North Bay

EASTERN
ONTARIO

Cornwall

Ottawa

Kingston

LAKE ONTARIO'S
HEARTLAND

Peterborough

Oshawa

METROPOLITAN
TORONTO

Niagara Falls

Welland

NIAGARA

Barrie

Owen
Sound

LAKELANDS

Guelph

FESTIVAL
COUNTRY

Woodstock

SOUTHWESTERN
ONTARIO

Chatham

Windsor

THE FAR NORTH

Timmins

Thunder
Bay

Contents

THANKS! vii

AGRI-FOOD NETWORK viii

INTRODUCTION ix

SOUTHWESTERN ONTARIO 1

NIAGARA 27

FESTIVAL COUNTRY 57

METROPOLITAN TORONTO 85

LAKE ONTARIO'S HEARTLAND 115

EASTERN ONTARIO 143

LAKELANDS 166

THE CANADIAN SHIELD 193

THE FAR NORTH 218

FARMERS' MARKETS 245

SELECTED EXHIBITIONS, TOURS AND FESTIVALS 252

RECIPE INDEX 255

Thanks!

We extend our sincere appreciation to Diane Wetherall of the Agri-Food Network. Her enthusiasm has consistently driven this project forward.

Thanks also to Iain Aitken and Wayne Stewart for being superb travelling companions, particularly when we had "just one more stop" before heading homeward or back to the campsite. Thanks must go as well to Carolyn Gall, whose sterling work in the test kitchen helped to ensure that all our recipes taste great and work perfectly. Our gratitude goes to the editorial staff at *Homemaker's Magazine* for their help and support. They took on extra work above and beyond the call of duty while Julia was joyfully eating her way around the province. Thanks, too, to Macmillan Canada's wonderful managing editor, Susan Girvan, whose cheerfulness, sense of humour and expertise we truly appreciate.

Further thanks are due to the following organizations, which provided funding to assist with the research and recipe development:

By Ward Market—Ottawa
Dairy Farmers of Ontario
Farmers' Markets Ontario
Ontario Cattlemen's Association
Ontario Chicken Producers' Marketing Board
Ontario Egg Producers' Marketing Board
Ontario Greenhouse Vegetable Producers' Marketing Board

Agri-Food Network

EVERYONE EATS! SO IT IS NATURAL TO HAVE QUESTIONS ABOUT our food and the systems that bring it to our provincial tables. However, the incredible diversity of the agriculture and food industry makes finding answers challenging. In response, a coalition of agriculture and food organizations established the Agri-Food Network in 1991 to improve public awareness of the entire food system. The implementation of programs such as an information referral service, educational workshops and exhibits, a bureau of expert agri-food speakers, a directory of all agricultural organizations and companies, and, of course, publications such as this one, achieve this goal.

We at the Agri-Food Network take great pleasure in being the sponsor of *The Ontario Harvest Cookbook*. We hope this book will encourage producers and consumers alike to a new awareness of the great bounty and the magnificent possibilities that are on our doorsteps daily.

For further information contact: Agri-Food Network, Research Park Centre, Suite 103, University of Guelph Research Park, 150 Research Lane, Guelph, Ontario N1G 2W1 Tel: 519 767 5008 Fax: 519 837 8721.

Introduction

AS THE WATERS OF THE LAST GREAT GLACIER SLOWLY MELTED INTO the lakes and oceans, the first peoples trekked the most northerly reaches of the land we now call Ontario. For ten millennia, they built a scattered but well-organized culture. A thousand years before Christ, they had a trading system that spanned Turtle Island, the continent of North America. They flourished. A multitude of tribes ebbed and flowed across the land, many with specific territories and all with a faith that bound them to their earth.

In the very early 1600s three European travellers came to their land: Henry Hudson, Etienne Brûlé and Samuel de Champlain, the founder of North America's first feasting society. This was the beginning of alliances between the Indians and the explorers that shattered some bands and lent power to others. Ontario was *the* link between the fur-trading posts of Quebec and the rich river lands in the heart of the continent. Forts were built at strategic locations—Frontenac (Kingston), Fort Niagara, Fort Détroit and Fort Michilimackinac. Not until the late 1700s did the British finally gain a foothold in the province, when they sacked and burned Frontenac and Niagara. Then, when the native allies of the French were defeated in 1763–64, the British effectively took control.

From this refuge, protected by Lake Ontario, the most easterly of the Great Lakes, and by several wide, rapids-filled rivers, the British and a group of Loyalists used the region as a base during the American War of Independence. It is not surprising, then, that the second large group of immigrants came from the south. In short order an estimated six to ten thousand Americans loyal to the British Crown settled in southern Ontario. And by 1812, eighty percent of the population had roots that spoke of their American origin. Many were Pennsylvania Dutch, and names that are still common in the Amish sections of the northeastern United States can be easily found from Niagara to Toronto.

The War of 1812 changed little. Boundaries remained the same. However, there *was* peace. Word spread, and with continued famine and oppression in Europe, a flood of immigrants arrived. Sixty percent were Irish, often dirt poor and sick. The islands of the St. Lawrence became quarantine stops and mass grave sites. The rest, roughly twenty percent each, were hardy and a little wealthier Scots and English. The journey into a land so unlike their own must have been at once thrilling and terrifying. There were few roads; waterways and narrow trails had to suffice, all heading into the bush—

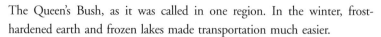

The Queen's Bush, as it was called in one region. In the winter, frost-hardened earth and frozen lakes made transportation much easier.

Some founded settlements beside fast-flowing rivers and used their stone-masons' skills to build sturdy, oftimes towering mills and villages. South-western and Eastern Ontario are filled with great mill towns and cities. By 1851 the population had grown to 952,000.

Upper Canada, as it was then called, was agricultural, in many ways as it is today. Dairy, fruit and vegetable farming predominated. But farmers needed implements and other services, so urban centres became industrialized. In 1867, with Confederation, Ontario became a province of Canada. Toronto, the hub of transportation and commerce, became its capital.

In the following decades, the news spread that Canada welcomed immigrants and that there was good land and real opportunity. Italians, Chinese, Portuguese, Eastern Europeans—they all came. Ontario became a microcosm of the world, Toronto the most ethnically diverse city on earth. Toronto *is* Ontario decked out in urban finery.

Ontario's culinary regions are gradually solidifying. Ethnicity, land use, climate—they all play a part. In this book, we begin the process of defining who we are, sometimes in historical terms, sometimes in terms of the future. The people of Ontario, be they immigrants from ten thousand years ago or ten months ago, have built a province. Our culture is hospitable. Our foods are delicious. We can drink the water from our wells. Our air is clean and our skies are clear. While the financial and manufacturing expertise in our cities is well documented, the contribution of rural Ontarians is often overlooked. Agriculture is the second largest industry in the province, employing one in five. Today's single family farm feeds 120 people, compared to only 47 a mere fifteen years ago. And best of all, our agricultural researchers are developing new plants, better crop management and techniques of agriculture, which will help feed the world.

Enjoy our culinary odyssey. We hope it inspires and guides you on one of your very own.

South-western Ontario

Fishing boats plow through the white-capped cobalt-coloured water. Vineyards are bathed in early morning lake mists. Greenhouses dot the landscape. The infinite summer sun radiates in waves from the land and is mirrored in the lakes—Erie and Huron and St. Clair. This is southwestern Ontario, our hottest region and one that is, for many crops, our most productive.

To really understand southwestern Ontario you must travel it not on an expressway but by driving into its heart. Wind your way along Lake Erie from the Niagara region to Windsor on Highway 3, through peach orchards, dusted pink in the springtime and laden with golden fruit in the summer. The Bluewater Highway (Highway 21) cruises past long Lake Huron sand beaches and bean fields drying in the sunshine. Through small towns and past hundreds of farm-gate markets and pick-your-own berry farms, these two routes provide a feast for the true traveller.

This is the region where a picnic is a must! Bring a knife, a skillet and a bit of butter to cook up a few fillets of fresh yellow perch from Rudy Krause Fisheries in Leamington, or simply share some fresh fruit and cheese. There are wineries and at least one ciderie en route, so remember the corkscrew. Sit beside the lake with your only worry how to make the day last forever.

Makes **about 46**

Preparation time: **20 minutes**

Cooking time: **1 hour**

*C*aviar . . . the word conjures up extravagant thoughts and visions of luxury. In Lake Erie, Pelee Treasures of Kingsville harvests golden whitefish caviar. Early in the season it has a soft texture (Pelee Gold); later on it is renowned for the firmness and clarity (Pelee Diamonds). Whitefish swim in most northern freshwater lakes. In Lake Erie, at the southern extremity of their range, they spawn on the shoals near Pelee Island. The roe is taken, lightly salted and then immediately frozen. After it is defrosted, refrigerated shelf life is one week. The company has recently added yellow sturgeon to its list (Pelee Sapphires) and a line of smoked whitefish, sturgeon, rainbow trout and salmon.

MINI BAKED POTATOES WITH WHITEFISH CAVIAR AND CRÈME FRAÎCHE

One of Ontario's best-kept secrets is the wonderful whitefish caviar harvested and processed by Pelee Treasures of Kingsville. Here at home we may only be just catching on to this bounty from Lake Erie, but farther afield its fame has already spread. According to Gary Penner of Pelee Treasures, the company shipped seven tons of their caviar to Finland in 1995 to be served on Finnish cruise ships plying the Baltic Sea. The frozen product is available in 40 g and 125 g jars. Once it arrives, you can try this delectable appetizer, created for us by recipe tester Carolyn Gall. Choose tiny potatoes not more than 1 inch (2.5 cm) in diameter.

3 tbsp	whipping cream	45 mL
⅓ cup	sour cream	75 mL
1 tbsp	each chopped fresh parsley and snipped fresh chives	15 mL
1 lb	baby new potatoes, scrubbed	500 g
2 tbsp	canola or corn oil	25 mL
½ cup	whitefish caviar	125 mL

In small bowl, whip whipping cream just until it thickens and is the consistency of yogurt. Gently stir in sour cream, parsley and chives until well combined. Refrigerate crème fraîche, covered, until ready to serve.

Preheat oven to 375°F (190°C). Prick potatoes with fork. In large bowl, combine potatoes and oil; toss until potatoes are coated with oil. Arrange potatoes on baking sheet; bake for 1 hour or until very tender. Let cool on baking sheet until cool enough to handle.

With tip of a paring knife, cut an X in top of each potato. Pinch base of potato to expose pulp. Divide crème fraîche evenly among potatoes. Top each potato with about ½ tsp (2 mL) caviar. Serve at once.

ESSEX COUNTY FIELD TOMATO SOUP

This is a terrific way to use aromatic Ontario field tomatoes. The soup freezes well, so you can enjoy a fresh taste of summer later in the year, and it is equally good served chilled.

3 lb	ripe tomatoes (about 10)	1.5 kg
1 cup	chicken stock	250 mL
6	green onions, chopped	6
2 tbsp	packed fresh basil leaves	25 mL
2 tbsp	packed brown sugar	25 mL
1 tbsp	Worcestershire sauce	15 mL
2	cloves garlic, sliced	2
1	bay leaf	1
½ tsp	salt	2 mL
¼ tsp	black pepper	1 mL
4	fresh basil sprigs for garnish	4

Cut tomatoes in half; cut out any tough pieces at stem ends. In large stainless steel or enamel saucepan, combine tomatoes, stock, onions, basil, sugar, Worcestershire sauce, garlic, bay leaf, salt and pepper. Bring to boil over high heat, stirring occasionally. Reduce heat to medium-low; simmer, covered, for 30 to 40 minutes, stirring occasionally, until tomatoes are very soft. Remove from heat; let cool slightly. Discard bay leaf.

In blender, process soup in 2-cup (500 mL) batches until smooth. Rub through a sieve to remove tomato skins and seeds. Return to rinsed-out saucepan; heat over medium-high heat, stirring occasionally. When hot, ladle into warm soup bowls; float a basil sprig in each bowl.

Makes **4 servings**

Preparation time: **20 minutes**

Cooking time: **35 to 45 minutes**

*W*ith such long, voluptuous summers, it's understandable that farms in the Leamington, Windsor and Chatham area grow some of the ripest and juiciest tomatoes in the nation. Kent County alone produces forty-eight percent of Ontario's tomatoes. H.J. Heinz set up their manufacturing plant in Leamington in 1908 and still is one of the major processors, while Aylmer processes Essex and Kent county tomatoes at their Dresden facility. So, when you crack open that next bottle of ketchup, the chances are you're tasting last summer's sun-drenched Kent and Essex harvest.

Makes **8 to 10 servings**

Preparation time: **20 minutes**

Cooking time: **15 to 20 minutes**

*C*rowds gather early beneath a row of blooming ancient horse chestnut trees to savour the foods at the Leamington Mennonite Sale and Auction. Vendors sell deep-fried *rollkuchen*, thin, golden pastries topped with all sorts of home-made jams and a thick wedge of water-melon on the side. Around the auditorium of the United Mennonite Educational Institute (UMEI) booths sell traditionally prepared foods. Taste cabbage borscht; *plumi moos* (stewed dried fruits); small meat turnovers known as *fleisch perishky*, buns baked with smaller topknots called zwieback (see recipe p.72) and huge pans filled with fruit *platz* (see recipe p.22), sold in pieces so that buyers can choose a variety of fruits. It's a day of feasting, for as organizer Paul Enns says, Mennonites use "any excuse to get together to eat." There's a quilt sale, and tables laden with the early fruits and vegetables from the region's fields and greenhouses, from hothouse cucumbers to slender stalks of asparagus.

Leamington-Style Cabbage Soup

This hearty soup is a delicious blend of Russian Mennonite culinary tradition and some of the best vegetables in all of Canada—those of Kent and Essex counties! It's a great soup to serve to a crowd. Simply increase the amount of stock and vegetables to accommodate more people.

6 cups	chicken, beef or vegetable stock	1.5 L
2 cups	each diced onions, diced carrots, cubed potatoes and peeled, chopped tomatoes (2 medium onions, 5 medium carrots, 2 medium potatoes and 2 large tomatoes)	500 mL
2 tbsp	granulated sugar	25 mL
4 cups	finely shredded green cabbage (half a small cabbage)	1 L
¼ cup	chopped fresh dill	50 mL
	Salt and black pepper	
	Chopped fresh dill for garnish	

In large pot, bring stock to boil over high heat. Add onions, carrots, potatoes, tomatoes and sugar; return to boil. Reduce heat to medium-low; simmer, covered, for 10 minutes, or until vegetables are almost tender. Stir in cabbage and dill; return to boil over high heat. Reduce heat to medium-low; simmer, covered, for 5 to 10 minutes, until vegetables are tender. Season with salt and pepper to taste. Ladle into soup bowls; sprinkle with chopped dill. Serve at once.

Grandma Brown's Salad Dressing

When Jeff and Cathy Cardiff fire up their homemade mobile barbecue each summer to grill Huron County's finest venison, beef and pickled pork roasts, they serve a huge variety of homemade salads dressed with good old-fashioned dressings. Cathy combines this concentrated base—named for Jeff's grandmother—with prepared whipped dressings, but we like it mixed with an equal quantity of buttermilk and poured over young lettuce leaves, or spread as is on crisp bacon and field tomato sandwiches.

2	eggs	2
1 cup	granulated sugar	250 mL
3 tbsp	all-purpose flour	45 mL
1 tsp	each salt and dry mustard	5 mL
1½ cups	water	375 mL
½ cup	white vinegar	125 mL

In small bowl, beat eggs lightly; set aside.
In heavy medium saucepan, stir together sugar, flour, salt and mustard. Whisk in water and vinegar until smooth. Bring to boil over high heat, whisking constantly. Beat a little of the mixture into beaten eggs. Return mixture to saucepan; bring to boil, whisking constantly. Reduce heat to medium; cook, whisking constantly, for 2 minutes, until thickened and bubbly. Strain through a sieve into lidded container; let cool, then refrigerate, covered, for up to 2 weeks.

Makes **3 cups (750 mL)**

Preparation time: **15 minutes**

Cooking time: **4 minutes**

*F*armers wear many hats in order to earn a living. Take Jeff Cardiff from Brussels. We first met at Taste of Country, a food show in the town of Blyth. He was wrestling with the sheets of steel covering a huge barbecue. Turns out he built the barbecue, and inside, over grey-coloured coals, he was spit-roasting Huron County venison, rolled roasts of beef and sweet pickled pork roasts from his own farm, home to 1,700 hogs. Every summer weekend, as the head of Cardiff Catering—which means his family works alongside him—he drives the trailer and truck to events that serve great country food to small groups or, as when we met, groups of nine hundred or more. Throughout the summer, as produce ripens, the menu changes. In August, there'll be corn on the cob cooked in a big old cast iron kettle suspended from a tripod over a fire. And because Jeff and his wife, Cathy, are bean farmers, there'll often be a pot of baked beans, or at the very least a delicious white bean salad.

Makes **4 to 6 servings**

Preparation time: **15 minutes**

*M*annina Cheese in Windsor makes and markets marvellous ricotta and whole milk mozzarella, small *provelette* and *primo sale* to delicatessens around the city and east to London. The public is welcome at their Crawford Street plant and, although there are no tours, all the styles and shapes of Mannina cheese are for sale.

SIMPLY THE BEST TOMATO SALAD

In the summer when Ontario tomatoes are at their best, there's nothing finer than this easy salad. Don't even think of making it in the winter! Use an Ontario mozzarella, such as Mannina mozzarella from Windsor, or substitute crumbled goat cheese.

1 lb	beefsteak tomatoes (2 large)	500 g
6 oz	mozzarella cheese, thinly sliced	175 g
1 tbsp	canola, corn or olive oil	15 mL
	Black pepper	
8 to 10	fresh basil leaves	8 to 10

Slice tomatoes into ¼-inch (5 mm) slices. On large serving platter, arrange tomatoes, overlapping slices slightly. Arrange mozzarella over tomatoes. Drizzle with oil; sprinkle generously with black pepper.

Just before serving, stack basil leaves one on top of the other. With sharp knife, slice leaves into thin strips; scatter evenly over tomatoes and cheese. Serve at room temperature.

PASTA TOSSED WITH HEAT-WAVE BRUSCHETTA TOPPING

There's little dispute that the very best tomatoes are those sun-ripened to perfection in late summer, but throughout the rest of the year, there's an excellent alternative. If you allow hothouse tomatoes to ripen at room temperature until they are red and luscious, you will be surprised at how juicy and sweet they are. The flavourful tomato mixture in this recipe is equally good served the traditional way: atop slices of lightly toasted crusty Italian bread.

3	large ripe tomatoes, chopped	3
½	sweet red pepper, seeded and finely chopped	½
3	green onions, finely chopped or ½ cup (125 mL) minced red onion	3
¼ cup	slivered fresh basil leaves or 1 tbsp (15 mL) dried basil	50 mL
2	cloves garlic, minced	2
½ tsp	each salt and freshly ground black pepper	2 mL
4 cups	penne pasta	1 L
1	bay leaf	1
3 oz	crumbled goat cheese	75 g
	Fresh basil sprigs for garnish	

In medium bowl, combine tomatoes, pepper, onions, basil, garlic, salt and pepper; set aside.

In large pot of boiling salted water, cook pasta with bay leaf for 6 to 7 minutes, until al dente (tender but still with a bite). Drain pasta well, discarding bay leaf; return pasta to pot. Add tomato mixture and goat cheese to pasta; toss well. Serve at once, garnished with basil.

Makes **4 servings**

Preparation time: **15 minutes**

Cooking time: **6 to 7 minutes**

*O*ver the past decades Italian cuisine has blossomed in Windsor. Immigration reinforced the community before and after World War II to twenty-six thousand families. Erie Street, or "Via Italia," is lined with Italian shops and restaurants serving pasta and pizza and crusty, country-style breads. As in any Little Italy, there are excellent greengrocers. The city is also the pizza capital of Canada, with more pizzerias per capita than in any other Canadian city. Franco's, the largest in the city, sells more than 300,000 pizzas per year. Windsor's pizzas are baked in a style all their own, thick crusted and topped with locally made mozzarella, local pepperoni and thick, spicy sauce. Essex and Kent County tomatoes are the only ones used in Primo sauces.

Makes **6 servings**

Preparation time: **20 minutes**

Standing time: **1 hour**

Cooking time: **about 4½ hours**

*I*n this province, food-related success stories are legion! One of the most exciting occurs when a group of producers bands together to form a dynamic co-operative to market their produce. The Hensall District Cooperative (HDC) specializes in white and coloured beans—cranberry, black turtle, Dutch brown, adzuki, dark red, light red and white kidney. The cooperative, with sales of more than $110 million, just built a brand new $1.5 million drying facility. From there, beans are shipped all over the country. To make sure you're buying HDC beans you'll have to head to their retail store on the main street of Exeter. Sadly, at this writing, there is no such thing as a "Grown in Ontario" label, so it's impossible to know whether you're buying locally or supporting farm communities thousands of miles from home.

LAMB SHANKS BRAISED WITH HURON COUNTY WHITE BEANS

Lamb and beans have a special affinity, and in this recipe economical lamb shanks are braised until meltingly tender along with beans and vegetables. This one-pot supper takes a while to cook but needs little attention and no accompaniment, save perhaps some good bread to mop up the delicious juices. Use a shallow casserole large enough to hold lamb shanks in a single layer or (and this is what we do) use a shallow roasting pan and cover it with foil. Cubed lamb shoulder or leg can be substituted for the shanks if you prefer; reduce the cooking time to 1 hour before adding the beans.

1 lb	white pea beans (2½ cups/625 mL)	500 g
2	large onions	2
6	whole cloves	6
3	bay leaves	3
6	lamb shanks	6
2 tbsp	canola or corn oil	25 mL
3	medium carrots, chopped	3
6	large cloves garlic, peeled	6
1 cup	red wine	250 mL
1	can (19 oz/540 mL) tomatoes, undrained	1
1 tsp	each salt, dried marjoram and thyme	5 mL
½ tsp	black pepper	2 mL
½ cup	dry bread crumbs	125 mL
¼ cup	chopped fresh parsley	50 mL
2 tbsp	melted butter	25 mL

Rinse beans; pick over, discarding any grit. In large pot, combine beans with 8 cups (2 L) cold water. Cover; bring to boil over high heat. Boil for 2 minutes. Remove from heat; let stand, covered, for 1 hour. Drain. Return beans to pot, along with 8 cups (2 L) cold water. Peel 1 onion; stick with cloves. Add onion to pot, along with 1 bay leaf. Bring to boil over high heat. Reduce heat to

medium-low; simmer, covered, for 45 minutes to 1 hour, until beans are tender. Drain well, discarding onion and bay leaf.

While beans are cooking, preheat oven to 350°F (180°C). Pat lamb shanks dry with paper towels. In shallow flameproof casserole large enough to hold lamb shanks in single layer or in shallow roasting pan, heat 1 tbsp (15 mL) oil over medium-high heat. Cook lamb shanks in batches for 3 to 5 minutes, turning often, until browned on all sides, adding more oil as necessary. Remove shanks to a plate as each batch browns.

Peel and chop remaining onion; add to casserole, along with carrots and garlic. Cook, stirring, over medium heat for 3 to 5 minutes, until onion is soft but not brown. Add wine to casserole; bring to boil over high heat, scraping up brown bits from bottom of casserole. Stir in tomatoes, salt, marjoram, thyme, pepper and remaining bay leaves, breaking up tomatoes with the back of a spoon. Return lamb shanks to casserole; bring to boil. Cover with lid or foil; cook in oven for 2 hours.

Add drained beans to casserole, stirring gently so that beans are well distributed. Cover with lid or foil; cook for 1 hour or until lamb shanks are very tender.

In small bowl, combine bread crumbs, parsley and butter; sprinkle evenly over lamb and beans. Cook, uncovered, for 20 to 30 minutes, until bread crumbs are golden. Discard bay leaves; serve in wide soup bowls, making sure everyone gets a clove of garlic.

*B*eans are big in Huron County. More than 45,000 acres are planted yearly. For more than three decades, Zurich, a small village of nine hundred people right in the heart of the county, has held a Bean Festival on the final Saturday of August. More than a ton of local white beans is donated by the three local mills and cooked during the week. From 11 a.m. to 7 p.m., Zurich-baked beans, barbecued pork chops, coleslaw and at least a thousand pies provide the twenty thousand visitors with a real country feast. The festivities really begin on Friday night with a huge antique car parade. (In 1995 eight hundred oldies cruised the town.) On Saturday downtown is closed to vehicles to create a giant street market. But the real highlight, other than the bean dinner, is the annual frog-jumping contest.

Makes **4 servings**

Preparation time: **15 minutes**

Cooking time: **about 1 hour**

$\mathcal{T}$he Maitland Valley Conservation Authority and the Ecological Farmers Association of Ontario have pooled their resources to establish an alternative Agricultural Lending Library (books, articles, videos and journals). The MVCA is also the Canadian resource centre for Community Shared Agriculture (CSA), a program whereby consumers purchase pre-crop shares from a local organic farmer. More CSAs have sprung up in Ontario than in any other province in Canada. Throughout the year, produce is delivered to the shareholder's home, and during the wintertime planning sessions, direct input into new crops or better methods allows the consumer to communicate directly with their grower, who oftimes becomes their friend.

SHEDDEN RHUBARB FESTIVAL PORK CHOPS

The village of Shedden, the other Rhubarb Capital of Ontario (see page 132 for more on this contentious issue), celebrates Rosy Rhubarb Days on the second weekend in June. In 1994 the Rosy Rhubarb Cookbook Committee published Favourite Rhubarb Recipes *to raise funds to build a new community centre. Shedden residents Marilyn Lunn and Nancy Smith contributed this comforting main-course recipe to the book, and they kindly consented to share it with us. Fresh or frozen rhubarb can be used for the recipe; thaw frozen rhubarb only partially and pat it dry on paper towels before using.*

1 tbsp	canola or corn oil	15 mL
4	centre-cut or butt bone-in pork chops (¾ inch/2 cm thick)	4
3 tbsp	butter	45 mL
2½ cups	soft bread crumbs	625 mL
3 cups	sliced rhubarb (about ¾ lb/375 g trimmed)	750 mL
½ cup	packed brown sugar	125 mL
¼ cup	all-purpose flour	50 mL
1 tsp	cinnamon	5 mL
¼ tsp	each salt and black pepper	1 mL

Preheat oven to 350°F (180°C). In large heavy skillet, heat oil over medium-high heat. Add pork chops; cook for 2 minutes on each side, until lightly browned. Remove chops from skillet; set aside.

Add butter to skillet; melt over medium heat, stirring to combine with pan drippings and scraping up any brown bits from bottom of skillet. Remove skillet from heat; stir in bread crumbs until well combined. Set aside ½ cup (125 mL) bread-crumb mixture; sprinkle remaining bread-crumb mixture over base of 13- by 9-inch (3 L) baking dish.

In medium bowl, stir together rhubarb, sugar, flour and cinnamon until well combined. Spoon half of rhubarb mixture over bread crumbs in baking dish. Arrange chops on top of rhubarb mixture; sprinkle with salt and pepper. Top evenly with remaining rhubarb mixture. Bake, covered, for 45 minutes. Sprinkle reserved bread-crumb mixture over chops; bake, uncovered, for 10 to 15 minutes, until chops are tender and bread crumbs are golden brown.

An excellent guide to agriculture in Windsor, Essex and Pelee Island is available from the regional Convention and Visitors Bureau. The small booklet will lead you to all sorts of farms, from a pheasant farm that holds the annual Pelee Island Shoot to a hothouse that grows English (seedless) cucumbers. It lists all the fairs, festivals and area museums, as well as complete hours of operation for the region's pick-your-own stands and farmers' markets, including the great Windsor City Market. One word of advice: call ahead to individual farmers, otherwise you may find no one at home save the yappy family dog.

Makes **6 servings**

Preparation time: **20 minutes**

Cooking time: **40 to 50 minutes**

*T*he VQA region known as Lake Erie North Shore spans the flat, former sea bed between Windsor and Blenheim. Dominated by heavy clay soil, this region has the most heat units in all of Canada. But the lake is so shallow, it has little to no moderating effect. "When it freezes, it's just cold," says Pierre LeBlanc, co-owner of LeBlanc Estate Winery near Harrow. There the Brookston clay soil stresses the vines, encouraging low yields and hence concentrated flavour. Lyse LeBlanc, winemaker and mother of four, creates lush, rounded vintages with very limited production of Pinot Gris, Riesling, Gewurztraminer, Vidal, Pinot Noir and Cabernet Sauvignon.

Pelee Island, another designated wine region floating a few miles offshore in Lake Erie, has a climate so unique that according to winemaker/manager Walter Schmoranz, the harvest must be completed within twenty-four to forty-eight hours.

ROAST CHICKEN BREAST WITH FRESH BASIL AND SUMMER PEACH SAUCE

Celebrate the summer with this easy main dish that's special enough for company.

1½ cups	late-harvest Riesling wine	375 mL
3	firm ripe peaches, peeled, pitted and sliced	3
6	boneless skinless chicken breasts (1¾ lb/875 g)	6
1 tbsp	grated gingerroot	15 mL
½ cup	chilled butter, cubed	125 mL
2 tbsp	slivered fresh basil leaves Basil leaves for garnish	25 mL

Preheat oven to 350°F (180°C). In medium saucepan, combine wine and peach slices; bring to boil over high heat. Reduce heat to medium-low; simmer, covered, for 2 to 3 minutes, until peaches are just tender. With slotted spoon, transfer peaches to bowl; keep warm. Reserve cooking liquid in saucepan.

Heat large oiled nonstick skillet over medium-high heat; cook chicken breasts in batches for 1 to 2 minutes on each side, until golden brown. As each batch browns, transfer chicken to lightly buttered 11- by 7-inch (2 L) baking pan; cover with foil or lid. Bake for 20 to 25 minutes, until chicken is no longer pink inside; keep warm.

While chicken is baking, add gingerroot to saucepan containing reserved poaching liquid; bring to boil over high heat. Boil, uncovered, for 12 to 15 minutes or until liquid is reduced to about ½ cup (125 mL). Remove saucepan from heat. Whisk in butter, a few cubes at a time, until it's all incorporated. Stir in basil.

To serve, pour some sauce onto each of 6 dinner plates. Cut each chicken breast crosswise into 5 slices; arrange on top of sauce. Garnish chicken with peach slices and basil leaves.

Variation: If you grow begonias in your garden, here's a tasty way to use them. Omit basil from the recipe and replace gingerroot with 1 cup (250 mL) loosely packed tuberous begonia blooms, making sure you use organically grown flowers. Break begonia flowers apart, cutting away the lighter-coloured base. Chop petals finely. Add petals to reserved cooking juices after reducing juices to ½ cup (125 mL). Whisk in butter and continue as above.

*T*here are growers like Susan and Stan Christie, who in addition to their cash crop operation cultivate 20 acres of the finest garlic in the province. The huge, strong-flavoured bulbs are available in only a handful of local grocery stores or by ordering directly from Flat Creek Farms Inc.

*Makes **6 servings***

Preparation time: **15 minutes**

Cooking time: **about 15 minutes**

*T*he humble rutabaga is a much-maligned vegetable, but there are few products so economical, tasty and versatile. One of Canada's most passionate rutabaga advocates is Susan Sutherland, former national director of promotions for the Canadian Produce Marketing Association in Ottawa. A couple of years ago Sutherland launched a one-woman campaign to make the rutabaga Canada's national vegetable. Why? It's obvious, claims Sutherland. Rutabaga's very name is bilingual, the chunky vegetable is hard to separate, it's good for our constitution (being packed with vitamin C), and it's distinct: some provinces wax their rutabagas, others, such as Quebec, do not!

The village of Blyth is the capital of Ontario's rutabaga production. It was here that the first precision seeder was developed, and in 1939 rutabaga pioneer Russ Dougherty opened a waxing plant. Despite an on-again, off-again Rutabaga Festival, the area still boasts more than three hundred acres in production, most of which is shipped to the United States.

APPLE-GLAZED HURON COUNTY RUTABAGA

In southwestern Ontario, growers have discovered that our climate suits the humble rutabaga just fine. In fact, the area produces around ninety million pounds of the vegetable each year, which translates into a farm-gate value of more than $7 million! The rutabaga is tasty and low-cal and lends itself particularly well to sweet glazes such as the one in this recipe. Serve it with your Thanksgiving turkey and celebrate a great Canadian vegetable.

1	small rutabaga, peeled and cut into ½-inch (1 cm) cubes (about 5 cups/1.25 L)	1
2 tbsp	each butter, apple cider and maple syrup	25 mL
¼ tsp	each nutmeg, salt and black pepper	1 mL
2	apples, peeled, cored and sliced	2
2 tbsp	chopped fresh parsley	25 mL

In medium saucepan, combine rutabaga with enough cold water to just cover it. Bring to boil over high heat. Reduce heat to medium-low; simmer, covered, for 10 to 12 minutes, until rutabaga is tender. Drain well. Spoon into serving dish; keep warm.

Meanwhile, in separate saucepan, combine butter, apple cider, maple syrup, nutmeg, salt and pepper; heat over medium heat until butter has melted. Add apples; increase heat to medium-high. Cook, uncovered, stirring occasionally, for 3 to 5 minutes, until apples are tender but not broken up and liquid is reduced and syrupy.

Pour apple mixture over rutabaga; toss gently to combine. Sprinkle with parsley; serve at once.

OLD-FASHIONED CREAMED CORN WITH WHISKY

Here's a new twist on traditional creamed corn that combines the corn of southwestern Ontario with Canadian whisky. Windsor is home to the Hiram Walker Canadian Club distillery, which has a fascinating tour available (there's lots of walking, so wear comfortable shoes).

This recipe is best made with fresh Ontario corn that has been rushed from field to kitchen as quickly as possible. For not-so-fresh corn you may want to add ½ tsp (2 mL) granulated sugar when you're cooking the corn in the butter.

3 cups	fresh corn kernels (about 4 large ears)	750 mL
1 tbsp	butter	15 mL
1	small sweet red pepper, seeded and finely chopped	1
¼ cup	Canadian whisky	50 mL
½ cup	whipping cream	125 mL
	Salt and black pepper to taste	

Remove kernels from shucked ears of corn by standing the ears on one end and running a sharp knife down between kernels and ear. In large heavy skillet, melt butter over medium heat. Add corn and red pepper; cook, stirring, for 8 to 10 minutes, until corn is tender.

Add whisky; cook, stirring, until almost all the whisky has evaporated. Add cream; increase heat to high. Cook, stirring, for 1 minute, until cream has reduced and thickened a little. Remove from heat; season with salt and pepper to taste.

Makes **4 servings**

Preparation time: **15 minutes**

Cooking time: **10 to 12 minutes**

*C*hatham is in corn country, with roughly 145,000 acres seeded in Kent County and 165,000 acres seeded in neighbouring Middlesex. But try to buy local cornmeal! Unless you grind it yourself, it's impossible to find. Corn is shipped, and that's the last time it is identifiable. Chances are you're buying Ontario corn, but like the bean crop in our province, the products are not named as being grown here because they are often blended with foreign product. The other main crop of the region is soft winter wheat, for which Ontario is becoming widely known. Here consumers have better luck, because Dover Mills in Cambridge buys much of it to grind into cake-and-pastry flour. Just look for the Dover Flour brand name.

Makes **one 9-in (23 cm) corn bread**

Preparation time: **20 minutes**

Cooking time: **30 to 35 minutes**

*T*he Elgin Settlement, now known as the village of Buxton, was the final stop for blacks from the south on the Underground Railway to freedom. Founded in 1849 by the Reverend William King on 4,300 acres, the region was settled by freed and fugitive black slaves. It soon became a thriving community of nearly two thousand whose success in education and industry is proudly documented at the regional archives. The area is rich with black history including the North American Black Historical Museum and Cultural Centre, the cabin of Reverend Josiah Henson (1789–1883), the man who was the basis for Harriet Beecher Stowe's *Uncle Tom's Cabin,* and the small Baptist church in the village of Sandwich, the destination of the first slaves to settle permanently. The African-Canadian Association of Chatham proudly recalls their local heritage by cooking up soul food for summer motor-coach travellers. Chicken is pan-fried while the ham bakes; collard and turnip greens are simmered with ham hocks; potatoes are scalloped and coleslaw is heaped into large family-size bowls. There may be a strawberry short-cake, and often there's old-fashioned lemon pie and butter tarts.

CORN BREAD STUDDED WITH CRISP BACON

You'll taste a version of this delicious corn bread at the African-Canadian Association's soul-food dinners in Chatham. When two people write a cookbook, lively discussion over some recipes is inevitable, and this corn bread is a perfect example. Anita likes her corn bread on the sweet side and adds ⅓ cup (75 mL) sugar to this recipe; Julia's tooth is not so sweet and she prefers 2 tbsp (25 mL). We compromised and used ¼ cup (50 mL), but please feel free to use more or less sugar according to your personal taste.

6	slices side bacon, chopped	6
1 cup	all-purpose flour	250 mL
¾ cup	cornmeal	175 mL
¼ cup	granulated sugar	50 mL
1 tbsp	baking powder	25 mL
½ tsp	salt	2 mL
1¼ cups	buttermilk	300 mL
2	eggs, well beaten	2
2 tbsp	canola or corn oil	25 mL

Preheat oven to 400°F (200°C). In medium skillet, cook bacon over medium-high heat for 3 to 5 minutes until crisp. With slotted spoon, remove bacon from skillet, reserving drippings. Drain bacon on paper towels; set aside.

In large bowl, stir together flour, cornmeal, sugar, baking powder and salt. In glass measure, whisk together milk, eggs and oil. Add milk mixture to flour mixture, along with bacon. Stir gently just until dry ingredients are moistened (batter should be lumpy). Grease a 9-inch (2.5 L) square cake pan with some of the reserved bacon drippings; pour in batter, spreading evenly. Bake for 25 to 30 minutes, until golden brown and risen and a toothpick inserted in centre of corn bread comes out clean. Serve warm or cold, cut into squares.

OLD-FASHIONED BLACK CURRANT PRESERVES

Anita's mother, Anne MacDonald, made these delectable preserves when Anita was a child. The mixture is so runny that Anita remembers having to balance it on top of buttered toast to keep it from dripping. But her favourite way of eating it was in the winter, when Mom spooned it into a large mug and added boiling water, leaving the spoon in so that little Anita could devour the currants that collected at the bottom of the mug. If you prefer a firmer preserve, boil the mixture for up to 30 minutes. The recipe works equally well with fresh or frozen black currants.

2 cups	black currants (¾ lb/375 g)	500 mL
4 cups	granulated sugar	1 L
2 cups	cold water	500 mL

If necessary, strip black currants from their stems by running tines of a fork down stems; rub off the flower ends. In large heavy saucepan, combine black currants, sugar and water. Bring to boil over high heat. Reduce heat to medium; simmer, uncovered, for 10 to 15 minutes, stirring occasionally. Skim off any foam.

Immediately ladle into 4 hot, sterilized ½-pint (250 mL) jars, leaving ¼ inch (5 mm) headspace. Wipe jar rims to remove any excess preserves; seal with two-piece lids, tightening screw bands until just fingertip tight. Process in hot-water bath for 5 minutes. Remove jars from canner; let cool for 24 hours. Check jar seals (sealed lids curve downwards). Remove screw bands; label jars. Store preserves in cool, dark place.

Makes **4 half-pint (250 mL) jars**

Preparation time: **15 minutes**

Cooking time: **10 to 15 minutes**

Processing time: **5 minutes**

*I*t shouldn't be surprising that Huron County, a major agricultural centre, is loaded with direct-to-the-consumer farm produce. A well-organized pocket guide has been compiled by the County's Planning and Development Department, listing names, locations and contact numbers for more than eighty producers who sell everything from corn to wild boar; there are also listings for farm vacation homes, markets and farm tours.

Makes **2 loaves**

Preparation time: **30 minutes**

Rising time: **3 hours**

Cooking time: **35 to 40 minutes**

*L*ondon has been the home of Say Cheese for twenty-six years. Owner Hilary Alderson searches out not only Ontario's best but the finest cheeses from across Canada and around the world—from Forfar and Jensen's Cheddar to Pinneau's creamy Quark cheese ("the best made in Canada," according to Ms Alderson) and Woolwich Dairy's prizewinning goat's milk cheeses. The Say Cheese restaurant has two faces, the first being the original menu from twenty-five years ago. Customers still come in for cheese soup and Welsh rarebit—once outrageous and trendy, now old-fashioned and a bit nostalgic. Their second menu, a list of the season's finest produce, is fully updated every six weeks.

SOURDOUGH-CARAWAY RYE BREAD

The rye breads of Ontario's farmers' markets are among the best in the nation. German and other eastern European bakers have immigrated to Ontario, bringing with them their love of good bread: light and dark rye, pumpernickel, sunflower seed rye. The list is long, the breads delicious.

2 cups	Grey County Sourdough Starter (see recipe on page 192)	500 mL
1½ cups	very warm water (125°F/52°C)	375 mL
⅓ cup	molasses	75 mL
¼ cup	canola or corn oil	50 mL
2 tbsp	cocoa	25 mL
2 tsp	salt	10 mL
3½ cups	all-purpose flour	875 mL
2½ cups	rye flour, preferably organic	625 mL
1 tbsp	instant yeast	15 mL
2 tbsp	caraway seeds	25 mL
	Additional flour for kneading	
2 tbsp	cornmeal	25 mL

In large bowl, stir together sourdough starter, water, molasses, oil, cocoa and salt until well combined. Add 1½ cups (375 mL) all-purpose flour and 1 cup (250 mL) rye flour. Whisk until mixture is well blended. Add yeast; beat for 2 minutes or until very smooth. Stir in remaining all-purpose and rye flours and the caraway seeds, mixing until no dry spots remain.

Turn out onto floured surface; knead for 5 minutes, working in up to 1 cup (250 mL) additional flour to keep dough from sticking. Form dough into ball; place in lightly oiled bowl, turning dough to coat with oil. Cover loosely with plastic wrap; let rise in warm, draft-free place for 1½ hours or until doubled in size.

Punch dough down; divide in half. Pat out each half into a rectangle; shape each rectangle into a loaf by rolling it up jelly-roll style, pinching edges together to seal. Grease 2 baking sheets; sprinkle with cornmeal. Place loaves seam-side down on baking sheets; with sharp knife, cut slashes in tops of loaves. Cover with damp towel; let rise at room temperature for 1½ hours or until doubled in size. Preheat oven to 350°F (180°C). Bake loaves for 35 to 40 minutes until well risen and golden brown, and loaves sound hollow when tapped on bases.

*M*ost southwestern Ontario towns have good bakeries. Try the Lakeside Home Bakery in Leamington or the Down Home Bakery & Deli in Shedden. At the Portuguese-run European Bakery in Leamington, their potato bread is available only on Wednesdays and Fridays.

Makes 12 muffins

Preparation time: 20 minutes

Cooking time: 25 to 30 minutes

*N*o other garden in Ontario addresses the food basket the way researcher Dr. Gordon Scheifele's Alternative Crops Garden at Ridgetown College does. More than eight hundred new and unusual plant varieties are represented in the one and a half acres under cultivation. Chinese vegetables like bitter melon and okra; grains like kamut and spelt that hail from ancient civilizations; industrial hemp; herb plants by the dozen, twenty-four different garlic varieties along with medicinal herbs like ginseng, May apple, evening primrose and goldenseal. It's one of the few places to see stevia growing. This plant, known in China for years, is many hundreds of times sweeter than sugar. From June until the end of September, from dawn to dusk, visitors are encouraged to take the self-guided tour through the garden.

RHUBARB-CRISP MUFFINS

This is one of our favourite muffins—reason enough to dig up a flower bed and start your very own rhubarb patch! If you wish, stir a handful of chopped pecans or walnuts into the batter before baking. Frozen rhubarb can be used in the recipe, although the finished muffins will be a little more moist. Thaw the rhubarb only partially, then blot with paper towels to remove as much liquid as possible.

Topping:

⅓ cup	brown sugar	75 mL
1 tbsp	softened butter	15 mL
1 tsp	cinnamon	5 mL

Muffins:

1½ cups	packed brown sugar	375 mL
½ cup	softened butter	125 mL
1	egg	1
1 tsp	vanilla	5 mL
½ tsp	almond extract	2 mL
3 cups	all-purpose flour	750 mL
1 tsp	each baking powder and baking soda	5 mL
1 cup	buttermilk	250 mL
3 cups	finely diced rhubarb (about ¾ lb/375 g trimmed)	750 mL

Topping: In small bowl, combine sugar, butter and cinnamon until crumbly. Set aside.

Muffins: Preheat oven to 375°F (190°C). In medium bowl, cream together brown sugar, butter, egg, vanilla and almond extract until mixture is light in colour. In separate bowl, stir together flour, baking powder and baking soda.

Add flour mixture to sugar mixture alternately with buttermilk, stirring just until dry ingredients are moistened. Do not overmix—batter should be lumpy. Fold in rhubarb. Divide batter among 12 paper-lined or well-greased muffin cups; muffin cups will be very full. Sprinkle each muffin generously with sugar mixture. Bake for 25 to 30 minutes, until a toothpick inserted into centre of muffin comes out clean.

According to Shalin Khosla, the greenhouse expert at the Harrow Research Station near Windsor, the province of Ontario is the largest centre for greenhouse growing in all of North America. The Leamington area alone has two hundred acres under glass and last year saw a thirty percent increase. Bright red and sweet cluster tomatoes, English seedless cucumbers (the bigger the better), a few acres of red peppers, butterhead lettuce and some fresh herbs are all being cultivated.

Makes **10 to 12 servings**

Preparation time: **20 minutes**

Cooking time: **45 to 50 minutes**

*P*aul Glatt, of Glatt Bros. Brewing Company in London, calls his approach to beer making "craft-brewing." His latest offering, Harvest Ale, is Ontario's first all-organic brew. Using a blend of grains grown near London, the small brewhouse has recently released its first organic Harvest Ale. Framboise is another of their unusual offerings. It's a cream ale with a "ridiculously high amount of fresh raspberry juice" (twenty percent by volume). Their Green Chillie Beer is a premium lager with a blast of, yes, green chili peppers.

FRUIT PLATZ

Peaches, pears, apricots and cherries all flourish along Lake Erie's hot northern shoreline, where the sun pours down like honey onto mile after mile of tender fruit. The area's Russian Mennonite community brought to Canada one of their most typically eastern European desserts, platz. A light cakelike base is studded with whatever seasonal or home-frozen fruit is available, then is sprinkled with a sweet crumb topping before being popped into the oven to bake. This is a great dessert to serve when you have a houseful of guests!

Crumb Topping:

½ cup	granulated or brown sugar	125 mL
½ cup	all-purpose flour	125 mL
¼ cup	softened butter	50 mL

Base:

½ cup	granulated sugar	125 mL
½ cup	softened butter or shortening	125 mL
2	eggs	2
1 tsp	vanilla	5 mL
1½ cups	all-purpose flour	375 mL
2 tsp	baking powder	10 mL
¼ cup	milk	50 mL
1½ cups	pitted and sliced peaches or apricots, whole blueberries or pitted sweet cherries	375 mL

Crumb Topping: In small bowl, combine sugar and flour. Cut or rub in butter until mixture is crumbly; set aside.

Base: Preheat oven to 350°F (180°C). Generously grease a 13- by 9-inch (3.5 L) baking pan.
In medium bowl, beat together sugar, butter, eggs and vanilla until mixture is light in colour.
In separate bowl, stir together flour and baking powder. Add to creamed mixture alternately with milk until a smooth batter forms.

Spread batter evenly in base of prepared pan. If using sliced fruit, arrange in neat rows on top of base; if using blueberries or cherries, scatter them evenly over base. Sprinkle crumb topping evenly over fruit. Bake in oven for 45 to 50 minutes, until golden brown around edges and puffy. Cut into squares; serve warm with milk, cream or ice cream.

Variation: For rhubarb or gooseberry *platz*, combine 3 cups (750 mL) diced rhubarb or whole gooseberries and ⅓ cup (75 mL) water in heavy saucepan. Bring to boil over medium heat; simmer 3 to 4 minutes, until fruit is softened. Stir together 1 cup (250 mL) granulated sugar and 3 tbsp (45 mL) cornstarch. Add to simmering fruit; cook, stirring, for 2 to 3 minutes, until thickened. Remove from heat; let cool for 30 minutes before using in above recipe.

*T*he Harrow Research Station is responsible for much of the work being done on new pear and apple cultivars. Jonagold is a firm full-flavoured large apple with a delicate blush on its sun cheek. Fuji, in spite of its less than gorgeous appearance, has lots of full apple flavour. Gala, with its pretty red stripes, is coming to market now, but because of the supply will probably only be available in the autumn for the next few years. Pears like Flemish Beauty and Bosc are rapidly replacing the older varieties. Look for the novel Ontario-grown red Bartletts and brand-new varieties bearing the name Harrow. We picked up a bag of ultra-sweet Harrow Delight pears at The Apple Place in Simcoe.

Makes **12 servings**

Preparation time: **20 minutes**

Cooking time: **50 to 60 minutes**

*T*he Harrow Fall Fair is one of the largest country fairs in southwestern Ontario, attracting upwards of 50,000. The 120-foot-long craft table is full. There are dozens of prizes, ranging from the very best apple pie to the finest blueberry dessert, awarded by Klassen Blueberry Farm, just outside the town.

*A*nn McColl's Kitchen Shop is another London institution, and Hilary Alderson of Say Cheese says it is "the most beautiful store in the world." With modest beginnings in the 1960s (we still remember Ann cooking in her tiny kitchen behind the store while waiting on customers), the store now fills a former Massey Harris tractor showroom, a massive, high-ceilinged building constructed in the late 1800s. Cooking classes are held in the light-filled atrium. From rosette irons to shortbread stamps to cookbooks, this is what a kitchen store should be—filled with all an adventurous cook could ever desire.

BLUEBERRY COFFEE CAKE

In 1994, Sandra Lott of La Salle won first prize in the Best Blueberry Dessert Competition at the Harrow Fair with this wonderful coffee cake. She's made the recipe for years, ever since her husband, Larry, planted a few blueberry plants and the Lotts found themselves blessed with an overabundance of the little purple berries.

Topping:

1 cup	packed brown sugar	250 mL
¼ cup	softened butter	50 mL
2 tsp	cinnamon	10 mL

Cake:

¾ cup	granulated sugar	175 mL
¾ cup	softened butter	175 mL
1	egg	1
1 cup	sour cream	250 mL
1 tsp	vanilla	5 mL
2 cups	all-purpose flour	500 mL
1 tsp	each baking powder and baking soda	5 mL
¼ tsp	salt	1 mL
2 cups	fresh blueberries	500 mL

Topping: In small bowl, using a fork, stir together sugar, butter and cinnamon until well combined and crumbly; set aside.

Cake: Preheat oven to 350°F (180°C); lightly grease a 9-inch (2.5 L) springform pan.

In medium bowl using electric mixer, cream together sugar and butter until light and fluffy. Beat in egg on low speed until well combined. Stir in sour cream and vanilla.

In separate bowl, stir together flour, baking powder, baking soda and salt. Gradually stir flour mixture into sugar-butter mixture until well combined (batter will be stiff).

Spoon two-thirds of cake batter into prepared pan, spreading evenly. Top evenly with blueberries. Drop remaining batter by spoonfuls on top of blueberries; spread evenly to more or less cover blueberries. Sprinkle evenly with topping.

Bake for 50 to 60 minutes or until well risen, golden brown and firm to touch. Let cool in pan on wire rack. Release sides of pan; place cake on serving plate. Serve warm or cold.

*W*indsor chef, caterer and entrepreneur Vince Del Duca, a passionate supporter of locally grown ingredients, proudly states, "We take the regional products and develop them as a cuisine." From Mannina cheeses to superb local veal, he uses them all. His soups use ingredients grown or manufactured right in Essex County—ripe red sweet peppers, huge garlic cloves . . . even the orzo (rice-shaped pasta), is locally manufactured with Prairie durum wheat flour.

His bakery, the Pastry Table, is famous for its mocha tortes. Chiffon-like and flavoured with dark roasted coffee, these incredibly light cakes are layered with ultra-rich (forty percent) whipped cream. Two to four hundred are sold weekly. You'll find freshly baked biscotti; Sicilian-style cannoli stuffed with Mannina's ricotta; handmade rolled-fondant-iced wedding cakes and delicate petits fours. The truffles are generously spiked with all the Hiram Walker liquors from Canadian Club to Kahlùa.

Makes **6 to 8 servings**

Preparation time: **20 minutes**

Cooking time: **about 5 minutes**

*W*indsor is more than Italian, and the global village's influence is very strong. Try the *paczki*, a rich jelly dough-nut made during Lent, at Blak's Bakery or visit Schwab's Bakery for a loaf of pumpkin seed or flax bread baked with flour they've ground themselves, or Adler's for their famous five-pound loaf of Russian rye bread, or the Mid-East Bakery for freshly baked pita. And if you're in the mood for perogies, St. Vladimir's Ukrainian Orthodox Cathedral opens its doors every Wednesday to sell the traditionally prepared sauerkraut-filled and potato-and-cheese-stuffed packets. Finish off with a tub of Peanut Toffee Ice Cream or a single hand-dipped truffle from the copper kettles at Walker's Fine Candies.

CHILLED SPICED PEACH SOUP

Serve this unusual but refreshing dessert only when peaches are at their ultimate best. A couple of Ontario Nut Lace Cookies (see recipe on page 186) are a perfect accompaniment.

2 lb	peeled, pitted and sliced fresh peaches (about 7 large peaches)	1 kg
1½ cups	water	375 mL
½ cup	granulated sugar	125 mL
1	2-in (5 cm) cinnamon stick	1
1 cup	off-dry Riesling or other slightly sweet Niagara white wine	250 mL
2 tbsp	cornstarch	25 mL
1 cup	whipping cream	250 mL
¼ tsp	almond extract	1 mL
	Fresh mint sprigs for garnish	

In large heavy saucepan, combine peaches, water, sugar and cinnamon stick; cover and bring to boil over medium-high heat. Reduce heat to medium-low; simmer, covered, for 1 to 2 minutes, until peaches are tender but not broken up. With slotted spoon, remove peaches and cinnamon stick to large bowl, reserving cooking liquid in saucepan. Set peaches aside.

In small bowl, combine ¼ cup (50 mL) wine and the cornstarch, stirring until smooth. Stir cornstarch mixture into reserved cooking liquid. Bring to boil over medium-high heat; cook for 1 minute, stirring constantly, until smooth and slightly thickened. Remove from heat; pour over peaches. Let cool completely. Discard cinnamon.

Add remaining wine, the cream and almond extract to peaches; stir gently until well combined. Chill well before serving.

To serve, ladle into small chilled soup bowls; garnish with fresh mint leaves.

"We can grow anything here except tropical fruit!" Over and over you'll hear these words from producers in this lush region that stretches from Niagara-on-the-Lake over the Niagara Escarpment and westward along Lake Erie to Simcoe. From pecans to figs, from persimmons to white peaches, the region characterizes the possibilities that form Ontario's culinary reality. There's even one small grower who is attempting greenhouse-raised lemons. However, it's this region's tender fruit with which most are familiar. Apricots, peaches, grapes, pears and plums ripen throughout the long, oftimes very hot, summers.

From its most humble beginnings, Niagara's wine industry has gained a spot on the world stage. Its foods will surely do the same.

Begin any exploration of the region by shopping its roadside stands and sipping your way through The Wine Route.

Niagara is one of three legally defined wine-growing regions in the province—Lake Erie North Shore and Pelee Island being the others. Within Niagara, however, are other definable areas. The Bench, for instance, sweeps along the Niagara Escarpment's craggy outcroppings from St. Catharines. It plateaus into a narrow, fertile band of well-drained, shallow silty clay loam over limestone bedrock. There the climate is the coolest of the Niagara peninsula. Riesling grapes flourish here. Allan Schmidt, winemaker at Vineland Estates, characterizes the grapes as having a "racy acidity."

Throughout the lower Niagara region, from the Lakeshore through Queenston to St. Davids, the soil varies from sandy loam to coarse and gravelly deposits. It's these potential subappellations that are challenging the expertise of winemakers like Jean-Laurent Groux of Hillebrand. "In France," he says, "the job of finding out what grows best and where took two thousand years. Here we are trying to do it in ten to twenty."

Niagara

Makes **4 servings**

Preparation time: **15 minutes**

Cooking time: **20 to 25 minutes**

*N*owhere in Canada is there more asparagus grown than in Norfolk County. The sandy soil is perfect for the tender shoots. More than 2,500 acres are harvested yearly—by hand!

ROASTED ASPARAGUS SOUP WITH GOAT CHEESE

Roasting asparagus is easy to do and it seems to intensify its flavour wonderfully. This soup, with its creamy topping of goat cheese combined with the season's first chives, is equally delicious served hot or chilled. Using a blender to puree the soup results in a smoother texture than using a food processor.

1½ lb	slender asparagus	750 g
1 tbsp	melted butter	15 mL
4 cups	chicken stock	1 L
1 cup	chopped onion (1 medium)	250 mL
	Salt and black pepper	
2 oz	goat cheese	50 g
1 tbsp	snipped fresh chives	15 mL

Preheat oven to 400°F (200°C).

Trim woody ends from asparagus by snapping each stalk where it breaks naturally. Rinse under cold running water; drain well. Spread asparagus out more or less in a single layer (it doesn't matter if it overlaps somewhat) on a baking sheet; drizzle evenly with melted butter.

Bake asparagus for 15 to 18 minutes, depending on thickness, turning once or twice with a spatula, until very tender. Remove from oven. Cut off eight of the best-looking tips; reserve for garnish. Roughly chop remaining asparagus.

In medium saucepan, combine chicken stock and onion. Bring to boil over high heat. Reduce heat to medium-low; simmer, covered, for 5 minutes, until onion is tender. Add asparagus.

In blender, puree soup in batches until fairly smooth. If serving hot, return to rinsed-out saucepan; heat over medium-high heat until simmering. Season with salt and pepper to taste. To serve chilled, refrigerate, covered, until chilled. Season with salt and pepper to taste.

In small bowl, combine goat cheese and chives. To serve, ladle soup into 4 individual soup bowls; place a spoonful of goat-cheese mixture in centre of each bowl. Top each portion of goat cheese with two reserved asparagus tips.

*H*ome economist and cooking school owner Elaine Duffy has married her love of great wine and great food by founding a regional cuisine touring company. Few people have such an understanding of local ingredients or have greater access to them. The Niagara region is her culinary playground. She guides her clients to a variety of places as diversified as the region itself—an orchard that dries its own fruit, a winery and its restaurant, an ostrich farm or a nut farm.

Makes **6 to 8 servings**

Preparation time: **20 minutes**

Cooking time: **25 to 30 minutes**

$\mathcal{E}$very Thursday vendors from all around the region set up their wares at the Simcoe Farmers' Market. It's a jewel! Local produce is heaped onto the tables. The region is known as "the horn of plenty," and it's obvious why. Vendors sell melons of every description, bushels of squash—neatly labelled with cooking instructions on each—organic blackberries, paper dragon hot peppers, high bush blueberries, baskets of newly dug potatoes, garlic, smoked fish and Jensen's cheeses, buttery Dutch pastries and crusty Portuguese breads. And we can't forget the apples, peaches, pears, apricots, grapes . . . !

VELVETY BUTTERNUT SQUASH SOUP

Butternut squash may be replaced by hubbard or acorn, or the one with the best name of all, sweet mama! Ontario peanuts are a new crop in this province, taking the place of many fields of tobacco. They are fresh-tasting and, although not widely available, Picard's has an outlet near Simcoe, which stocks a wide assortment of different peanut products.

1 tbsp	butter	15 mL
2	large onions, chopped	2
2	cloves garlic, minced	2
1 tsp	curry powder	5 mL
6 cups	peeled and cubed squash (1 small butternut)	1.5 L
2½ cups	chicken or vegetable stock	625 mL
1½ cups	milk or half-and-half cream	375 mL
¼ cup	chopped fresh parsley Salt and black pepper	50 mL
¼ cup	sour cream	50 mL
¼ cup	chopped roasted unsalted peanuts (skins on)	50 mL

In large saucepan, melt butter over medium heat. Add onions and garlic; cook, stirring, for 3 to 5 minutes, until softened. Add curry powder; cook, stirring, for 30 seconds. Add squash and stock; bring to a boil over high heat. Reduce heat to medium-low; simmer, covered, for 15 to 20 minutes, until squash is tender.

Remove saucepan from heat; stir in milk. Let cool slightly.

In blender, puree soup in batches until smooth. Return soup to rinsed-out saucepan; heat over medium-high heat (do not boil). Stir in parsley; add salt and pepper to taste. Ladle soup into heated soup bowls. Garnish each serving with a spoonful of sour cream and a sprinkling of peanuts.

*W*hen summer ripens into autumn, the International Plowing Match and Farm Machinery Show sets up its massive tent city and turns the region it has chosen to be that year's venue into the largest, most colourful outdoor agricultural and country living show in the nation. Huge displays range from antique farm machinery to the latest in conservation; from sheep shearing to a myriad of country household arts like quilting; from Charolais cattle to ostrich. Foods reflect the autumnal harvest. The spacious roadways that line the displays are filled with the aromas of barbecued meat and frying potatoes. You can taste this season's apple butter and buttery corn on the cob. Ongoing food demonstrations in the life-styles tent run the culinary gamut from whole-grain bread baking to celebrity cooking demos with some of the province's best-known personalities. The IPM is an authentic, joyous rural Ontario celebration!

Makes **4 to 6 servings**

Preparation time: **20 minutes**

Cooking time: **12 to 17 minutes**

$\mathcal{S}$uccess stories in Ontario agriculture are legion. New varieties, better farming practices, higher yields, they all hark back to one critical component, research and development. The Ontario Ministry of Agriculture, Food and Rural Affairs OMAFRA) Simcoe Horticultural Research Station has been instrumental in much of what has happened in the past two decades. In the sandy soils of Norfolk County, crops are tested for adaptability to the rigours of southern Ontario's climate and for specific qualities that will allow them to be more widely used by processors. "We can grow anything," says Dr. Arthur Loughton, former director of the station. And they do. Eighty-nine varieties of corn, twenty-one of Spanish onions, ten varieties of sweet potatoes, including one with purple skin and golden flesh. There are peppers coloured from black to yellow, and dozens upon dozens of apple trees being tested in every imaginable way.

MARINATED SUMMER VEGETABLES WITH MINT

This colourful make-ahead salad combines fresh summer vegetables with fresh mint; it goes well with any barbecued meat or fish.

2	ears corn, shucked	2
2 cups	sugar-snap peas (about ½ lb/250 g), trimmed	500 mL
1 cup	sliced zucchini (1 medium)	250 mL
1 cup	thinly sliced carrot (1 large)	250 mL
¼ cup	canola or corn oil	50 mL
2 tbsp	chopped fresh mint	25 mL
2 tbsp	cider vinegar	25 mL
	Salt and black pepper	

In large pot of boiling water, cook corn for 10 to 15 minutes or until tender. Remove from pot. When cool enough to handle, run a knife down ears of corn to remove kernels. Place kernels in large serving bowl.

Bring pot of boiling water back to boil; add sugar-snap peas, carrot and zucchini. Cook for 2 minutes. Drain vegetables well; add to corn in serving bowl.

Drizzle oil over vegetables; sprinkle with mint, cider vinegar, and salt and pepper to taste. Toss well; serve at room temperature. Recipe can be prepared ahead; refrigerate, covered, up to 24 hours. Bring to room temperature, then toss well before serving.

RAINBOW-PEPPER SALAD

A combination of green, red and yellow peppers makes this salad really pretty. The peppers are broiled to bring out their sweet, subtle flavour, but you can also prepare them on the barbecue; grill them over medium heat for 15 to 20 minutes, turning often.

1	each sweet red, green and yellow pepper	1
2 tbsp	canola or corn oil	25 mL
1 tbsp	cider vinegar	15 mL
½ tsp	each granulated sugar and finely minced hot pepper	2 mL
Pinch	salt	Pinch
2 tbsp	shredded fresh basil leaves	25 mL

Preheat broiler to high. Broil peppers 2 inch (5 cm) from broiler (place baking sheet on lower shelf to catch any drips), for 20 to 30 minutes, turning often, until skins are blackened all over. Place peppers in brown paper or plastic bag; let stand for at least 10 minutes or until cool enough to handle.

Carefully peel off skin from peppers. Cut peppers in half; discard seeds, stems and any thick membrane from insides. Cut peppers into ½-inch (1 cm) wide strips; arrange on serving platter.

In small bowl, whisk together oil, vinegar, sugar, hot pepper and salt, until sugar has dissolved. Pour dressing over peppers; sprinkle evenly with basil leaves. Serve at room temperature.

Serves **4 to 6**

Preparation time: **20 minutes**

Cooking time: **15 to 20 minutes**

Standing time: **10 minutes**

*T*he menu is a page out of a field naturalist's checklist: mulled sumac, maple wine, cattail hearts, elk with black currant sauce and glazed wild leeks, Jerusalem artichoke chowder, Muskoka cranberry bread, wild ginger tart. Every year, in late September, the Royal Botanical Gardens (RBG) in Hamilton holds this fund-raising Botanical Buffet. Jack Lord, lecturer, master forager and the RBG's Manager of Education Programs, leads diners through the evening meal from wild mushroom canapés to spice bush tea.

The RBG, located on the northern outskirts of Hamilton, is one of the largest botanical gardens in North America, with 2,700 acres of formal gardens, natural protected areas and wetlands. There are thirty miles of hiking trails, many of which are self-guided explorations of the magnificent flora that has been collected from all over the world or from the forests of southern Ontario. Check out the Herbe Faire in late August, where you can register for a herb-related course, buy some plants and watch a herbal cooking demonstration.

Handle all hot peppers with care. Always wear plastic or rubber gloves, and never touch your face with your hands while you prepare them.

Makes **4 servings**

Preparation time: **20 minutes**

Marinating time: **at least 1 hour**

Cooking time: **10 to 12 minutes**

About a kilometre south of Vittoria is Kernal Peanuts, the peanut farm, processing plant and sales room of Ernie and Nancy Racz. There is no comparison between just-roasted, Ontario-grown peanuts and the musty, less-than-fresh variety sold in most stores. Actually legumes, peanuts need well-drained sandy soil and lots of heat units. Norfolk County provides both. On the 160-acre Racz farm, the small Valencia-style nuts are harvested using a Canadian-designed machine. After a thorough scrub, the whole nuts are kiln-dried for five days before sizing and shelling. Then they are roasted and seasoned in a myriad of ways (salted/with garlic/with hot spices); ground, with the skins on for extra dietary fibre, into peanut butter; or made into Nancy's fabulous peanut brittle and chocolate-coated peanut crisp. All the shells are composted, and the smallest peanuts are sold for birdseed. To watch the harvest you'll have to be there in mid-September to late October, but to sample and taste, the small store is open seven days a week: Monday through Friday 9 a.m. to 5 p.m.; Saturday 10 a.m. to 5 p.m. and Sunday 1 to 5 p.m. Factory tours can be arranged if you call in advance.

JUMP-FRIED CHICKEN WITH SUMMER VEGETABLES AND SIMCOE PEANUTS

Lemon thyme is a great substitute for fresh lemons. It's easy to grow, needs little attention and spreads like wildfire. If you don't have lemon thyme in your garden, substitute 2 tbsp (25 mL) regular thyme leaves plus the juice of half a lemon in this tasty stir-fry.

1 lb	boneless, skinless chicken breasts, cut into ½-inch (1 cm) strips	500 g
3 tbsp	cider vinegar	45 mL
½ tsp	freshly ground black pepper	2 mL
2 tbsp	peanut oil	25 mL
3 cups	broccoli florets and chopped stems	750 mL
½ lb	baby carrots, halved lengthwise, or 2 cups (500 mL) thinly sliced carrots	250 g
¼ cup	water	50 mL
3	green onions, cut diagonally into 1-inch (2.5 cm) pieces	3
2 tbsp	fresh lemon thyme leaves	25 mL
1 tsp	cornstarch	5 mL
2 tbsp	light soy sauce	25 mL
⅓ cup	roasted unsalted Ontario peanuts	75 mL

In shallow nonmetallic dish, combine chicken, cider vinegar and pepper; refrigerate, covered, at least 1 hour or up to 8 hours.

With slotted spoon, remove chicken from cider vinegar; discard vinegar. Heat wok or very large skillet over high heat. Add 1 tbsp (15 mL) oil; heat over high heat. Add chicken to wok; stir-fry for 4 to 5 minutes or until chicken is no longer pink inside. Remove chicken from wok; set aside. Wipe out wok with paper towels.

Heat wok over high heat. Add remaining 1 tbsp (15 mL) oil to wok; heat over high heat. Add broccoli and carrots; stir-fry for 30 seconds. Add water; cover wok. Reduce heat to medium; cook for 4 to 5 minutes, until vegetables are tender-crisp. Stir chicken, green onions and lemon thyme into vegetables.

In small bowl, stir cornstarch into soy sauce until smooth. Add cornstarch mixture to wok; cook for 1 to 2 minutes, stirring constantly, until sauce is thickened and bubbly. Stir in peanuts; serve at once over steamed or boiled rice.

*J*ust around the corner from the Racz peanut farm is The Cider Keg, a small, family-run business on Highway 24 that makes and sells superb sparkling and sweet apple ciders, blends of Tolman Sweets and Russets from their own orchards. But for us, the most interesting find was the locally pickled Norfolk County asparagus. Fabulous!

Makes **4 servings**

Preparation time: **20 minutes**

Cooking time: **12 to 14 minutes**

*T*he Bosc family's château, a magnificent structure set into the vineyards sweeping up to the escarpment's southern expanse, is the showplace of Niagara. Their chardonnays and *méthode champenoise* sparkling wines are exceptional.

Stonechurch Vineyards, one of the newcomers in the Lower Niagara, came into the limelight by winning Ontario a Grand Gold at VinItaly for their 1991 Icewine. Nearby are the perfectly groomed vineyards of Herbert Konzelmann. Little wonder his wine-competition medals are of the highest order: a Grand Gold at VinItaly and three golds at InterVin in 1993.

LAMB KEBABS WITH FRESH PEACH MINT SAUCE

This is a great way to use up a few slightly overripe peaches. Pork works very well in this recipe, but we love the old-fashioned combination of lamb and mint. The peach sauce can be prepared up to one day ahead, covered and refrigerated, but don't add the fresh mint to the sauce until shortly before serving.

Lamb:

½ cup	dry white wine	125 mL
¼ cup	chopped fresh mint	50 mL
2 tbsp	canola or corn oil	25 mL
1	clove garlic, minced	1
½ tsp	black pepper	2 mL
1½ lb	boneless Ontario lamb, trimmed of excess fat and cut into 1-inch (2.5 cm) pieces	750 g

Fresh Peach Mint Sauce:

1 tbsp	butter	15 mL
1½ cups	peeled, pitted and sliced peaches (about 3 medium)	375 mL
1	clove garlic, minced	1
2 tbsp	chopped fresh mint	25 mL
1 tbsp	honey	15 mL

Lamb: In shallow nonmetallic dish, whisk together wine, mint, oil, garlic and pepper. Add lamb, stirring to coat with marinade. Refrigerate, covered, at least 8 hours or overnight, stirring occasionally. Remove lamb from fridge 30 minutes before cooking.

Preheat barbecue to medium-high. Remove lamb from marinade; discard marinade. Thread lamb onto 4 metal skewers, dividing evenly. Place on oiled barbecue grill; grill for 6 to 8 minutes, turning often, for medium-rare. Serve kebabs with Fresh Peach Mint Sauce.

Fresh Peach Mint Sauce: In small skillet, melt butter over medium heat. Add peaches and garlic; cook for 5 minutes, stirring often, until garlic is softened and peaches start to disintegrate. Remove from heat; let cool slightly.

In food processor, process peach mixture until smooth. Spoon into small bowl; stir in mint. Add honey 1 tsp (5 mL) at a time, tasting as you go, until sauce has a sweet-tart flavour.

*I*t takes a sheet of legal-size paper with single-spaced typing to list all the apple varieties at Pomona Orchards near Rockton. They begin with Amasia and end with Zuccalmaglio's Reinette. From very early in the summer, tables are set up in the shed and, as they ripen, apples are arranged on them in baskets, ready for appreciative tasters. The Jansons are usually on site to give a running commentary on each apple's personal pedigree. For gardeners especially, Pomona is a find. Their book exchange deals with pomology and horticulture. There are out-of-print books and reference volumes available for sale. If you plan on visiting them, allow yourself ample time to both taste and buy.

To peel peaches, bring a saucepan of water to the boil. Add peaches; bring back to boil. Boil 1 minute. Remove peaches with slotted spoon; place immediately in bowl of cold water. When peaches are cool enough to handle, skins should slip off easily.

Makes **6 servings**

Preparation time: **25 minutes**

Cooking time: **1¼ hours**

*T*he Old Gun Club Pheasantry in Simcoe has a huge array of game birds. Guinea fowl or *pintade,* a pretty black bird with white polka dots, are meatier than pheasant. Owners Howard and Mary Richmond also raise ring-necked pheasant, rock Cornish hens and quail, which are prized for their tiny mottled eggs. Every Saturday, the Richmonds travel to Toronto's St. Lawrence Market to set up their stall, where they also sell other regional delicacies, from shiitake mushrooms to frozen Simcoe sour cherries.

ROAST PHEASANT WITH SPICED SOUR CHERRY SAUCE

If you always thought roast pheasant to be rather dry, you'll be pleasantly surprised by our version. The flesh stays beautifully moist and the spicy-sweet sauce is the perfect accompaniment. This is a great impress-your-dinner-guests dish! If sour cherries aren't available, the Prizewinning Rosemary Apple Cider Jelly on page 114 also goes well with the pheasant.

Pheasant:

2	pheasants (3 lb/1.5 kg each)	2
1	small onion, quartered	1
1	apple, quartered	1
2	bay leaves	2
2 tbsp	softened butter	25 mL
½ tsp	each salt and black pepper	2 mL
6	slices bacon	6

Spiced Sour Cherry Sauce:

2 cups	sour cherries, drained	500 mL
½ cup	red wine	125 mL
¼ cup	packed brown sugar	50 mL
4	whole cloves	4
2	¼-inch (5 mm) slices fresh gingerroot	2
1	2-inch (5 cm) cinnamon stick	1
1 tbsp	cornstarch	15 mL

Pheasant: Preheat oven to 400°F (200°C). Pat pheasants dry with paper towels. Place 2 onion quarters, 2 apple quarters and a bay leaf in cavity of each pheasant. Place pheasants on rack in shallow roasting pan. Smear butter evenly over each pheasant; sprinkle with salt and pepper. Cut bacon slices in half crosswise; arrange, overlapping slightly, over breast and legs of each pheasant.

Roast for 1 hour or until internal temperature registers 185°F (85°C). Remove pheasants to board; cover loosely with foil and let stand for 10 minutes before carving. Discard bacon; carve pheasants as you would chicken. Serve with Spiced Sour Cherry Sauce.

Spiced Sour Cherry Sauce: In small saucepan, combine sour cherries, all but 1 tbsp (15 mL) of red wine, sugar, cloves, gingerroot and cinnamon stick; bring to boil over high heat. Reduce heat to low; simmer, covered, for 10 minutes for flavours to blend.

In small bowl, combine cornstarch with remaining red wine. Stir cornstarch mixture into sour-cherry mixture; simmer, stirring constantly, for 2 to 3 minutes, until sauce bubbles and has thickened slightly. With fork, fish out and discard cloves, gingerroot and cinnamon stick. Spoon sauce into serving bowl; serve with pheasant.

*S*tokes Seeds in St. Catharines was originally an American company. The company fell upon hard times during the Great Depression, and their young salesman, W.H. Gale, whose territory was "all of Canada," snapped it up for $4,000 and brought it north. Since then, research and diversification have created a huge, multinational company that specializes in supplying market gardeners and commercial greenhouse operations across Canada and the northeastern United States. The most interesting part of their operation is the company farm on Lakeshore Road between Fifth and Seventh Streets. Thousands of annuals are grown there for their own tests as well as for the All-America Trials. Visitors are most welcome during July and August from 8 a.m. to 4:30 p.m. The seed store on James Street is open year round, Monday through Saturday.

*Makes **4** servings*

Preparation time: **15 minutes**

Cooking time: **8 to 10 minutes**

*T*here is no doubt that Niagara's
Cuvée is one of the most prestigious
wine events in Canada. It is held yearly
in early March when the winemakers
gather to give their blessings and award
medals to the previous year's finest.
Accompanied by Cuvée en Route, a
specially orchestrated series of private,
educationally oriented tastings on site at
the wineries, the weekend is one glorious celebration of Ontario's excellence
in the art of winemaking.

*O*ntario's wine industry has made
monumental strides in the past decade.
Scores of medals now hang proudly in
winery showrooms. Much of this international success is directly attributable
to a group of committed visionaries led
by Donald Ziraldo and Karl Kaiser, the
founders of Inniskillin Wines; Peter
Gamble, Executive Director of the
Vintners' Quality Alliance (VQA); and
Len Pennachetti, the current chair of the
VQA. With the establishment of the
VQA in 1988, it finally became possible
for consumers to identify wines that are
Ontario grown, and even the specific
region in which they are produced.

SHORTHILL'S TROUT BAKED WITH RIESLING, RED ONION AND THYME

*Three years ago, Ontario's first winery restaurant
opened at Cave Spring Cellars in Jordan. On The
Twenty, named for nearby Twenty-Mile Creek, specializes in dishes that use locally grown ingredients,
such as this outstanding trout recipe. Chef Michael
Olson proudly claims that all the ingredients for the
recipe come from within a ten-minute drive of the
restaurant, including the trout, which Michael buys
from nearby Shorthill's Trout Farm. Baking fish in
parchment paper helps to seal in the flavours and
juices and also looks quite dramatic. After cooking,
place each package on a dinner plate and have your
guests cut them open at the table. If you prefer, the
fish can be baked in aluminum foil.*

4	6- to 8-oz (175 to 250 g) trout fillets	4
	Salt and black pepper	
1	small red onion, sliced	1
8	sprigs fresh thyme	8
½ cup	Riesling, such as Cave Spring Cellars	125 mL
1 tbsp	butter	15 mL

Preheat oven to 375°F (190°C). Cut four 14-inch
(35 cm) squares of parchment paper or aluminum
foil. Fold each in half diagonally; unfold paper.
Place trout fillet on one half of each piece of paper;
sprinkle lightly with salt and pepper. Divide onion
slices among trout fillets; place 2 thyme sprigs on
each fillet. Drizzle wine evenly over each fillet; dot
evenly with butter.

Fold paper over to enclose each trout fillet.
Double-fold the edges of each package, twisting
and crimping edges to seal package completely.

Place packages on baking sheets. Bake for 8 to 10 minutes, until packages puff up with steam and fish flakes easily with a fork (open your package to check fish). Place a package on each of four dinner plates; open packages at the table. Serve with rice and vegetables.

*T*he VQA recognizes three distinct viticultural areas: Niagara Peninsula, Pelee Island and Lake Erie North Shore. The VQA represents a wide range of professions within the wine industry, from researchers and growers to academics and government. An independent panel of experts evaluates every wine presented for designation. The VQA sticker on any bottle of wine sold anywhere in the world guarantees that:

- only vitis vinifera and French hybrids such as Chardonnay, Riesling, Vidal and Baco Noir have been used;
- the wine in the bottle has been produced with one-hundred-percent Ontario-grown grapes;
- for varietals, eighty-five percent of the wine is made with the variety named on the label and must exhibit the predominant characteristic of that particular variety; if a vineyard is designated on the label, the site must be within a recognized viticultural region and one-hundred percent of the grapes must be from that vineyard;
- "estate-bottled"wines must be made with grapes one-hundred percent owned or controlled by the winery in a specific viticultural area, and the grapes must reach a specified level of ripeness.

Makes **6 servings**

Preparation time: **25 minutes**

Cooking time: **55 to 65 minutes**

*M*ike Columbus is the deputy mayor of the Township of Delhi. He also happens to be the Crop Innovation Advisor at the Simcoe Office of the Ontario Ministry of Agriculture, Food and Rural Affairs (OMAFRA) and is one of the most interesting men we've met. There's not a farmer in Norfolk County who doesn't know Mike on a first-name basis. Wandering through the Simcoe Farmers' Market with him took ages because everyone wanted to chat. Mike's a mover and shaker, encouraging growers and coaching them through the trials of establishing alternative crops like ginseng, sweet potatoes and peanuts. With great common sense, he advises on new methods of adding value to their crops and has put together a directory of Haldimand–Norfolk farm products, including where and how to find them.

SPAGHETTI SQUASH SMOTHERED IN CHEESE SAUCE

Jensen Cheddar cheese has been recognized for its quality since the founder of the company began selling cheese from the trunk of his Model T in the 1920s. Today the cheese is manufactured at the Jensen plant near Belleville, but the head office is still in Simcoe. Use a medium Cheddar in this scrumptious vegetable dish so as not to mask the flavour of the vegetables.

1	spaghetti squash (about 3 lbs/1.5 kg)	1
2 tbsp	canola or corn oil	25 mL
2	stalks celery, chopped	2
1	small sweet red pepper, seeded and finely chopped	1
1	small onion, chopped	1
2	cloves garlic, minced	2
2 cups	chopped mixed vegetables (such as snow peas, broccoli, green beans and/or mushrooms)	500 mL
2 tsp	minced fresh marjoram or thyme leaves or ½ tsp (2 mL) dried	10 mL
¼ tsp	each salt and black pepper	1 mL
¼ cup	whipping cream	50 mL
2 cups	shredded medium Cheddar cheese (½ lb/250 g)	500 mL
2 tbsp	bread crumbs	25 mL
¼ cup	chopped hazelnuts	50 mL

Preheat oven to 350°F (180°C). Cut squash in half lengthwise; place cut-side down on baking sheet. Bake for 25 to 30 minutes or until tender. Alternatively, pierce whole squash in several places with a fork. Place on paper towel; microwave on High (100%) for 10 minutes, turning over halfway through cooking time. Then cut squash in half lengthwise; microwave, covered, on High (100%) for 7 to 9 minutes, until tender, rotating twice. Let stand for 10 minutes.

In large skillet, heat oil over medium-high heat. Add celery, red pepper, onion and garlic; cook, stirring, for 3 to 5 minutes, until onion is soft but not brown. Stir in mixed vegetables, marjoram, salt and pepper. Cook, stirring, for 3 to 5 minutes or until vegetables are tender-crisp; set aside.

Preheat oven to 350°F (180°C). Scoop out and discard seeds from squash. With a fork, remove spaghetti-like strands from squash and place in a large bowl. Add cooked vegetables; toss well. Season with salt and pepper to taste.

Spoon mixture into a deep 10-inch (25 cm) pie plate. Pour whipping cream evenly over vegetables; sprinkle evenly with cheese, bread crumbs and hazelnuts. Bake for 20 to 25 minutes or until topping is golden and bubbly.

*T*o combine a great day of cycling and a wonderful feast of Lake Erie perch, park your car in Simcoe and bike along the twelve-kilometre Lynn Valley Trail to Port Dover along the abandoned but refurbished railway line to the old Erie Beach Hotel.

Makes **one 9-in (23 cm) square cake; 8 to 10 servings**

Preparation time: **25 minutes**

Cooking time: **about 50 minutes**

*I*cewine—no grape harvest in the world could be colder than this. Winemakers wait until the winter temperatures dip to well below freezing. Then, in the middle of the night, dressed in thermal layers and carrying clippers, they head to the vineyards where the grapes hang in hard, frozen clusters. All night long pickers clip Vidal and Riesling grapes that have been dried and sweetened by months on the vine. Pressing occurs immediately, and the precious golden drops are collected and vinified with due respect.

Canada is the world's largest producer of this magical wine, a wine that tastes of apricots and honey and late autumn sunshine.

It is appropriate that it was an icewine, Inniskillin's 1989 Vidal, that brought Canada its first serious medal in world wine competition: the Grand Prix d'Honneur at VinExpo in Bordeaux. In 1994 Stonechurch's Vidal Icewine won another Grand Gold, this time at VinItaly in Verona, another of the world's great competitions.

It's a risky venture for growers to leave acres unpicked. They may be picked clean by ingenious birds adept at avoiding nets or become subject to noble rot, *Botrytis cinerea*, which pierces the skin, allowing the juice to evaporate prematurely. However, Ontario's vintners have a serious competitive edge that works in their favour year after frosty year: Ontario always, always, always has winter, and plunging temperatures provide the potential for some of the finest and most exotic wines in the world. It truly is liquid gold in a crystal glass.

UPSIDE-DOWN HAZELNUT-APRICOT CAKE

Apricots and hazelnuts thrive in the more temperate regions of Ontario and team up in this recipe as the topping for an easy cake that was created for us by recipe tester Carolyn Gall. Served warm with ice cream or softly whipped cream, it's special enough for company.

Apricot Layer:

¼ cup	butter	50 mL
¾ cup	packed brown sugar	175 mL
½ cup	toasted chopped hazelnuts	125 mL
16	fresh apricots, peeled, pitted and cut in half	16

Cake:

¾ cup	granulated sugar	175 mL
½ cup	softened butter	125 mL
2	eggs	2
1 tsp	vanilla	5 mL
1½ cups	all-purpose flour	375 mL
2 tsp	baking powder	10 mL
1 tsp	baking soda	5 mL
¼ tsp	salt	1 mL
1 cup	sour cream	250 mL
¼ cup	milk	50 mL

Apricot Layer: Preheat oven to 350°F (180°C). Place butter in 9-inch (2.5 L) square cake pan; place in oven for 2 minutes or until butter melts. Remove pan from oven; sprinkle sugar and hazelnuts evenly over bottom of pan. Arrange apricots cut sides down in pan; set aside.

Cake: In large bowl, cream sugar and butter until light and fluffy. Beat in eggs one at a time, beating well after each addition. Beat in vanilla.

In medium bowl, stir together flour, baking powder, baking soda and salt. Beat flour mixture into sugar mixture alternately with sour cream until well combined. Beat in milk.

Spoon batter evenly over apricots to cover completely, smoothing batter to edges of pan. Bake for 40 to 50 minutes, until toothpick inserted into centre of cake comes out clean. Let cool in pan on wire rack for 15 minutes. Turn out cake onto serving plate; serve warm.

Anita reminisces, "My first memory of Women's Institutes being mentioned was hearing loving remarks about how my grandmother was a great Institute worker. It seemed as high a mark of respect as any woman could have had at that time. Then, later, when I was beginning to cook and when my mother wanted to pickle or can anything from our small market garden in the countryside north of Toronto, she'd turn to the well-worn Women's Institute cookbooks, soft-sided and small and always spattered with beet juice, black currant jam or something tomato. Although neither my mother nor I were ever members, we benefited immensely from the culinary knowledge that was so liberally shared. It was only later that I learned the prime mandate for the WI was education, particularly as it related to women and issues affecting women."

Founded officially in Stoney Creek, Ontario, in 1877 by Adelaide Hoodless, the Women's Institute quickly spread across Canada. Today there any many thousands of members from coast to coast to coast.

To toast hazelnuts, preheat oven to 350°F (180°C). Spread hazelnuts on ungreased baking sheet; bake for 5 to 7 minutes, until skins are dark brown and nuts are fragrant. Remove nuts from oven; wrap in clean tea towel. Let cool for 5 minutes, then rub vigorously in towel to remove loose skins.

Makes **6 to 8 servings**

Preparation time: **20 minutes**

Cooking time: **45 to 55 minutes**

*I*n Port Dover, Lynne Van Wyck has been called the presiding priestess of all things related to ginger. Lynne, with her family, holds court in a seventeen-room Victorian home, The Gingerbread House, in which she began selling antiques a number of years ago. A superb baker, she tempted her customers with ginger cookies, and the rest is history. To the bakery, in which she sells four kinds of ginger squares, twelve varieties of ginger cookies, ginger muffins and the inevitable ginger people, she has added a tea room—she does international tea tastings—and finally a full-service restaurant, where she concentrates on serving the best local ingredients she can find. Ontario smoked duck breast may be topped with a dried cherry sauce; there are pork and bison from the region, as well as all the seasonal vegetables Lynne can harvest from local farms.

PEAR AND CANDIED GINGER TART WITH ALMOND CRUST

Kate Greenland of Compton and Greenland Fine Foods and Catering prepared this fabulous tart for a fund-raiser for the Royal Botanical Gardens in Hamilton in 1995. Called "a party on the wild side," the evening had a menu that featured dishes made from local wild foods, such as artichoke chowder, cattail casserole and glazed wild leeks. Wild ginger grows throughout the southern part of eastern Canada in shaded deciduous woodlands. Its kidney-shaped, fuzzy leaves grow in pairs, and in the summer the plant sports an unusual brownish-maroon flower. Although wild ginger is not botanically related to the gingerroot we buy in supermarkets, it is similar in appearance and has a flavour that's a combination of ginger and cloves. Our adaptation of Kate's recipe uses preserved ginger in syrup, which is available in jars in specialty food stores and at bulk food stores.

Base:

1 cup	all-purpose flour	250 mL
½ cup	unsalted butter	125 mL
⅓ cup	granulated sugar	75 mL
¼ cup	sliced almonds	50 mL

Filling:

¼ lb	cream cheese (half a 250 g pkg)	125 g
½ cup	granulated sugar	125 mL
2	eggs	2
½ cup	table cream	125 mL
¼ cup	preserved ginger syrup (drained from preserved ginger)	50 mL
2 tbsp	finely chopped preserved ginger	25 mL
½ tsp	vanilla	2 mL
3	ripe pears, peeled, cored and sliced	3

Base: Preheat oven to 400°F (200°C). In food processor, combine flour, butter, sugar and almonds. Process, using on/off pulses, until mixture is well combined and resembles coarse crumbs. Turn mixture into 10-inch (25 cm) tart pan with a removable base; press evenly over base and up sides of pan. Bake for 15 minutes until pale golden; set aside. Reduce oven temperature to 350°F (180°C).

Filling: In medium bowl, beat cream cheese until smooth; beat in sugar until well combined. Beat in eggs one at a time, beating well after each addition. Stir in cream, ginger syrup, preserved ginger and vanilla. Arrange pear slices neatly in tart pan; pour cream-cheese mixture evenly over pears. Place pie on baking sheet; bake for 30 to 40 minutes or until pears are tender and filling is golden.

*P*aron Cheese is an artisanal cheese manufacturer on the Niagara Escarpment near Hamilton. The village of Hannon, although that's Paron's address, isn't even on our map. In 1955 Louis Paron took over from his father, who had been making cheese since the 1930s. Today, although he distributes across Canada, aficionados have to travel up over Hamilton mountain to buy his black-encrusted Parmesan, a magnificent cheese and one that has claimed many Canadian prizes, triumphing over all other cheeses from all categories many times. Medals hang around the tiny ultra-clean store that doubles as a packing room and sales office. Paron Cheese is a must for anyone who loves cheese!

Makes **16 squares**

Preparation time: **20 minutes**

Cooking time: **35 to 40 minutes**

*T*here is a distinct possibility that, in not too many years, Ontario will be the home of a healthy tree-nut industry. Most growers, who could be best characterized as infinitely patient people, advertise locally, and their crops sell out as soon as they have finished harvesting. In fact there are waiting lists for many varieties. What is truly astounding is the variety of nuts our climate will sustain. On one farm near Wainfleet, there are six varieties of pine nuts alone. Edible sweet chestnuts, sweet kernel apricots, hazelnuts, heart nuts and shellbark hickory, all are reaching maturity, as are northern pecans, almonds and walnuts.

NIAGARA NUT AND MAPLE SQUARES

Choose any variety of locally grown nuts—hazel, heart, northern pecan, black walnut or hickory—for these yummy squares. Shell them, then use whole or chop coarsely if you prefer.

Base:

1 cup	all-purpose flour	250 mL
¼ cup	packed brown sugar	50 mL
½ cup	softened butter	125 mL

Topping:

1 cup	maple syrup	250 mL
⅔ cup	packed brown sugar	150 mL
2	eggs, beaten	2
2 tbsp	all-purpose flour	25 mL
½ tsp	vanilla	2 mL
1 cup	nuts	250 mL

Base: Preheat oven to 350°F (180°C). In small bowl using a fork, stir together flour, sugar and butter until well combined and crumbly. Pat firmly into 9-inch (2.5 L) square pan. Bake for 5 minutes; set side. Increase oven temperature to 425°F (220°C).

Topping: In small saucepan, combine maple syrup and sugar. Cook over medium heat for 5 minutes, stirring occasionally, until sugar has dissolved. Remove from heat; let cool 10 minutes. Whisk in eggs, flour and vanilla until mixture is smooth; stir in nuts. Pour topping evenly over base; bake for 10 minutes. Reduce temperature to 350°F (180°C); bake for 15 minutes, or until firm. Let cool slightly before cutting into squares. Let cool completely in pan.

NIAGARA WINE-BERRY SAUCE

Make this sauce with one of Ontario's lusty VQA red wines, such as Maréchal Foch or Baco Noir. If you like, fold additional raspberries, Tay berries, blackberries or lightly sweetened sour cherries, sliced ripe peaches, apricots or nectarines into the sauce just before serving, or strew the fruit around each serving. We love this sauce poured over cheesecake, angel food cake or ice cream.

4 cups	fresh or frozen and thawed unsweetened raspberries (about 1 lb/500 g)	1 L
1	bottle (750 mL) red wine	1
1¼ cups	granulated sugar	300 mL

In large skillet, combine berries, wine and sugar; bring to boil over high heat. Reduce temperature to medium-high; simmer, uncovered, for 25 to 30 minutes, stirring occasionally during the final 15 minutes, until sauce is reduced to about 2½ cups (625 mL). Rub sauce through fine sieve to remove seeds. Refrigerate, covered, up to 5 days.

Makes **2 cups (500 mL)**

Preparation time: **15 minutes**

Cooking time: **30 to 35 minutes**

*F*ounded on the solid base of Loyalist ancestry, the E.D. Smith family's history parallels that of the Niagara region. They arrived after the War of Independence, barely survived, then fought in the War of 1812. The family went on to found a fruit-processing company specializing in jam so pure that the federal department of agriculture uses the Smith standard as its base measure. Now, well into its fourth generation of family ownership, the company employs some men and women whose great-grandparents worked for the founder, E.D. Smith. The company's products, E.D. Smith Jams & Pie Fillings, HP Sauce, Lea & Perrins sauces, President's Choice sauces, Pizza Pizza pizza sauce, A&P's ketchup and various food service brands, have become the backbone of this enterprise as it faces the twenty-first century. E.D. Smith's stated mission is "to be the best, independent, family-owned food company in North America." Seems they're well on their way—and they're still based in the small Niagara hamlet of Winona.

Makes **8 to 10 servings**

Preparation time: **30 minutes**

Cooking time: **35 to 40 minutes**

$\mathcal{V}$ision Niagara is an earnest attempt to link the region's artisan producers and their superb products with local chefs. Springing out of a new awareness of the merits of dining locally, particularly in such a lush area, Vision Niagara has published a well-documented directory of product resources for food service and retail industries. For a nominal fee they will send you a copy.

PEACH AND RASPBERRY HAZELNUT CRUMBLE

Choose freestone peaches, such as Redhaven or Loring, for this luscious dessert. The recipe comes from Erik Peacock, chef at the Wellington Court Café in St. Catharines. Erik uses stone-ground flour from Spring Creek Milling in Vineland, which gives the dessert an interesting nutty flavour. Most health-food stores stock stone-ground flour; if it's unavailable, substitute regular whole-wheat flour.

Fruit Layer:

8	ripe peaches, peeled, pitted and coarsely chopped	8
4 cups	raspberries (1 lb 6 oz/675 g)	1 L
1 cup	granulated sugar	250 mL
½ cup	stone-ground whole-wheat flour	125 mL

Crumble Topping:

2 cups	stone-ground whole-wheat flour	500 mL
¾ cup	granulated sugar	175 mL
½ cup	cold butter, cubed	125 mL
¼ cup	rolled oats	50 mL
½ cup	chopped toasted hazelnuts	125 mL

Fruit Layer: Preheat oven to 350°F (180°C). In large bowl, combine peaches, raspberries, sugar and flour; toss gently to coat fruit with sugar and flour. Arrange fruit mixture in shallow 13- by 9-inch (3 L) baking dish; set aside.

Crumble Topping: In food processor, combine flour, sugar and butter; process until mixture resembles cornmeal. In medium bowl, combine flour mixture and oats. Sprinkle topping evenly over fruit to cover completely. Sprinkle hazelnuts evenly over topping.

Bake for 35 to 40 minutes, until fruit is bubbly and topping is golden brown. Serve hot or warm with Maple-Whisky Cream (recipe on page 110), softly whipped cream or vanilla ice cream.

*S*toney Ridge Cellars is the quintessential country winery, with a pick-your-own orchard and flowers by the flat. It is situated on the northern extremity of the Beamsville Bench, and winemaker Jim Warren produces delightful albeit limited-edition specialty wines like Crystal, an iced apple dessert wine. Warren has a master's hand with Chardonnay.

To toast hazelnuts, preheat oven to 350°F (180°C). Spread hazelnuts on ungreased baking sheet; bake for 5 to 7 minutes, until skins are dark brown and nuts are fragrant. Remove nuts from oven; wrap in clean tea towel. Let cool for 5 minutes, then rub vigorously in towel to remove loose skins.

Makes **8 servings**

Preparation time: **20 minutes**

Cooking time: **25 to 30 minutes**

Standing time: **15 minutes**

*G*inseng (*Panax Quinquefolium*) is the new kid playing on the agricultural block, at least here in Ontario. It is native to North America and dates its "discovery" back to the Jesuit priests near Lake Huron in the very early 1700s. Its first shipment to China was in 1716. But it wasn't until recently that ginseng was cultivated as a horticultural crop. Ontario's growers had the vision to found the first ginseng growers' association in Canada and also, with the help of Agriculture and Agri-Food Canada, to establish the first ginseng research gardens in Delhi. At this writing there are more than three thousand acres of cloth-shaded ginseng fields in Norfolk County alone. Prized for its exceedingly high quality, Canadian ginseng is harvested in its third year of maturity. The roots are dried and sold at premium prices to the Asian market for herbal medicines, as an aphrodisiac and a restorative tea.

PEACH SHORTCAKE WITH CASSIS

Here's a new twist on a traditional favourite: rich shortcake filled with whipped cream and fresh peaches marinated in Cassis. Serve the rest of the bottle of Cassis as an accompaniment to the shortcake. If you can't find Southbrook Farms Cassis, substitute a fruit-flavoured liqueur in the filling and reduce the sugar to taste. The shortcake is best served while still slightly warm from the oven.

Shortcake:

2 cups	all-purpose flour, sifted	500 mL
2 tbsp	granulated sugar	25 mL
4 tsp	baking powder	20 mL
½ tsp	cinnamon	2 mL
	Pinch salt	
½ cup	cold butter, cut into pieces	125 mL
⅔ cup	cold milk	150 mL
1	egg	1
	A little extra sugar	

Filling:

2 cups	peeled, pitted and sliced peaches (about 4 peaches)	500 mL
3 tbsp	granulated sugar	45 mL
2 tbsp	Southbrook Farms Cassis	25 mL
¾ cup	whipping cream	175 mL

Shortcake: Preheat oven to 425°F (220°C). In medium bowl, stir together flour, sugar, baking powder, cinnamon and salt. With pastry blender or two knives, cut in butter until mixture resembles coarse crumbs with a few pea-size pieces of butter.

In small bowl, beat milk and egg with fork until well combined. Add all at once to flour mixture; stir with fork just until dry ingredients are moistened (do not overmix). Gather dough into ball; turn out onto very lightly floured work surface. Knead lightly 10 or 12 times until dough holds together.

Pat out dough to 8-inch (20 cm) round. Place on lightly buttered baking sheet. Brush with a little of the whipping cream (from filling); sprinkle with a little sugar. With sharp knife, score top of short-cake lightly to make eight even-size wedges (do not cut right through). Bake for 20 to 25 minutes, until golden brown and risen. Let cool on wire rack while you prepare the filling.

Filling: In medium bowl, stir together peaches, 2 tbsp (25 mL) of the sugar and the Cassis. Let stand at room temperature for 15 minutes, stirring occasionally.

In separate bowl, whip cream until stiff peaks form; fold in remaining sugar. Just before serving, carefully split shortcake in half horizontally using a serrated knife. Place bottom layer of shortcake on serving plate; spoon peaches and their juices over shortcake. Spread cream over peaches; cover with top layer of shortcake. Serve cut into wedges.

*D*riving along Highway 3 on the eastern outskirts of Simcoe, it's very easy to miss the entranceway of The Apple Place, a superb little shop specializing in all things apple—fresh apples, apple cider, vinegar, everything you need to bake an apple pie and even cinnamon-sugared apple-cider doughnuts. But there's more to The Apple Place than a retail store. The Apple Place is operated by The Norfolk Fruit Growers Association, the oldest such cooperative in Canada. Their huge (3.5 acre), state-of-the-art fruit storage facility holds, in a year, eighteen to twenty percent of all apples grown in Ontario—or one million bushels—at one time.

Makes **6 servings**

Preparation time: **15 minutes**

Cooking time: **35 to 40 minutes**

*I*n July, pails of chilled, pitted and partially sweetened sour cherries are available in many small-town grocery stores. Their season is so short it's well worth freezing them so you can enjoy a taste of summer later on in the year. To freeze, simply ladle cherries and their juices into plastic containers or large freezer bags in 4-cup (1 L) quantities, then store in the freezer for up to six months. To use them in a pie or as a cheesecake topping, place the contents of one container in a heavy saucepan; heat over medium heat until thawed, breaking apart the frozen fruit. Combine 1 cup (250 mL) granulated sugar and ¼ cup (50 mL) cornstarch; add to cherries. Bring to boil, stirring constantly; simmer for 2 minutes, until thickened and smooth. Remove from heat; cool slightly before using.

SOUR-CHERRY COBBLER

Since cherries, both sweet and sour, have just about the shortest season of any Ontario fruit (it lasts barely a month), we like to enjoy them to the max during July. In pies, muffins, as a topping for cheesecake or ice cream, there's no end to the ways you can use the ruby-red fruit. Here's one of our favourites; it's quick, easy and tastes great!

3 cups	drained pitted sour cherries	750 mL
¼ cup	granulated sugar	50 mL
½ tsp	almond extract	2 mL

Topping:

1 cup	all-purpose flour	250 mL
2 tbsp	granulated sugar	25 mL
2 tsp	baking powder	10 mL
¼ tsp	grated nutmeg	1 mL
Pinch	salt	Pinch
¼ cup	cold butter, cubed	50 mL
½ cup	buttermilk	125 mL

Preheat oven to 375°F (190°C). In 8-inch (2 L) square baking dish, combine cherries, sugar and almond extract; set aside.

Topping: In medium bowl, stir together flour, sugar, baking powder, nutmeg and salt. With pastry blender or two knives, cut in butter until mixture resembles coarse crumbs. Add buttermilk all at once; stir until soft, slightly sticky dough forms. Form dough into 8 even-size pieces; arrange in single layer over cherries (cherries won't be completely covered). Bake for 35 to 40 minutes, until topping is risen and golden brown and cherries are bubbly. Serve at once with softly whipped cream or vanilla ice cream.

SWEET AND SOUR MUSTARD

This mustard is fabulous with barbecued farmer's sausages or whisked into salad dressings. Try it as well in our Mustard-Glazed Ontario Leg of Lamb (recipe on p. 147). Although the mustard may be used immediately, we like to let it rest and mellow for a day or so. If you like, replace the brown sugar with ¾ cup (175 mL) liquid honey, and for best flavour, use Keen's dry mustard.

1 cup	brown sugar	250 mL
½ cup	dry mustard	125 mL
⅓ cup	cider vinegar	75 mL
2	eggs	2
2 tbsp	butter	25 mL

In small heavy saucepan, combine sugar, mustard and cider vinegar until smooth; beat in eggs. Cook over medium heat for 3 to 5 minutes, stirring constantly, until bubbly. Cook for 2 minutes, stirring constantly. Remove from heat; stir in butter until melted. Let cool to room temperature, stirring occasionally. Refrigerate in tightly covered container for up to 2 weeks.

Makes **about 1½ cups (375 mL)**

Preparation time: **10 minutes**

Cooking time: **5 to 7 minutes**

*C*anada is famous all over the world for the quality of our mustard seed. The grains are mainly prairie-grown and shipped to Ontario where G.S. Dunn and Co. in Hamilton grinds them into mustard powder. Anton Kozlik, a St. Catharines manufacturer, blends dry mustard with maple syrup to create what he calls "Canadian mustard," which has a perfect combination of sweet, hot and savoury flavours.

It's impossible to buy dry mustard with any sort of provincial pedigree. However, if you remember that we are a world leader when it comes to mustard production, the chances of a mustard being Canadian-grown and Ontario-ground are very good.

Makes **4 half-pint (250 mL) jars**

Preparation time: **30 minutes**

Cooking time: **about 1 hour**

Processing time: **10 minutes**

*Y*ellow varieties of plum, such as Early Golden, appear in farmers' markets in July and August, while the prune plums, such as Italian and Stanley, are available from August through October. Both yellow and prune plums can be used in this rich chutney, but to make preparation easier, choose freestone varieties such as those mentioned.

*L*arry Kormos is a young entrepreneur with a dream: to grow the sweetest, most delicious onions in the province. On five acres there are rows and rows of golden onions with their tops bent over awaiting the harvest. As a ginseng grower whose crops have to be free of moisture before shipping, Kormos understands how to dry crops, so he built himself an onion dryer. With the help of Mike Columbus at the Simcoe Research Station, he has bins filled and ready to ship under the label of The Incredible Norfolk Onion Company.

SPICED PLUM-RAISIN CHUTNEY

7 cups	pitted and quartered plums (2½ lb/1.25 kg)	1.75 L
3 cups	granulated sugar	750 mL
1½ cups	sultana raisins	375 mL
1½ cups	cider vinegar	375 mL
¾ cup	fresh lemon juice	175 mL
1	medium onion, finely chopped	1
3	large cloves garlic, minced	3
1 tsp	allspice	5 mL
½ tsp	hot pepper flakes	2 mL

In large stainless steel or enamel saucepan, combine plums, sugar, raisins, vinegar, lemon juice, onion, garlic, allspice and hot pepper flakes; cook, stirring, over medium heat until sugar has dissolved. Increase heat to high; bring to boil. Reduce heat to medium-high; simmer, uncovered, for 45 minutes to 1 hour, stirring often and making sure mixture doesn't stick to bottom of pan, until mixture is very thick. Watch carefully towards the end of cooking time; stir thoroughly and reduce temperature if necessary, as the chutney can scorch easily.

Immediately ladle into 4 hot, sterilized ½-pint (250 mL) jars, leaving ½ inch (1 cm) headspace. Wipe jar rims to remove any excess chutney; seal with two-piece lids, tightening screw bands until just fingertip tight. Process in hot-water bath for 10 minutes. Remove jars from canner; let cool for 24 hours. Check jar seals (sealed lids curve downwards). Remove screw bands; label jars. Store chutney in cool, dark place.

Hedgerows filled with wild apples and grapevines, highbush cranberries and chokecherries line the gravel roads.

The Grand River winds from its marshy headwaters in north Wellington and Dufferin counties. Settlement first occurred along its course, and many small hamlets were built around its tumbling waterfalls. Today, rather than milling grain and sawing lumber, the river provides a haven for fisherfolk fly casting for brown trout and northern pike. Canoeing, especially in late spring and early summer, is superb. Kayaking through the faster sections of the river in areas like the Elora Gorge can be downright hair-raising.

The name "Festival Country" says it all. There are dozens upon dozens of celebrations, from an old-fashioned "garden party" in Alma to the rip-roaring Germanic festivities at Kitchener's Oktoberfest.

Festival Country is also where much of the province's weighty agricultural research and education takes place. The University of Guelph oversees every aspect of the food chain from a state-of-the-art aquaculture station to an internationally recognized School of Hotel and Food Administration. The George Morris Centre, founded by Dr. George Morris, a beef farmer from Merlin, Ontario, is devoted to the independent study of agricultural economic policy and issues that affect the national agri-food industry.

Festival Country

Makes **4 servings**

Preparation time: **20 minutes**

Cooking time: **15 to 20 minutes**

*T*he Woodland Cultural Centre in Brantford is actively preserving the old ways of the Six Nations. All year long there are events, festivals and displays, and at all of them, food plays a major role. It's little wonder. Bertha Skye, the lady in charge of most of the food operations, joined Canada's national aboriginal culinary team in Frankfurt, Germany, and became part of history when they competed and won Gold. At home, Bertha's cooking is hearty and homespun. Corn soup and bannock are two of her most often asked for specialties. At the Snowsnake Tournament, the players of this ancient native game, wherein long poles or "snakes" are thrown along a snowy trench, all love to come inside out of the February cold for a bowl of her traditional soup. The corn is grown nearby and dried before being specially processed with ashes to make it puffy. A troop of volunteers labour all morning, roasting and carving turkey, preparing and baking the bannock and setting the tables. The second major event is the annual craft sale, and again Bertha's on board cooking up a storm. Finally, there's the annual Pow Wow, a magnificent celebration of drumming and dancing at nearby Ohsweken at the end of July. There, once again, food has a huge role. In the often hot sun, the dancers' thirst is quenched with Iroquois Strawberry Drink (p.84), and there are "Indian tacos," buffalo burgers and fry bread topped with jam.

THREE SISTERS SOUP

To the natives of eastern North America the Three Sisters of Life were beans, corn and squash. In fact, that trio of vegetables eaten together constitutes a "perfect" food, supplying the body with all the nutrients it needs. Bertha Skye, the award-winning chef from Ohsweken, begins her interpretation of this traditional soup over an open fire using pork meat and bones. Our updated version uses ready-made chicken or beef stock, but it's just as tasty.

4 cups	chicken or beef stock	1 L
2	medium potatoes, cut into ½-inch (1 cm) cubes	2
2 cups	peeled and cubed squash (¼ of a butternut squash)	500 mL
1 cup	fresh or frozen kernel corn (1 ear if using fresh)	250 mL
½ cup	each trimmed and sliced green and yellow wax beans (about ¼ lb/125 g)	125 mL
	Salt and black pepper	

In large saucepan, bring stock to boil over high heat. Add potatoes and squash; return to boil. Reduce heat to medium-low; cook, covered, for 10 minutes or until almost tender. Stir in corn, and green and yellow beans; return to boil over high heat. Reduce heat to medium-low; simmer, covered, for 5 to 10 minutes, until corn and beans are tender. Season to taste with salt and pepper. Ladle into warm soup bowls; serve with Bannock (see recipe on page 222).

BUTTERY BAKED GARLIC POTATO WEDGES

Choose Yukon Gold potatoes for this recipe and celebrate a great Ontario success story. The popular variety was created, developed and bred at the University of Guelph by Gary Johnson, plant breeder with Agriculture and Agri-Food Canada. Serve the crisp garlicky potato wedges as an appetizer with sour cream for dunking, or as a side dish with meat or fish.

2 tbsp	butter	25 mL
¼ cup	freshly grated Parmesan cheese	50 mL
2	cloves garlic, minced	2
½ tsp	each salt, black pepper, dried basil and oregano	2 mL
4	large baking potatoes (2½ lb/1.2 kg), scrubbed and each cut lengthwise into 8 wedges	4

Preheat oven to 450°F (230°C). On a large baking sheet with a good rim, heat butter in oven for 2 to 3 minutes, until butter has melted. Stir cheese, garlic, salt, pepper, basil and oregano into melted butter until well combined. Add potato wedges; stir to coat well with butter mixture.

Bake for 30 to 40 minutes, stirring every 10 minutes, until potato wedges are tender and golden brown. Serve at once.

Makes **4 to 6 servings**

Preparation time: **15 minutes**

Cooking time: **about 40 minutes**

*Y*ukon Gold, *the* success story of the potato world, was hybridized at the University of Guelph's Cambridge Research Station. The only potato to be sold under its authentic name, the yellow-fleshed spud is one of the finest all-round potatoes ever marketed. Several of its cousins, Royal Gold, Temagami and Rose Gold, are being carefully nurtured, and 1996 will mark their entry onto the seed potato market. Where to find them? As with most innovative crops, at first they'll likely be sold only at farmers' markets and at the farm gate.

Makes **4 servings**

Preparation time: **15 minutes**

Cooking time: **6 to 8 minutes**

*W*aterloo County is, in a word, dynamic! Each year, on the Saturday after Thanksgiving, the Waterloo Federation of Agriculture holds its annual Town and Country Farm Tour. It's a superb opportunity for families to visit with part of a farming team that generates more than $257 million in business yearly. Hop into your car and head across the West Montrose covered bridge or down a route so winding that it's called "snake road" into one of the beautiful townships that make up the county. Maps are supplied and the route is well signed with the familiar Conestoga wagon logo. Every year eight different regional farms open their gates to showcase their unique agriculture. You may see an equestrian centre, a milking dairy herd, a market garden that supplies cabbages to manufacture good old-fashioned Waterloo County sauerkraut or a cash crop operation with an alfalfa dehydration plant that presses pellets for pet food and has a collection of antique John Deere tractors on the side. There may be a beef farm or one that harvests maple syrup, a shiitake mushroom producer or an organic grain farm that mills its own wheat into flour. Registration begins at 9:30 a.m. and continues to 1:30 p.m. The tours begin at 9:30 and may last until 4:30 p.m.

WATERLOO COUNTY HOT SPINACH SALAD

In the springtime, this Waterloo County favourite is made with young dandelion leaves; in the autumn it works well with curly endive. Serve it immediately so that the greens stay fresh and unwilted.

6 cups	washed, dried and torn spinach (about 1 bunch)	1.5 L
2	slices side bacon, chopped	2
1 tbsp	all-purpose flour	15 mL
1 tbsp	granulated sugar	15 mL
1 tsp	dry mustard	5 mL
½ cup	half-and-half cream	125 mL
2 tbsp	cider vinegar	25 mL

Place spinach in large salad bowl; cover and refrigerate.

In heavy skillet, cook bacon over medium-high heat for 3 to 5 minutes, until crisp. With slotted spoon, remove bacon from skillet; drain on paper towels.

Add flour, sugar and mustard to bacon fat remaining in skillet; cook, stirring, over medium-low heat for 1 minute. Whisk in cream and vinegar; cook, stirring, for 2 minutes, until smooth and bubbly. Add dressing to spinach; toss well. Sprinkle bacon over top; serve at once.

CHILLED CUCUMBER SOUP

The secret of a good cold soup is not to serve too icy-cold (let it stand for 30 minutes at room temperature before serving) and to adjust the seasonings to taste immediately before ladling into bowls. This version with cucumber and mint is especially refreshing during a steamy Ontario summer.

1	large field cucumber	1
2 cups	plain yogurt	500 mL
¼ cup	packed mint leaves (no stems)	50 mL
1	clove garlic, sliced	1
½ cup	half-and-half cream	125 mL
¼ tsp	each salt and black pepper	1 mL
4	fresh mint sprigs	4
	Country-Style Croutons (see recipe on page 144)	

Trim ends from cucumber. Cut cucumber in half crosswise; remove peel with vegetable peeler or sharp knife. Cut each piece of cucumber in quarters lengthwise; scoop out seeds. Cut cucumber into ½-inch (1 cm) chunks.

In a blender, combine cucumber, yogurt, mint and garlic. Blend, using on/off pulses, until fairly smooth. Pour soup into a bowl or pitcher; stir in cream, salt and pepper. Refrigerate, covered, until well chilled. Taste and adjust seasoning before serving. Ladle into chilled soup bowls; garnish with sprigs of fresh mint and Country-Style Croutons.

Makes **4 servings**

Preparation time: **20 minutes**

*T*he Outdoor Farm Show sums up agri-business in Ontario. This show, states Dr. Arthur Loughton, director of the Simcoe Research Station, "gives us all an appreciation of the degree of capitalization required in agriculture. A tomato harvester can cost anywhere from $150,000 to $200,000. You don't get much of a tractor for $60,000." The show is held yearly in late summer on the Shur-Gain Research Complex near the small hamlet of Burford in south-western Ontario. Visitors are welcomed by smiling local service club members and the roar of heavy equipment. You'll see new crop varieties in the field, many of which are still identified only by a research number, log on to the Internet with University of Guelph staff, and rub shoulders with several thousand Ontario farmers who are checking out the latest in equipment, seed planting and harvesting techniques. There's even a demonstration of forestry equipment.

*F*irst Line Seeds, a five-thousand-acre farm east of Guelph, has an open-door policy, so visitors, if they call a few days in advance, can tour the inordinately huge bean farm and seed company. Their primary crops are corn and soybeans. One of their more interesting crops is a small-seeded soybean that is used in the production of *natto*. People have been making *natto* near Nagasaki since the 1700s. Soybeans are cooked, inoculated and then fermented, to be eaten as is or over rice.

Makes **4 to 6 servings**

Preparation time: **20 minutes**

Cooking time: **1 hour, 40 minutes**

$\mathcal{T}$he Seagram Museum in Waterloo forms a special link between the region's past and the mighty distilling empire of the Seagram family. Exhibitions are held throughout the year, as are workshops, wine appreciation classes, school programs and an annual "Spirit Walk." Each Saturday, for a nominal fee, The Canadian Whisky Tasting Experience allows visitors to learn the techniques involved in whisky making and even taste a couple. The annual Grape and Grain Harvest Festival in late September or early October allows amateurs to compete in winemaking and bread baking. Displays on grape crushing and destemming and on wine production occur in the Discovery Room.

WHISKY-BRAISED BEEF WITH CELERY

Whisky adds depth of flavour and a slight sweetness to this rich beef stew. If whisky's not your tipple and you don't want to buy a whole bottle, two of the miniature-size bottles contain ½ cup (125 mL).

2 lb	stewing beef, trimmed of excess fat and cut into 1½ -inch (4 cm) cubes	1 kg
	Canola or corn oil (about 2 tbsp/25 mL)	
1	large onion, sliced	1
3	cloves garlic, minced	3
¾ cup	beef stock	175 mL
½ cup	Canadian whisky	125 mL
2 tbsp	horseradish	25 mL
6	sprigs fresh thyme or 1 tsp/5 mL dried thyme	6
1	bay leaf	1
½ tsp	salt	2 mL
¼ tsp	black pepper	1 mL
2 cups	sliced celery (about 3 stalks)	500 mL
½ cup	chopped fresh parsley	125 mL

Pat beef dry on paper towels. In large heavy saucepan or Dutch oven, heat 1 tbsp (15 mL) oil over medium-high heat. Cook beef in batches for 2 to 3 minutes, until browned, adding more oil as necessary. Remove with slotted spoon; set aside on plate. Add onion and garlic to saucepan; cook, stirring, for 3 to 4 minutes, until onion is softened. Add stock and whisky; bring to boil over high heat, stirring to scrape up any brown bits from bottom of saucepan.

Return meat to saucepan, along with horseradish, thyme, bay leaf, salt and pepper. Reduce heat to medium-low; simmer, covered, for 1 hour. Stir in celery; cook, covered, for 30 minutes, until meat and vegetables are tender.

With slotted spoon, remove meat and vegetables to heated serving dish; keep warm. Bring liquid remaining in saucepan to boil over high heat; boil, stirring occasionally, for 3 to 5 minutes, until reduced and thickened slightly. Remove bay leaf and thyme sprigs. Spoon sauce over meat and vegetables; sprinkle with chopped parsley.

*A*round the Guelph area there are many fine butchers. But few raise the meat themselves. John Rowe does—and he's very proud of it. Natural aging adds to the flavour of his beef, which is fed a diet of organic corn silage and barley. His apple butter and honey garlic sausages are superb, as are his classic, juicy versions of ham and pastrami. John sells his meat in Guelph and at various farmers' markets, including Toronto's St. Lawrence Market (north building) every Saturday.

Makes **6 servings**

Preparation time: **20 minutes**

Cooking time: **2¼ hours**

*T*he Mennonite Relief Sale & Quilt Auction at New Hamburg is held yearly on the last Saturday of May. Congregations from all over Ontario donate quilts, pieced and stitched over the long winter, and great traditional foods for a sale that now raises upwards of $300,000 for the Mennonite Central Committee's relief efforts all over the world and here at home. Everything is donated, from the auctioneer's time to the maple syrup for the pancake breakfast. The preview begins at the New Hamburg Fair Grounds on Friday evening, when the food booths open. All around the arena in which the quilts hang prior to auction, visitors taste an enormous variety of country foods— cream buns, shoofly pie and summer sausage, locally made apple butter and huge monster cookies. While the quilts are being sold, buyers savour slices of strawberry pie and coffee or treat themselves to a crisp rosette.

SPARERIBS WITH CARAWAY SAUERKRAUT AND DUMPLINGS

This is a favourite fall dish in Mennonite homes all over Wellington County. It's hearty and filling, and oh-so-good! Choose a good Ontario-made beer for this recipe—as an ingredient and to serve along with the meal.

4 lb	lean back ribs	2 kg
¾ cup	beer	175 mL
1	can (28 oz/796 mL) sauerkraut	1
1 tsp	caraway seeds	5 mL
4 cups	water	1 L
¾ cup	all-purpose flour	175 mL
1½ tsp	baking powder	7 mL
¼ tsp	salt	1 mL
1	egg	1
¼ cup	milk	50 mL

Preheat oven to 325°F (160°C). Cut ribs into serving-size pieces; place in large roasting pan. Pour in beer; add sauerkraut, along with its juices. Sprinkle caraway seeds over top. Cover pan with foil. Bake for 2 hours, or until ribs are tender.

With slotted spoon, remove ribs and sauerkraut to heated serving platter, reserving cooking juices in the roasting pan. Cover platter; keep warm. Place roasting pan over medium heat. Add water; bring to boil.

Meanwhile, in medium bowl, combine flour, baking powder and salt. In glass measure, whisk together egg and milk. Stir egg mixture into flour mixture just until dry ingredients are moistened; do not overmix. The dough should be stiff enough to hold its shape when dropped into the boiling cooking juices. Drop spoonfuls (1 tbsp/15 mL) of dumpling batter into boiling cooking juices. The surface will be almost covered with dumplings. Reduce heat to low; cook, covered and without looking, for 12 minutes, until dumplings have risen. Pile dumplings over and around ribs and sauerkraut. Serve at once.

Stratford is the home of the annual Ontario Pork Congress, a June meeting of the province's producers. Perth County is known for both the quality and quantity of its pork. There are more than a thousand producers in the county, and in 1994 they produced more than six hundred thousand hogs. The Pork Congress welcomes the public, but its focus is on the high-tech side of the business, particularly animal health and the protection of the environment.

Makes **4 main-course or 6 side-dish servings**

Preparation time: **20 minutes**

Cooking time: **6 to 10 minutes**

*H*illside Festival is *the* summer folk music festival in the region. Held in the rolling hills on the shore of Guelph Lake, it celebrates local and national talent. But it has also become known as a super place to nosh down the best fast food the area has to offer. In recent years Guelph has seen numerous small cafés and ethnic restaurants open and flourish. Lebanon is represented with Emir's falafels. There's a fantastic salsa variation made by a Chilean who now lives in Wellington County. Diana's sells an East Indian tandoori-baked naan with vegetable curry. The Greek family from Basket Case serves gyros and spanokopita, the Kanata Native Cultural Society dishes up prairie chicken stew with sunflower corn bread, and Latino's offers their popular black bean burritos and vegetarian chili.

WOK-BRAISED MUSHROOMS AND BOK CHOY

Among the new crops appearing in the more fertile regions of the province is a cornucopia of Oriental vegetables. From bean sprouts to bok choy, these stir-fry stars are available from July to October. Here, we combine crunchy bok choy with Ontario mushrooms in a quick dish to serve over rice as a main course, or as a vegetable accompaniment.

2 tbsp	each chicken stock, oyster sauce* and sherry	25 mL
1 tbsp	soy sauce	15 mL
1	clove garlic, minced	1
1 tsp	granulated sugar	5 mL
1 tbsp	water	15 mL
2 tsp	cornstarch	10 mL
1 tbsp	canola or corn oil	15 mL
6 cups	sliced bok choy (about 1 small head)	1.5 L
½ lb	assorted sliced mushrooms (button, shiitake, portobello, oyster)	250 g
4	green onions, chopped	4

In small bowl, combine chicken stock, oyster sauce, sherry, soy sauce, garlic and sugar; set aside.

In separate small bowl, combine water and cornstarch until smooth; set aside.

Place wok or very large skillet over high heat until very hot. Add oil. When haze appears over oil, add bok choy and mushrooms. Stir-fry over high heat for 2 minutes. Add chicken-stock mixture; bring to boil. Reduce heat to medium; simmer for 3 to 5 minutes, stirring occasionally, until bok choy is tender-crisp and mushrooms are tender.

Stir in cornstarch mixture; simmer until thickened. Spoon onto serving platter; sprinkle with green onions.

* Available in Oriental section of most large supermarkets.

College Royal—the name says it all. For one mid-March weekend every year, the entire University of Guelph holds a gala open house. From all seven colleges, students, professors and staff guide visitors through the halls, labs and fields of higher learning. This particular university is renowned for its leading-edge agricultural research, and there are a multitude of demonstrations, displays, hands-on workshops and free lectures. From wild birds to surfing the Net, from discovering the joys of edible insects to a full-fledged livestock show, there is something for absolutely every age.

Makes **8 servings**

Preparation time: **5 minutes**

Cooking time: **8 minutes**

*D*rayton Farmers' Market is a tiny, Saturday-morning gem of a market held at the old arena in this lively theatre town northeast of Waterloo. Dutch syrup cookies are made on a well-used waffle press. Karen Adele Kurg's stall is filled with bouquets of fresh herbs, bags of dried herbs and small jars of herbal glazes. You can buy a local sausage heaped with sauerkraut on a bun to enjoy while stocking up on the best in local produce.

WELLINGTON COUNTY SMOKED PORK CHOPS WITH MAPLE GLAZE

Smoked pork chops are available at many farmers' markets throughout the province, but especially at those in Wellington County. They're fully cooked so need only a brief grilling. The maple glaze is also wonderful drizzled over chicken portions on the barbecue.

⅓ cup	maple syrup	75 mL
1 tbsp	Sweet and Sour Mustard (see recipe on page 55) or honey mustard	15 mL
2 tsp	horseradish	10 mL
8	¾-inch (2 cm) thick smoked pork chops Canola or corn oil	8

In small bowl, whisk together maple syrup, mustard and horseradish. Lightly brush both sides of each pork chop with oil. Preheat barbecue to medium-high. Grill chops for 8 minutes, turning once and basting frequently with maple-syrup mixture.

Alternatively, broil chops 4 inch (10 cm) from hot broiler for 8 minutes, turning once and basting frequently with maple-syrup mixture.

STAFFA TOASTED OATMEAL CRISPS

These are so easy, you'll never have to buy cookies again. If we happen to have some chocolate chips in the cupboard, we like to add a handful to the batter.

½ cup	each shortening and softened butter	125 mL
½ cup	each granulated sugar and packed brown sugar	125 mL
1	egg	1
1 tsp	vanilla	5 mL
1½ cups	all-purpose flour	375 mL
1 tsp	baking soda	5 mL
½ tsp	salt	2 mL
1½ cups	rolled oats	375 mL
½ cup	each sultana raisins and chopped walnuts	125 mL

Preheat oven to 350°F (180°C). In medium bowl, cream together shortening, butter, granulated and brown sugars, egg and vanilla until fluffy.

In separate bowl, stir together flour, baking soda and salt. Stir flour mixture into shortening mixture until well combined. Work in rolled oats, raisins and nuts (we use our hands for this).

Form mixture into small balls about the size of a walnut; arrange 2 inch (5 cm) apart on ungreased baking sheets. Flatten with tines of a fork. Bake for 10 minutes, until just starting to colour around edges. Let cool completely on wire racks; store in airtight container.

Makes **about 50 crisps**

Preparation time: **15 minutes**

Cooking time: **10 minutes**

*T*he tiny hamlet of Staffa is the home of Hilton Whole Grain Millers. Barry and Karen Mahon are entrepreneurs in the truest sense. Their rolled and toasted oats may be found in most local stores. But that's still a fairly limited market. So the Mahons set up stalls at various farmers' markets across the province, created a mailing list and founded a highly successful mail order business. Now, consumers across North America can purchase the complete product line, including oat groats, a superb rice substitute far more nutritious than rice and very high in protein.

Makes **4** loaves

Preparation time: **30 minutes**

Rising time: **4 hours**

Cooking time: **25 to 30 minutes**

*F*or more than twenty years the small community of Wellesley has held its Apple Butter and Cheese Festival in late September. Stacks of pancakes and locally made sausages with lots of apple-sauce are the festival's official breakfast. The street is lined with vendors selling apple dumplings (the pastry-encased Waterloo County specialty), apple frit-ters and, of course, apple pie with aged Cheddar cheese. There's a quilt auction, apple butter and cider mill tours, an antique car and tractor show. Then, more food! At the smorgasbord din-ner—here "dinner" means the noon meal—feast on pigtails, rolled spareribs, sauerkraut, roast beef, salads and a table-ful of homemade pies. Bast Cheese opens its original store for this single day of the year, so you'll have a chance to purchase their specially aged Cheddar.

BRAIDED PORTUGUESE SWEET BREAD

Over the years, many Portuguese immigrants have settled in the Cambridge area, bringing with them their traditions of brightly painted homes and a love of great baking. These richly glazed braids are won-derful sliced and spread with butter. If you wish, you can drizzle the baked loaves with a thin icing made by stirring together 1⅔ cups (400 mL) icing sugar, ¼ cup (50 mL) milk and 1 tsp (5 mL) vanilla. The recipe makes four loaves, and each loaf will yield 12 to 14 slices, so make a batch and pop a couple of loaves in the freezer; well wrapped, they'll stay fresh for up to three months.

½ cup	warm water (105°F/41°C)	125 mL
2 tsp	granulated sugar	10 mL
2 tbsp	active dry yeast	25 mL
1 cup	milk	250 mL
½ cup	butter	125 mL
2 tsp	salt	10 mL
1½ cups	granulated sugar	375 mL
6	eggs, at room temperature	6
	All-purpose flour (about 8 cups/2 L)	
1½ cups	each sultana raisins and chopped walnuts	375 mL

Topping:

1	egg white	1
1 tbsp	milk	15 mL
¼ cup	coarse sugar	50 mL

In small bowl, combine warm water and sugar; sprinkle yeast over surface and set aside in warm place for 10 minutes or until puffy.

In small heavy saucepan, combine milk, butter and salt; heat over medium heat until butter has melted. Remove from heat; let cool until luke-warm.

In large bowl, beat together sugar and eggs until light in colour. Stir in milk mixture and yeast. With wooden spoon, gradually beat in 3 cups (750 mL) flour. Beat in raisins and nuts. Beat in more flour, 1 cup (250 mL) at a time, mixing well after each addition, until soft but not sticky dough forms.

Turn dough out onto a floured surface; knead for 10 to 12 minutes, until smooth and elastic, adding more flour as necessary (raisins and nuts will start popping out when dough is kneaded sufficiently). Form dough into a ball; place in oiled bowl, turning to oil dough on all sides. Cover loosely with plastic wrap; let stand in warm, draft-free place for 2 hours or until doubled in size.

Punch dough down; let dough rest for 10 minutes. Cut into four even-size pieces; roll each into 12-inch (30 cm) long rectangle. Cut each rectangle into three strips lengthwise, leaving about 1 inch (2.5 cm) uncut at the end of each rectangle. Braid the three strips together, pinching ends together to seal. Transfer to greased baking sheets. Cover with damp towel; let rise at room temperature for 2 hours or until doubled in size. Preheat oven to 350°F (180°C).

Topping: In small bowl, whisk together egg white and milk. Brush loaves lightly with egg-white mixture; sprinkle with coarse sugar. Bake for 25 to 30 minutes, or until loaves are well browned and sound hollow when tapped on bases.

*O*ntario grain, particularly soft wheat, is noted for its high quality. It stands to reason that the finest, most delicate of all cake flour is ground at Dover Mills in Cambridge and is named (what else?) Swan's Down. From their small red brick office, they sell ginormous bags of freshly milled flour of all types—and old-fashioned boxes of Swan's Down.

Makes **48 buns**

Preparation time: **30 minutes**

Rising time: **3 hours**

Cooking time: **12 to 15 minutes**

$\mathcal{W}$oolwich Dairy, a multi-award-winning dairy specializing in goat's milk cheese, is run by an energetic young couple, Tony and Olga Dutra. The dairy is located northwest of Guelph, and their cheeses can be found in many of Ontario's grocery stores and at the Saturday St. Lawrence Market in Toronto. Tony's the cheese maker and is constantly experimenting and perfecting. He can taste the milk and tell whether it comes from northern or southern Ontario. He explains that northern goat's milk has a slightly lower butterfat content and hence is fuller-flavoured. Certain milk is at its best in their creamy fresh cheeses, while other shipments are made into tangy feta or aged Cheddar. Small fluffy rounds of chevre are rolled in herbs or crushed pepper or matured till hard so they can be grated.

Olga suggests that the soft unaged chevres should be allowed to stand at room temperature so it becomes creamy and spreadable. Grate Gaisli, a firmer ripened cheese, and use it as you would mozzarella. It has a distinctive, delicious flavour when used on pizza or melted on bruschetta.

ZWIEBACK

These little buns with a top-knot are rich in butter and slightly salty and are superb with any of the soups in this book. The recipe makes a big batch of buns, but they freeze well and take very little time to thaw. Zwieback are a tradition of the Mennonite regions of southwestern Ontario, where you'll find them at church suppers and at community auctions like the New Hamburg Relief Sale.

1 cup	warm water (105°F/41°C)	250 mL
⅓ cup plus 2 tsp	granulated sugar	85 mL
2 tbsp	active dry yeast	25 mL
2 cups	warm milk (105°F/41°C)	500 mL
½ cup	butter, melted and cooled	125 mL
3	eggs, lightly beaten	3
¼ cup	shortening, melted and cooled	50 mL
4 tsp	salt	20 mL
	All-purpose flour (about 9 cups/2.2 L)	

In large bowl, combine water and 2 tsp (10 mL) of the sugar, stirring to dissolve sugar; sprinkle yeast over surface and set aside in warm place for 10 minutes or until puffy. Stir in milk, butter, eggs, shortening, salt and remaining sugar. Beat in flour 1 cup (250 mL) at a time until smooth dough forms.

Turn dough out onto lightly floured surface; knead in remaining flour until soft but not sticky dough forms. Knead for 10 to 12 minutes until dough is smooth and elastic. Form dough into ball; place in lightly oiled bowl, turning dough to coat with oil. Cover loosely with plastic wrap; let rise in warm, draft-free place for 1½ hours or until doubled in size.

Punch dough down; let rest for 15 minutes. Pinch off pieces of dough the size of an egg and shape into smooth rolls. Pinch off small pieces of dough (about 1 tsp/5 mL) and press them into the tops of the larger rolls. Place on greased baking sheets. Cover with damp towel; let rise at room temperature for 1½ hours or until doubled in size. Preheat oven to 375°F (190°C).

Bake rolls for 12 to 15 minutes until well risen and golden brown, and rolls sound hollow when tapped on bases. Let rolls cool on wire racks.

Wellington County Brewery in Guelph was a decade old in 1995. Founded to brew traditional Real Ale, the small company is uncompromisingly product driven. Now, they are making a bit of history by becoming the first micro-brewery on the Internet. Surf the Net and join brewmaster Jake Mckay in his cellar.

Makes 24 buns

Preparation time: 30 minutes

Rising time: 3 hours

Cooking time: 12 to 15 minutes

*W*aterloo County Farmers Market near St. Jacobs owes its genesis to the dispute over the destruction of the old Kitchener Market building to make way for a parking/market/shopping centre complex. Many Mennonite vendors simply pulled out, bought a chunk of land and set up shop north of the city of Waterloo. And it has worked! The area bustles from very early morning till mid-afternoon. Lamb, turkey in all its forms, superb summer sausage, rosettes, maple sugar and syrup are there year round. There's hardly a better place to shop for the freshest seasonal produce in all of the county.

Refrigerate leftover egg yolks, with enough water to cover them, in a covered container for up to 2 days. Or freeze them, adding ½ tsp (2 mL) salt or sugar for every six yolks, for up to 3 months.

RELIEF SALE CREAM BUNS

Some Mennonite bakers fill these light buns with sweetened whipped cream; others use the filling that follows. We like them with homemade preserves and a final dusting of icing sugar. Without the cream filling, the buns make great dinner rolls.

Buns:

1¼ cups	milk	300 mL
½ cup	granulated sugar	125 mL
1 tbsp	shortening	15 mL
1 tsp	salt	5 mL
½ cup	warm water (105°F/41°C)	125 mL
1 tbsp	active dry yeast	15 mL
1	egg, well beaten	1
4½ cups	all-purpose flour	1.15 L

Cream Filling:

3 cups	icing sugar	750 mL
2 tbsp	milk	25 mL
2	egg whites	2
⅓ cup	softened shortening	75 mL
2 tsp	vanilla	10 mL
	Strawberry or other fruit preserves	
	Icing sugar	

Buns: In heavy saucepan, heat milk over medium heat. Add ⅓ cup (75 mL) sugar, the shortening and salt, stirring until sugar is dissolved and shortening melted. Pour into large bowl; let cool until lukewarm.

In small bowl, stir together water and remaining sugar, stirring to dissolve sugar; sprinkle yeast over surface. Let stand in warm place for 10 minutes, until puffy. Whisk egg and yeast mixture into milk mixture. Beat in flour 1 cup (250 mL) at a time until smooth dough forms.

Turn dough out onto lightly floured surface; knead in remaining flour until soft but not sticky dough forms. Knead for 8 to 10 minutes until dough is smooth and elastic. Form dough into ball; place in lightly oiled bowl, turning dough to coat with oil. Cover loosely with plastic wrap; let rise in warm, draft-free place for 1½ hours or until doubled in size.

Punch dough down; let dough rest for 10 minutes. Divide dough into 24 even-size pieces; shape into buns. Place on greased or parchment-paper-lined baking sheets. Cover with damp towel; let rise at room temperature for 1½ hours or until doubled in size. Preheat oven to 375°F (190°C).

Bake buns for 12 to 15 minutes until well risen and golden brown, and buns sound hollow when tapped on bases. Let buns cool on wire racks.

Cream Filling: In large bowl, beat together sugar, milk and egg whites until smooth. Beat in shortening and vanilla until smooth and creamy. Split cooled buns, spread with filling and preserves and sift icing sugar over tops.

*G*ay Lea is far more than a brand name on a pound of butter or tub of yogurt. Gay Lea is a highly successful cooperative that represents nearly 4,000 members, 1,500 of them active milk producers. They banded together in 1958 to form a common voice, which enabled farmers to make their wishes known in an industry that needed a common-sense approach to doing business. Now, with six plants scattered across the province, Gay Lea makes a huge variety of dairy products with milk produced on farms from Yonge Street to Owen Sound to London. All the butter, including our favourite, known as Sweet Rose Bud, is made in the state-of-the-art Guelph plant; sour cream, table cream, lactose-reduced milk and yogurt are made in Weston, while cheeses, from mozzarella to Edam and Gouda, are manufactured in Baden. Although the plants themselves have no retail sales outlets, if you're on a country ramble, the entire line of cheeses may be purchased at Egli's, a local Baden meat market.

Makes **6 servings**

Preparation time: **25 minutes**

Cooking time: **20 to 25 minutes**

$\mathcal{W}$e often think of the Kitchener Farmers' Market as our province's Christmas market. Even if it's drizzling and foggy, the spirit and the aromas of the season fill the place, as they have every year for more than a century. Foodstuffs are fresh from the farm and crafts take over an entire floor of the building. On market days all year round the bustle begins about 5 a.m., and by 9 a.m. the aisles are full of shoppers. This is a market steeped in tradition. Many vendors have been coming since their parents and grandparents brought them decades ago. The faces behind the stalls tell the story. The foods smack of German and Mennonite cooking—homemade sour cream, Brethren egg noodles, golden yellow capons, freshly dug potatoes, crisp rosettes and poppyseed strudels. Bast Cheeses age their personally selected Cheddar to mellow ripeness for up to six years. There's always fresh apple butter and honey and Seleda's homemade fudge, the best we've tasted outside our own kitchens. At Mary Roth's stand, you can purchase homegrown dried beans, fresh herbs, heritage tomatoes and her husband Mahlon's handmade cherrywood rolling pins.

BLUEBERRY AND GOAT CHEESE PHYLLO PARCELS

Quebec native Louise Duhamel has been chef at Langdon Hall Country Hotel near Cambridge for three years. Louise tries to use local ingredients wherever possible and makes this pretty dessert with Woolwich goat cheese, which is produced nearby. For best flavour, she recommends using wild blueberries if you can get them.

Peach Sauce:

2 cups	water	500 mL
3	ripe peaches	3
2 tbsp	fresh lemon juice	25 mL
1 tsp	minced fresh gingerroot	5 mL
	Liquid honey to taste	

Phyllo Parcels:

12	sheets phyllo pastry, thawed	12
½ cup	unsalted butter, melted	125 mL
2	pkgs (4.5 oz/140 g each) goat cheese	2
2 cups	blueberries (¾ lb/375 g)	500 mL
2 tbsp	liquid honey	25 mL
2 tbsp	granulated sugar	25 mL
6	mint sprigs	6

Peach Sauce: In large saucepan, bring water to boil over high heat; add peaches. Reduce heat to medium-low; simmer, covered, for 10 to 12 minutes, until peaches are soft. Remove peaches with slotted spoon. When cool enough to handle, slip off skins; cut peaches in half and remove pits.

In food processor, process peaches until smooth; transfer to bowl. Stir in lemon juice and ginger; sweeten to taste with honey. Set aside.

Phyllo Parcels: Preheat oven to 400°F (200°C). Keeping remaining phyllo sheets covered with damp towel, lay one sheet on work surface; brush with butter. Place another sheet on top; brush with butter. Place one-sixth of goat cheese in one corner of phyllo sheet, leaving 2-inch (5 cm) border. Top goat cheese with one-sixth of blueberries; drizzle with 1 tsp (5 mL) honey. Wrap goat cheese and blueberries in phyllo to make a neat parcel, tucking in edges. Place seam-side down on greased baking sheet. Brush with butter; sprinkle with sugar. Repeat with remaining phyllo, goat cheese, blueberries and honey to make six parcels in all. (Do not crowd baking sheet; use two baking sheets if necessary.) Bake for 10 to 12 minutes, or until phyllo is golden brown.

To serve, spoon a little peach sauce onto each of six dessert plates. Place phyllo parcel in centre of each pool of sauce; serve warm garnished with mint.

"*G*et out of town!" Every summer Monday, Perth County farms, from emu and elk to dairy and grain, open their gates to individual visitors and even a few busloads to allow urbanites to become reconnected with the reality of Ontario's farming community. A different pair of farm families plays host each week. There are guided tours that sometimes last far longer than the allotted thirty minutes because, for many visitors, it's an opportunity to revisit their personal heritage. The season is capped with an annual Harvest Day held on the first Sunday in October. A map of a mystery tour is sold for the cost of printing. Then visitors set off to any number of locations. Build a scarecrow, bob for apples, discuss how rural Ontarians deal with the challenges of protecting the environment, or learn directly from the technical experts how to manage a large dairy herd. Being "in town" will never be quite the same.

Thaw phyllo pastry according to instruction on the box but don't unwrap it until ready to use; once uncovered, it dries out quickly.

Makes **6 to 8 servings**

Preparation time: **25 minutes**

Cooking time: **25 minutes**

$\mathcal{T}$he culinary synergy in Stratford is unequalled in any other region in Canada, partly because of the Shakespearean Festival but mainly because the city is home to an exceedingly fine, privately operated chefs' training school. The Stratford Chefs' School teaches the culinary arts for the love of them. Consequently the city can boast a whole cadre of superb restaurants—Rundles, The Old Prune, The Church, Down the Street, Bentley's…. Choose a style from sophisticated to casual—dining in Stratford is a joy. Because of the school, two of Canada's finest chefs, Neil Baxter and Bryan Steele, have been able to stay in an otherwise seasonal city. They understand that fine cookery must be close to the land. In Stratford, these needs are being fulfilled.

ONTARIO BERRY CLAFOUTIS

A clafoutis is a French dessert of fruit baked in a light batter. It's traditionally made with cherries, but Bryan Steele, chef de cuisine at Stratford's The Old Prune restaurant and senior cookery instructor at the Stratford Chefs' School, says that any Ontario berry is good in his version of the simple dessert; Bryan uses raspberries, blackberries or wild blueberries. Quark is a low-fat soft cheese, similar in consistency to a smooth cottage cheese. If quark is unavailable, substitute pressed cottage cheese.

2 tbsp	butter, softened	25 mL
1 tbsp	granulated sugar	15 mL
1 lb	quark cheese	500 g
4	eggs, separated	4
2 cups	icing sugar, sifted	500 mL
¼ cup	whipping cream	50 mL
3 tbsp	cornstarch	45 mL
2 tbsp	fresh lemon juice	25 mL
½ tsp	grated lemon rind	2 mL
2 cups	fresh berries	500 mL
	Whipped cream	

Preheat oven to 450°F (230°C). Use about ½ tbsp (7 mL) of the butter to butter an 8-cup (2 L) square baking dish; sprinkle with granulated sugar.

If quark seems moist, place in sieve; press with back of a spoon to remove as much moisture as possible. In large bowl using electric mixer, beat together quark and remaining butter until well combined. Beat in egg yolks one at a time, beating well after each addition. Gradually beat in icing sugar; continue beating until mixture is very light. Beat in cream, cornstarch, lemon juice and rind.

In separate bowl with clean beaters, beat egg whites until stiff peaks form. Gradually fold whites into quark mixture until well combined.

Arrange fruit in bottom of prepared dish. Spoon quark mixture over top. Bake for 25 minutes or until a toothpick inserted into centre of dessert comes out clean. Serve warm with whipped cream.

*T*he Stratford Chefs' School has nurtured a community of creative producers. Antony John is a perfect example. Antony, according to James Morris, owner of Rundles and co-founder of the Stratford Chefs' School, is part of the "renaissance of the market gardener." His business, Soiled Reputation, provides little edible posies and a huge variety of herbs and vegetables for most of the year. "Artisanal" would describe Robert Smith, who raises goats and makes small batches of delightful fresh goat's milk cheese on the farm on which he grew up. The Moss family grows berries of all descriptions, processing them into jam and encouraging people to come and pick their own. Ann Marie Moss, a graduate of the chefs' school, oversees much of the farm's imaginative culinary development.

The school also offers one of the great dining values in Ontario. Throughout the winter term, for a nominal registration fee, the "Dinner Club," under the tutelage of resident chefs and guest "great" chefs from all over Canada and the world, allows students to prepare and execute absolutely superb meals, all matched with the appropriate wines and spirits.

Makes **4 to 6 servings**

Preparation time: **25 minutes**

Cooking time: **45 minutes**

*I*magine a world in which the yield of wheat in the most populous country could be boosted by nearly thirty percent. This is not a dream—it's reality! Our reality! In an era of exploding world population, Professor Rick Upfold and two other University of Guelph scientists, Dr. Ed Gamble and Dr. Neal Stoskopf, did just that. The Chinese government asked for help in increasing both the quantity and the quality of wheat in the northeastern province of Heilongjiang. Later their work expanded to include the western, desertlike provinces of Xinjang and Gansu. In all these regions, wheat is a major food source, noodles and steamed breads taking the place of rice. Working out of the Elora Research Station and the university, the team took over their expertise and their grain, namely, hard red spring wheat. They helped the Chinese farmers by applying their well-honed skills in agronomy and by introducing various Canadian grains as breeding stock. Across the board, in this region of more than seventy million people, yields increased consistently by twenty-eight percent.

BUCKWHEAT CREPES WITH MAPLE POACHED-APPLE FILLING

Buckwheat flour gives these crepes an interesting nutty taste. Choose apples that hold their shape well, such as Granny Smith or Northern Spy, for the filling.

Crepes:

⅔ cup	all-purpose flour	150 mL
⅓ cup	buckwheat flour	75 mL
1½ cups	milk or buttermilk	375 mL
2	eggs	2
3 tbsp	canola or corn oil	45 mL
	Canola or corn oil for frying	

Filling:

2 tbsp	unsalted butter	25 mL
4	large firm apples, peeled, cored and thinly sliced	4
1 cup	maple syrup	250 mL
1 cup	ricotta or cottage cheese	250 mL
1 tsp	vanilla	5 mL

Crepes: In large bowl, whisk together all-purpose and buckwheat flours, milk, eggs and oil until smooth and free of lumps. Let stand for 15 minutes.

Heat an 8-inch (20 cm) crepe pan or heavy skillet over medium-high heat. Brush pan with a little oil; pour ¼ cup (50 mL) batter into pan, tilting pan to spread batter evenly. Cook for 1 minute or until lightly browned on underside; turn and cook for 30 to 60 seconds or until crepe is lightly browned. Repeat until all batter is cooked. Stack crepes on heated plate as they cook; keep warm, loosely covered, in low oven.

Filling: In large nonstick skillet, melt butter over medium-high heat. Add apples; cook for 3 minutes, stirring gently. Pour in syrup; reduce heat to medium. Cook, uncovered, for 8 to 10 minutes, stirring occasionally, until apples are tender.

With slotted spoon, remove apples from skillet; set aside and keep warm. Pour syrup into heat-proof pitcher; keep warm.

In small bowl, blend ricotta cheese, vanilla and 2 tbsp (25 mL) of the warm syrup until fairly smooth. Spoon about 1 tbsp (15 mL) ricotta mixture onto each crepe; top with four apple slices. Roll up crepes; arrange on heated serving platter. Top with remaining apple slices; serve with hot syrup.

*T*he size and importance of the work being done at the Elora Research Station can be seen by looking at a few figures. At any given time during the growing season, the fields hold twenty thousand different lineages of cereal grains, thirty to forty thousand different soy beans, thirty to forty thousand different lines of canola, thousands of barley plants and a huge number of white and coloured beans. Of those plants that are successful and chosen for whatever merits the scientists desire, it still takes nine to twelve years from the time of breeding to get them to the farm field.

The Elora research station maintains an open-door policy for the public (8 a.m. to 4 p.m. Monday to Friday). Visitors can arrange a pickup tour about the fields from the farm manager.

Makes **6** pint (500 mL) jars

Preparation time: **30 minutes**

Standing time: **4 hours**

Cooking time: **20 minutes**

Processing time: **15 minutes**

*G*uelph Farmers' Market was founded in August, 1827, on a site a little to the east of the present market building. Since all county roads went through Guelph, the market quickly became a resounding success. The quarterly cattle and produce market was a celebration, a little like it is today. Herds of three to four hundred shorthorns were driven in from outlying settlements and sold in a sales arena. When the railway went through in the mid-1800s, the prosperity of the market was further enhanced. The produce market continued with even greater frequency, and a butter market ran weekly. Vendors trekked in from as far away as Bruce and Huron counties.

Today, Guelph Farmers' Market has the wonderful eclectic personality only a university city can lend—and a market clerk who fiercely protects her vendors. Bring a jug to fill with cider and a cloth bag to fill with herbs, produce and great breads! Try Gostel Bros. Meats' *nusschinken,* a dry-cured ham, or Doug Eiche's honey collected from the purple phlox and fields of goldenrod along the Grand River.

SPICED ZUCCHINI RELISH

Sheila Mickle of Mickle's Apples in Drayton describes this relish as "the world's best; it's so good on hot dogs that you don't need the wiener!" We agree, and also love it slathered on homemade hamburgers or in big crusty sandwiches. Sheila says to peel the zucchini only if they're not young and tender.

10 cups	shredded zucchini (about 3¼ lb /1.6 kg)	2.5 L
4	medium onions, finely chopped	4
2	large sweet red peppers, seeded and finely chopped	2
1 tbsp	pickling salt	15 mL
3 cups	white vinegar	750 mL
⅓ cup	all-purpose flour	75 mL
2 tbsp	dry mustard	25 mL
1 tbsp	each celery and mustard seed	15 mL
1 tsp	each allspice and turmeric	5 mL
½ tsp	each ground ginger and cloves	2 mL
Pinch	cayenne	Pinch
2 cups	granulated sugar	500 mL
1 cup	water	250 mL

In large bowl, combine zucchini, onions, peppers and pickling salt. Let stand, covered, at room temperature for 4 hours. Drain well; set aside.

In large stainless steel or enamel saucepan, combine 1 cup (250 mL) vinegar, the flour, dry mustard, celery and mustard seeds, allspice, turmeric, ginger, cloves and cayenne; stir until mixture is smooth. Stir in sugar, water and remaining vinegar. Cook over medium-high heat for 10 minutes, stirring often, until thickened and smooth.

Add zucchini, peppers and onions; bring to boil over high heat. Reduce heat to medium; simmer, stirring often, for about 10 minutes, until thickened.

Immediately ladle into 6 hot, sterilized 1-pint (500 mL) jars, leaving ½ inch (1 cm) headspace. Wipe jar rims to remove any excess relish; seal with two-piece lids, tightening screw bands until just fingertip tight. Process in hot-water bath for 15 minutes. Remove jars from canner; let cool for 24 hours. Check jar seals (sealed lids curve downwards). Remove screw bands; label jars. Store relish in cool, dark place.

*I*t's unusual to find a small village with its own personal cottage brewery, but the "best beer by a dam site" is being produced in Elora, "the hub of Wellington County," according to those who live there. The Taylor & Bate story began in 1834 when James Taylor built his first brewery in St. Catharines. When he took Thomas Bate as a partner in 1857, the name was added to the label. The label fell out of family ownership. Then Crozier Taylor, four generations removed from James, bought the label back and continued the family tradition by brewing Elora Pale Ale and Elora Grand Porter beside the Elora Mill Inn and a beautiful dam on the Grand River. True to tradition, Mr. Taylor has recently reinstated the Elora version of the Ancient Order of Froth Blowers. Besides two pints of T&B, members receive a T-shirt, a membership card and the knowledge that in becoming part of the club, they join the ranks of those who call themselves "typhoon, cloudburst, grand hurricane, sou'west gale, gentle zephyr and welcome breeze." This is Elora, after all, rarely dull and never, ever conservative!

Makes **about 6 cups (1.5 L)**

Preparation time: **10 minutes**

Standing time: **15 minutes**

*T*he old saying "the fruits of one's labours" has a special meaning for crop scientist and berry specialist extraordinaire Dr. Allan Sullivan. A patient man, as plant hybridizers must be, Dr. Sullivan is leading the charge into the next millennium with raspberry hybrids that, at this writing, are called only by a number. The sturdy canes at the University of Guelph's Cambridge Research Station droop with truly huge, juicy raspberries from mid-June until frost. Within the next decade his first cultivars will begin to show up at pick-your-own farms throughout the province.

IROQUOIS STRAWBERRY DRINK

This is our favourite drink at the annual Six Nations Pow Wow at Ohsweken outside Brantford. On a hot summer's day, its clean fresh taste is more thirst-quenching than any carbonated beverage. Using a blender rather than a food processor to puree the strawberries makes an extra-smooth drink.

4 cups	sliced fresh strawberries or frozen and thawed unsweetened strawberries (about 1½ lb/750 g)	1 L
¼ cup	granulated sugar	50 mL
4 cups	water	1 L
	Mint or lemon balm sprigs for garnish (optional)	

In medium bowl, combine strawberries and sugar; let stand for 15 minutes, stirring occasionally, until sugar has dissolved.

In blender, process strawberries and their juices in batches until smooth. In pitcher, stir together strawberry puree and water. Pour over ice in tall glasses; garnish with sprigs of mint or lemon balm. Strawberry drink can be refrigerated, covered, for up to 5 days. Stir before serving.

Metropolitan Toronto

Toronto, especially in the gentle months of early summer, is an optimist's city. Throwing off the mantle of the chillingly damp Ontario winter, gardens burst into full bloom, and all summer long Torontonians and visitors alike take to the streets, revelling in dozens of festivals and countless openings.

Sprawling along Lake Ontario's northern shoreline, Toronto remains not only Canada's financial and publishing centre, but the third-largest theatre centre in the English-speaking world.

Yet, for all its sophistication, Toronto can boast the earthy delights of the St. Lawrence Market, one of the finest farmers' markets in Canada. If Toronto's exterior is that of concrete and gold-coated glass, its heart and soul are splashed with the multi-colours of racial diversity, a microcosm of ethnic communities and busy market areas. There are more Italians here than in any other city outside Italy. The city's two hundred thousand Chinese shop in three distinct Chinatowns among stores and restaurants owned by half a dozen other Asian minorities. There are Portuguese, Greek, Indian, Pakistani and West Indian communities, all with their traditions, celebrations, parades (every summer Sunday some street is closed) and foods.

Makes **4 to 6 servings**

Preparation time: **25 minutes**

Chilling time: **overnight**

*H*ot-pepper sherry is a spicy condiment made by steeping hot peppers in sherry. You can buy it at Southbrook Farms store, or make your own as follows. In a sterilized jar, place 2 seeded and chopped hot cherry peppers (wear rubber gloves when preparing hot peppers). Add 1 cup (250 mL) dry sherry; seal jar with lid. Refrigerate for 2 weeks for flavours to infuse. Strain sherry, discarding peppers. The sherry will keep indefinitely in the fridge and can be used in any recipe where you want to add a little zip; we like a dash added to a bloody Caesar!

SOUTHBROOK FARMS' GAZPACHO

Janette Keefe, the farm-store manager at Southbrook Farms, uses a mixture of green, red and yellow peppers in her dazzling soup, which is best made the day before serving. For best flavour, serve cool but not completely chilled.

3 cups	tomato juice	750 mL
1 cup	peeled and finely chopped cucumber	250 mL
1 cup	finely chopped tomatoes	250 mL
¾ cup	seeded and finely chopped sweet peppers	175 mL
2	small shallots, finely chopped	2
3 tbsp	hot-pepper sherry (see sidebar)	45 mL
2 tbsp	olive, canola or corn oil	25 mL
1 tbsp	each finely chopped fresh parsley and fresh coriander	15 mL
1 tsp	snipped fresh chives	5 mL
½ tsp	salt	2 mL
	Parsley or coriander sprigs for garnish	
	Plain yogurt	

In large nonmetallic bowl or lidded container, stir together tomato juice, cucumber, tomato, sweet peppers, shallots, hot-pepper sherry, oil, parsley, coriander, chives and salt until well combined. Refrigerate, covered, overnight for flavours to blend.

Ladle into soup bowls; garnish with parsley. Serve with plain yogurt to dollop on top.

THE BEST-EVER GREEK SALAD

The Greek community centred on Toronto's Danforth Avenue is one of the city's most colourful and well-established. Saunter along the Danforth on a summer evening and you could almost be in Athens. Sit at a sidewalk table when there's heavy traffic, and the pollution is almost as bad! This is positively the best Greek salad we've ever tasted. The recipe comes from Cheryl Embrett, a colleague of Julia's at Home-maker's Magazine, *where the recipe first appeared. Cheryl isn't Greek but she brought the recipe back from a visit to Greece some years ago, and it's become a classic. For best flavour, be sure to use perfectly ripe local tomatoes, a good Ontario feta, plus top-quality olive oil and olives.*

Makes **6 to 8 servings**

Preparation time: **20 minutes**

4	tomatoes (about 1 lb/500 g), cut into wedges	4
2	sweet green peppers, seeded and cut into rings	2
1	field cucumber, peeled, seeded and sliced	1
1	large red onion, sliced and separated into rings	1
⅓ cup	olive oil	75 mL
2 tbsp	fresh lemon juice	25 mL
1 tbsp	chopped fresh oregano	15 mL
¼ tsp	each salt and black pepper	1 mL
½ lb	feta cheese	250 g
15	Kalamata olives, pitted and halved	15

In large salad bowl, combine tomatoes, sweet peppers, cucumber and onion.

In small bowl, whisk together ¼ cup (50 mL) olive oil, the lemon juice, oregano, salt and pepper. Add dressing to salad; toss well.

Thinly slice feta cheese; arrange on top of salad. Sprinkle olives over cheese; drizzle with remaining olive oil.

*J*ules Verne's Phileas Fogg may have circumnavigated the globe in eighty days, but each summer in Toronto it's possible to do just that in a mere nine. In June, Festival Caravan kicks off when as many as forty different ethnic groups open the doors of their pavilions, dotted around Toronto, to share their culture and food. Caravan was founded in 1969 by Zena Kossar and has since become a summer tradition in the city. Less than $15 will buy you a nine-day passport, which becomes your round-the-world ticket to places as far-flung as Athens, Tokyo, Helsinki and Bridgetown. As you travel the world without even leaving the Greater Metro area, you can sample Philippino pizza (actually light and airy shrimp fritters), Korean barbecued beef with mouth-searing spicy *kimchi* (hot pickled cabbage) or Welsh leek and potato soup. With Caravan, Zena Kossar has achieved the impossible: economical—and delicious—travel without the jet lag!

Makes **6 appetizer servings**

Preparation time: **20 minutes**

Soaking time: **48 hours**

Cooking time: **6 to 8 minutes**

*T*he St. Lawrence Market is the foodie heart of Toronto! On Saturdays shoppers begin to arrive by 4 a.m.—cab drivers on their way home, night-shift workers and very early risers all in search of the special cut of meat or particular loaf of bread. The north market, the one that houses the farmers from the region, resounds with the sound of cleavers hitting the chopping blocks. The magnificent old south market building echoes with the rising crescendo of selling and buying.

Founded in 1803, the market was the historical trading centre of the city, and for tens of thousands, still is. Vendors in the building are permanently ensconced from Tuesday to Saturday: Alex Farm Products, where Alex Stroutzas sells cheeses from Spain, France, Italy, Great Britain and, of course, Ontario. Name a cheese and Alex will accept it as a personal challenge to find it for you. Great fresh seafood comes from Mike's, and at Whitehouse Meats the butchers make their own corned beef, pickled tongue and peameal bacon. There's rice from all over the world and specialty breads from all over Toronto.

ITALIAN SALT-COD SALAD

Italians the world over sit down to their Christmas feast on the evening of December 24. Stella Panacci and her husband, Liberato, came to Toronto from the town of Sora near Rome in 1964, and she has kept that Christmas custom alive for her children and grandchildren. In the Panacci family, tradition dictates that there must be as many different dishes of food on the table as people around it. This simple salad of baccala, *a salt-cured cod, is always on the Panaccis' festive menu, along with other rustic Italian fare, such as spaghetti tossed with anchovies and oil, cauliflower fritters and breaded smelt. The meal always ends with* crispella, *rings of deep-fried batter tossed in sugar, and roasted chestnuts. We've added a little wine vinegar to Stella's salad recipe, but you can leave it out if you prefer.*

1 lb	salted dried cod	500 g
½ cup	olive, canola or corn oil	125 mL
¼ cup	chopped fresh parsley	50 mL
3 tbsp	white wine vinegar	45 mL
1	clove garlic, minced	1
	Red-leaf lettuce	

Place cod in 13- by 9-inch (3 L) baking dish; add enough cold water to cover cod. Cover dish; let soak in refrigerator for 48 hours, changing water two or three times.

Drain cod well. In large skillet, bring 8 cups (2 L) water to boil. Add cod; reduce heat to medium. Simmer, uncovered, for 5 to 7 minutes, until cod flakes easily with a fork. Drain well. When cod is cool enough to handle, remove any skin and visible bones.

In medium bowl, using a fork, flake cod into bite-size pieces. Add oil, parsley, vinegar and garlic; toss gently. Serve at once on a bed of red-leaf lettuce, or refrigerate, covered, up to 4 hours. If refrigerated, let stand at room temperature for 30 minutes before serving.

*D*avid Cohlmeyer was a vegetarian chef. Now he's a gardener, growing, without question, the most unusual and highest quality salad greens in the nation. There's no one else who has made the connection between earth and table so thoroughly as Cohlmeyer. Period.

In his garden known as Cookstown Greens, Cohlmeyer raises specialty vegetables, herbs, edible flowers and seedlings of all sorts. His goal is to encourage a real bond between great chefs and great growers, in the interim helping to elevate the standards of taste in the Toronto area. So every week he personally delivers his crop. Heritage vegetables like the usually rough, bumpy, difficult-to-peel Jerusalem artichoke have a particular twist in the Cookstown garden—they're smooth and have either red or white skins "for roasting whole." He grows both black and white salsify, a rare vegetable with a delicious oyster-like flavour. Red Russian potatoes, German fingerling potatoes, extra-long leeks, incredible tomatoes, crisp celeriac and dahlia root are all on his list. Seedlings like onion, coriander, sweet corn and pea all add flavour to a mid-winter salad. His soil-only greenhouses produce herbs, flowers and salads all winter long, with a brief slowdown in January when light units are so very low. And in the summer, he harvests the wild for extras to bring his chefs: cattail shoots, wild grapes, milkweed pods and whatever else will add *cachet* to their dishes.

Makes **6 servings**

Preparation time: **30 minutes**

Cooking time: **about 2¼ hours**

*T*oronto, originally known as the town of York (founded in 1791), has long been known as "Hog Town." This extract from the York Town Meeting on March 3, 1800, helps to explain why:

> It is agreed by a majority of the inhabitants of the town that no hogs, of any description, shall be allowed to run at large within the limits of the city, and every person or persons shall be liable to pay the sum of five shillings lawful currency for each time and for each hog found running at large. It is also agreed that all persons who keep hogs shall cause them to be marked, which mark shall be registered with the Town Clerk.

Two years later the rules were altered to allow hogs up to three months old to run at large, while hogs over three months could be let loose only if they were "ringed and yoked."

These regulations seem comic in the late twentieth century; however, Toronto was the centre for cattle, pork and sheep sales in Upper Canada. Indeed, by the 1860s William Davies, Canada's first meat packer, had established a prosperous export business, primarily in smoked and cured hams, to the Old Country.

HEARTY STEAK, MUSHROOM AND SAUSAGE PIE WITH DARK ALE

Eat and drink your way through the province a pint and a plate at a time at The Bow and Arrow Pub. General Manager Keiron Meaney marries Ontario's micro-brews with regional ingredients for hearty daily specials like Ontario lamb braised in Conner's Best Bitter, steak, mushroom and sausage pie laced with Upper Canada Dark Ale and Niagara Gritstone and Maple Wheat venison ribs. At The Bow and Arrow the pie is prepared with a double crust, but we think it's just as good—and quicker to make—with only a top crust.

1½ lb	stew beef, trimmed of excess fat and cut into 1-inch (2.5 cm) cubes	750 g
2 tbsp	canola or corn oil	25 mL
1 lb	farmer's sausage, cut into 1-inch (2.5 cm) pieces	500 g
1	large onion, chopped	1
¼ cup	butter	50 mL
⅓ cup	all-purpose flour	75 mL
1	bottle (341 mL) Upper Canada Dark Ale	1
1 cup	beef stock	250 mL
2 tbsp	Worcestershire sauce	25 mL
½ tsp	each salt and black pepper	2 mL
1	bay leaf	1
½ lb	button mushrooms, cut into quarters	250 g
1	pkg (14 oz/397 g) frozen puff pastry, thawed	1
1	egg	1
1 tbsp	water	15 mL

Pat beef dry on paper towels. In large heavy saucepan or Dutch oven, heat oil over medium-high heat. Cook beef in batches for 3 to 5 minutes, until browned on all sides. With slotted spoon, remove beef to a medium bowl; set aside.

Add sausages and onion to fat remaining in saucepan; cook for 3 to 5 minutes, until sausages are browned and onion is softened. With slotted spoon, remove sausages and onion from saucepan; add to beef.

Add butter to saucepan; stir until melted. Stir flour into fat in saucepan; cook over medium heat for 1 minute, until golden. Gradually whisk in ale and stock; bring to boil over high heat. Return beef, sausages and onion to saucepan, along with Worcestershire sauce, salt, pepper and bay leaf. Reduce heat to medium-low; simmer, covered, for 45 minutes. Stir in mushrooms; cook for 30 minutes, until beef is tender. Adjust seasoning to taste; let cool completely. Remove bay leaf.

Preheat oven to 400°F (200°C). Spoon beef mixture into 10-inch (25 cm) deep pie plate or 6-cup (1.5 L) casserole; set aside.

On lightly floured surface, roll out puff pastry to 12-inch (30 cm) circle; place pastry over pie dish, sealing and fluting edges. Cut slits in top of pie for steam to escape. In small bowl, beat together egg and water; brush egg mixture over top of pie. Place pie dish on baking sheet; bake for 35 to 40 minutes, until golden brown. Let stand for 5 to 10 minutes before serving.

*O*ntario's 8,500 dairy farmers market about 2.3 *billion* litres of milk each year, enough to fill Toronto's SkyDome nearly twice!

Makes **4** servings

Preparation time: **25 minutes**

Marinating time: **24 hours**

Cooking time: **6 to 12 minutes**

*F*uture Bakery has been in business selling hearty, real bread for nearly fifty years. Their flagship location at 739 Queen Street West has a large, noisy café where you can dig into a bowl of beet borscht dolloped with M-C Dairy sour cream, cheese-stuffed crepes or a thick slice of fresh fruit pie; then take home a loaf of marble rye bread, a tub of yogurt and a paper-wrapped block of pressed cottage or Lithuanian cheese. Owner Boris Wrzesnewskyi is the third generation to personally supervise the now-booming business begun by his grandparents in 1952. His Polish grandfather earned his Master Baker's diploma in the Ukraine in 1906. After two world wars and a depression, he and his Ukrainian wife came to Canada, first to pick tobacco in the southwest of the province and then, after a brief sojourn in Winnipeg, they settled in Toronto. The little bakery has grown to the point that, at this writing, bakers are working around the clock, seven days a week, with one shift down for maintenance.

TANDOORI CHICKEN KEBABS

Wander along Toronto's Gerrard Avenue East between Coxwell and Greenwood on any summer evening and you'll smell the wonderful spicy aroma of tandoori chicken, for this is the area known as Little India. Traditionally, the chicken is baked in a tandoor, *or clay oven, where the intense heat cooks the chicken to perfection in very few minutes. It's hard to duplicate the exact cooking process at home, but this is a pretty good version. If you use the oven method, turn your extractor fan to high; there will be a lot of smoke.*

1½ lb	boneless skinless chicken breasts, cut into 1-inch (2.5 cm) pieces	750 g
3 tbsp	fresh lemon juice	45 mL
½ tsp	salt	2 mL
1	small onion, quartered	1
2	cloves garlic, sliced	2
1 in	fresh gingerroot, chopped	2.5 cm
1	chili pepper, seeded and chopped	1
¾ tsp	each ground coriander and black pepper	4 mL
¼ tsp	ground cumin and cardamom	1 mL
⅛ tsp	each ground mace and cloves	.5 mL
Pinch	grated nutmeg	Pinch
1 cup	plain yogurt	250 mL

In shallow nonmetallic dish, combine chicken, lemon juice and salt; stir to combine well. Set aside.

In food processor or blender, combine onion, garlic, gingerroot, hot pepper, coriander, black pepper, cumin, cardamom, mace, cloves and nutmeg; process until well combined and finely chopped. Add spice mixture to chicken, along with yogurt; stir well. Refrigerate, covered, for 24 hours, stirring occasionally.

Thread chicken onto 4 metal skewers, shaking off excess marinade. Preheat barbecue to medium-high; grill kebabs for 6 to 8 minutes, turning often, until chicken is golden brown and no longer pink inside.

Alternatively, preheat oven to its highest temperature. Place kebabs on foil-lined heavy baking sheet. Bake for 10 to 12 minutes, turning once, until chicken is golden brown and no longer pink inside. Serve with Faheem's Foolproof Basmati Rice (see recipe on page 100).

*I*n 1994 the Andrews family were named the Outstanding Farm Family in the Halton Region. On their 150-acre farm, Andrew's Scenic Acres on #10 sideroad off Highway 25 north of Milton, customers can pick everything from golden raspberries to sunflowers. Crops are staggered so there's always an interesting crop in the field. Asparagus, rhubarb, strawberries, blueberries, black-berries, raspberries, corn, gooseberries, currants of every colour, sweet and Indian corn, apples, gourds and, of course, pumpkins. There are festivals and fund-raisers all season long beginning with strawberries and ending with the Great Pumpkin Challenge. Super-sweet corn is boiled and sausages are barbecued under the big old maple tree in the yard ready to satisfy the inevitable hunger pangs that hit when you're out picking in the fresh country air. And the good news is that if you miss a particular crop, the chances are you'll be able to buy it from the Andrews' freezers.

Handle all hot peppers with care. Always wear plastic or rubber gloves, and never touch your face with your hands while you prepare them.

Makes **4 servings**

Preparation time: **20 minutes**

Marinating time: **at least 15 minutes**

Cooking time: **10 to 12 minutes**

*K*nives and Forks began as a chefs/ organic-growers coalition and has branched out to include a superb small public market in Mirvish Village on Markham Street. Every Saturday from 8 a.m. till 2 p.m. shoppers fill up their hampers with heirloom vegetables, fresh and smoked trout, seasonal wild vegetables, cultured shiitake mushrooms, a great variety of whole-grain organic breads and free-range poultry.

Note: *To make ginger wine, combine 2 parts rice wine or dry sherry and 1 part grated fresh gingerroot. Let stand for 15 minutes then strain.*

* Available in Oriental section of most large supermarkets.

SZECHUAN-STYLE CHICKEN AND EGGPLANT

Cantonese is now the third most widely spoken language in Canada, after English and French, so it's no wonder that Canada's largest city has not one but three major Chinatowns. This recipe comes not from a new Canadian but is an adaptation of a recipe by Hong Kong home economist Annie Wong of that city's Towngas Cooking Centre, and it's great for entertaining, as most of the preparation can be done ahead. Chicken thighs are best for stir-fries as the meat is juicier than breast meat.

4	chicken thighs, skinned and boned	4
1 tsp	cornstarch	5 mL
1 tsp	each ginger wine (see note in margin), soy sauce, canola or corn oil, and water	5 mL
¼ tsp	each salt, black pepper and granulated sugar	1 mL
¼ tsp	sesame oil*	1 mL
1	eggplant (¾ lb/375 g)	1
1	sweet red pepper	1
1 tbsp	minced fresh gingerroot	15 mL
2	cloves garlic, minced	2
1	green onion, chopped	1
½	chili pepper, seeded and chopped	½

Sauce:

½ cup	chicken stock	125 mL
1 tbsp	soy sauce	15 mL
2 tsp	Oriental chili sauce*	10 mL
½ tsp	granulated sugar	2 mL
½ tsp	each sesame oil* and red wine vinegar	2 mL
	Vegetable oil (about ¼ cup/50 mL)	

Cut chicken thighs into ¼-inch (5 mm) wide strips; set aside. In medium bowl, combine cornstarch, ginger wine, soy sauce, canola oil, water, salt, pepper, sugar and sesame oil. Add chicken; stir well. Refrigerate, covered, at least 15 minutes.

Cut eggplant crosswise into 2-inch (5 cm) slices. Then cut lengthwise into ½-inch (1 cm) thick slices, then cut each slice into ½-inch (1 cm) thick fingers; set aside. Cut pepper into 1-inch (2.5 cm) pieces, removing seeds and stem; set aside.

In small bowl, combine gingerroot, garlic, green onion and chili; set aside. All ingredients can be prepared ahead up to this point. Refrigerate, covered, up to 24 hours.

Sauce: In small bowl, combine stock, soy sauce, chili sauce, sugar, sesame oil and vinegar; set aside. Sauce can be prepared ahead up to this point. Refrigerate, covered, up to 24 hours.

To assemble: Place wok or very large skillet over high heat until very hot. Add 1 tbsp (15 mL) oil. When haze appears over oil, add red pepper; stir-fry over high heat for 1 to 2 minutes or until tender-crisp. Using slotted spoon, remove from wok and set aside. Add 1 tbsp (15 mL) oil to wok. When haze appears, add eggplant; stir-fry over high heat for 3 to 5 minutes or until golden brown and almost tender, adding oil as needed to prevent eggplant from sticking. Remove from wok and set aside.

Add 1 tbsp (15 mL) oil to wok. When haze appears over oil, add chicken and its marinade; stir-fry over high heat for 2 to 3 minutes or until no longer pink inside. Return eggplant and pepper to wok, along with gingerroot mixture and sauce. Cook over high heat for 2 to 3 minutes, stirring occasionally, until eggplant has absorbed most of sauce. Spoon onto serving platter; serve at once.

*F*or one marvellous late-summer Sunday, chefs, organic growers, vintners and brewers from the Toronto-based Knives and Forks coalition break out their picnic gear and head into the countryside to cook at the incomparable Feast of Fields. One year they'll be dotted over the rolling hills of a farm near Collingwood, another around the perimeter of a vineyard or perhaps in an orchard or a conservation area. Diners are given a map, a plate and a glass and encouraged to sample some of the land's most innovative ingredients from the tables of many of the region's best chefs. More than two dozen organic farmers are there to help and talk about their individual products, from red wattle pigs to Chinese silky chickens. It's a leisurely gastro-adventure into the world of great new foods, pleasant local wines and superb micro-brewed beers.

Handle all hot peppers with care. Always wear plastic or rubber gloves, and never touch your face with your hands while you prepare them.

Makes **6 servings**

Preparation time: **40 minutes**

Cooking time: **about 1 hour**

*U*sing Ontario organic soybeans, Soy City Foods has been producing tofu, tempeh and various "veggie burgers" since 1980. Although their products are sold in bulk to food services and institutions like various southern Ontario universities, the public may purchase them in small or case lots from their two Toronto restaurants. The West End Vegetarian Restaurant has a freezer showcase, but you'll have to ask what's available at The Vegetarian Restaurant. The food in these cafeteria-style dining rooms is firmly based on Soy City's own tofu, tempeh and grain products with a bent towards pure vegan vegetarianism. Spices and aromatic seasonings are used to their fullest in dishes like lemon-broiled tempeh with yogurt dill sauce or walnut-crusted tempeh that is crisp and ready for lashings of chutney.

POTATO-CHEDDAR VARENNYKY

When Maria Lozinski moved to Canada from her native Ukraine in 1953, she brought with her this traditional recipe for varennyky, *the Ukrainian version of Polish perogies. In the Ukraine, Maria used a pressed cottage cheese in the filling, but since discovering our great Ontario cheese, she prefers to use a mild Cheddar. To shape the* varennyky, *Maria rolls the dough into a long thin sausage, then cuts off small pieces and rolls each one separately. That way, she explains, no dough is wasted. For first-timers, we've given a simpler method.*

Filling:

2 tbsp	butter	25 mL
1 tbsp	canola or corn oil	15 mL
½ cup	chopped onion	125 mL
1 cup	cold cooked, mashed potato (1½ baking potatoes)	250 mL
¾ cup	shredded mild Cheddar cheese	175 mL
½ tsp	each salt and black pepper	2 mL

Dough:

2	eggs	2
2 tbsp	canola or corn oil	25 mL
1 tsp	salt	5 mL
½ cup	lukewarm water	125 mL
	All-purpose flour (about 2¼ cups/550 mL)	

Topping:

2 tbsp	butter	25 mL
1	medium onion, sliced	1
	Sour cream	

Filling: In large skillet, melt butter with oil over medium-high heat. Add onion; cook, stirring, for 5 to 7 minutes, until onion is golden brown and soft. Remove from heat.

In large bowl, combine onion, potato, cheese, salt and pepper until well combined; set aside.

Dough: In large bowl using electric mixer, beat together eggs, oil and salt; beat in water. Beat in the flour to form a soft but not sticky dough. Turn dough out onto well-floured surface; knead until smooth. Form dough into a ball. Place upturned bowl over dough; set aside for 30 minutes.

Divide dough in half. Roll out 1 piece of dough on lightly floured surface to ⅛ inch (3 mm) thickness; cut out rounds using a 3-inch (8 cm) cutter. Place 1 teaspoonful (5 mL) of filling on half of each round; fold dough over filling to enclose filling completely and form a half-moon shape. Seal edges by pinching together between your thumb and forefinger. Repeat with remaining dough and filling. (*Varennyky* can be prepared ahead up to this point; refrigerate, covered, overnight. If you make them ahead of time, they will seem quite sticky when you come to cook them but the texture will be fine after cooking.)

When ready to cook, bring large pot of salted water to boil over high heat. Add *varennyky* about 6 at a time; cook for 5 to 10 minutes, until *varennyky* rise to surface of water. Remove from pot with slotted spoon; keep warm in heated serving dish while you cook remaining *varennyky*.

Topping: While *varennyky* are cooking, melt butter in large skillet over medium heat. Add onion; cook, stirring, for 5 to 7 minutes, until golden brown and softened. Add onion to cooked *varennyky*; toss gently. Serve hot with sour cream.

*G*azing south over the lush fields that stretch away behind Southbrook Market Garden and Farm, it's hard to believe that the urban sprawl of Toronto begins just beyond the trees; on a clear day you can spot the CN Tower from the pick-your-own strawberry fields. At this oasis just fifteen miles north of Toronto, between Maple and Richmond Hill, Bill Redelmeier and his wife, Marilyn, farm 285 rolling acres and run a successful winery. The Market Garden store features many of the Redelmeier's own crops, such as peas, beans, squash, strawberries and raspberries. Of the rest of the fruits and vegetables on display Bill says, "If it's not produced in Ontario, we won't stock it."

Makes **4 to 6 servings**

Preparation time: **20 minutes**

Cooking time: **45 to 50 minutes**

$\mathcal{T}$oronto's 9,500-acre salad garden is located north of the city, in and around Holland Marsh, an area drained and made arable with a series of dikes built by early Dutch settlers between 1925 and 1930. The dark, almost black soil is light but laden with organic material. It holds the water beautifully so is perfect for celery and all sorts of lettuces. It's in these loamy fields that farmers produce forty percent of all Canada's carrots and one-third of the nation's cooking onions. Recently the rich earth has been yielding a series of Oriental vegetables from pak choi and nappa to Chinese broccoli and radishes. The Muck Research Station near Kettleby in the Holland Marsh is pioneering the cultivation of these crops for Ontario's very different conditions and plant pests. Commercial growers turn to the experts in this OMAFRA station to help identify problems that do not exist in their native lands.

CRISPY ROASTED PARSNIPS WITH BASIL

The bulk of Ontario's parsnip crop is grown in the Holland Marsh area north of Toronto, and although the humble vegetable has never really been welcomed with open arms in North America, it's well worth getting to know. Roasting brings out its natural sweetness, and a light coating of flour makes the parsnips nice and crispy. Choose small or medium-size parsnips; the larger they are, the woodier the texture.

2 lb	parsnips	1 kg
¼ cup	all-purpose flour	50 mL
½ tsp	each salt and black pepper	2 mL
¼ cup	canola or corn oil	50 mL
1 tbsp	dried basil	15 mL

Preheat oven to 425°F (220°C). Peel and trim parsnips; cut into 2- by ½-inch (5 by 1 cm) chunks. In large saucepan, combine parsnips and enough salted water to cover them; bring to boil over high heat. Reduce heat to medium-low; cook, covered, for 5 minutes. Drain well; set aside.

In large bowl, combine flour, salt and pepper. Add parsnips; toss to coat well.

Pour oil into 13- by 9-inch (3 L) baking pan; place in oven for 5 minutes until hot. Add parsnips to oil; sprinkle with basil. Turn parsnips to coat well with oil and basil. Bake for 35 to 40 minutes, turning occasionally, until golden brown and crisp. Drain on paper towels; serve hot.

HANUKKAH POTATO PANCAKES

Toronto food writer and confirmed potato-holic Julie Cohen shared her father's potato pancake recipe with us. Traditional potato pancakes are a dainty 2 inch (5 cm) in diameter, but Julie prefers these larger ones, finding them quicker to make. Rather than the usual applesauce or sour cream accompaniment, Julie serves her pancakes with butter, salt and pepper. Yum!

2½ lb	baking potatoes, peeled (about 5 potatoes)	1.25 kg
1	large onion	1
4	eggs	4
¼ cup	all-purpose flour	50 mL
½ tsp	salt	2 mL
¼ tsp	black pepper	1 mL
	Canola or corn oil (about ¼ cup/50 mL)	

In food processor or using a grater, grate potatoes and onion into large bowl. Add eggs one at a time, stirring well after each addition. Stir in flour, salt and pepper until well combined.

Preheat oven to 200°F (95°C). Brush nonstick skillet with oil; heat over medium heat. Spoon ½ cup (125 mL) potato mixture into skillet. With back of a spoon, spread potato mixture out to form a thin patty. Cook for 4 to 6 minutes, until underside is golden brown. Turn pancake over; cook 4 to 6 minutes, until golden brown. Remove pancake from skillet. Place on paper-towel-lined platter; keep warm in oven. Brush skillet with oil; cook remaining pancakes in same way. Serve at once.

Makes **9 large pancakes; 6 to 8 servings**

Preparation time: **10 minutes**

Cooking time: **8 to 12 minutes per pancake**

*C*hudleigh's is an Ontario success story. The late Eric Chudleigh saw the future in dwarf fruit trees, and in 1939 he became the first Canadian grower to import such rootstock from England. In 1956 he planted the present farm in the shelter of the escarpment just north of Milton, and by 1966, twenty-four thousand trees were in production. His son Tom, a graduate of the University of Guelph, and Tom's wife, Carol, started the pick-your-own concept. They believed that people might welcome a chance to tramp through their orchard, picking a few baskets of apples while enjoying the country air that flows down from the Niagara escarpment.

Today, the Chudleigh farm is rural entertainment at its best. Every weekend from early summer, the orchards are full of people intent on filling their baskets with the crunchiest of apples. There's a huge hay-bale maze for the children (but we've also seen some adults in it) and a store that sells Chudleigh's deep-dish fruit pies. Apple cider may be purchased by the glass or by the gallon; apples can be bought individually or by the bushel. As summer turns to autumn, there are squash, corn and pumpkins. In the winter, there are meat pies and chili and hot fresh muffins.

Makes **4 to 6 servings**

Preparation time: **20 minutes**

Standing time: **30 minutes**

Cooking time: **16½ to 21½ minutes**

*F*rozen tofu becomes chewier and more like meat after it's thawed. As the block thaws, press or squeeze out any excess water; the tofu will sponge up any marinade you choose to use. Usually tofu is soaked in a mixture of soy or tamari, cider vinegar, grated fresh ginger and minced garlic. Use it in stir-fries, tossed into stews and soups or as breaded "cutlets" with chutney, honey mustard or chili sauce.

FAHEEM'S FOOLPROOF BASMATI RICE

Faheem Ahmad came to Toronto from his native Pakistan in 1975. This is his mother's recipe, and it really is foolproof if you follow the instructions to the letter. Faheem says that when his mother cooks rice, she doesn't leave the stove, let alone the kitchen, while it boils. Timing is everything! Basmati rice is a very aromatic rice and well worth trying if you've never had it before. Most large supermarkets stock it in their international section, or look for it in Indian or Caribbean grocery stores.

| 2 cups | basmati rice | 500 mL |
| 1 tsp | salt | 5 mL |

Pick over rice, removing any grit or discoloured grains. In large bowl, combine rice with enough water to cover it. Swirl the rice with your hands, rubbing the grains lightly between your fingers. When the water becomes cloudy; drain the rice and cover with fresh water. Repeat the process until the water remains clear. Drain the rice. In the same bowl, combine rice with enough fresh water to cover; let stand for 30 minutes (the grains of rice will turn white and lengthen somewhat).

Bring large saucepan of water to boil over high heat; add rice and salt. Boil over high heat for 1½ minutes (no longer or rice won't be light and fluffy). Working quickly, drain rice then return it to saucepan. Form rice into cone shape in saucepan; make several holes in cone shape by poking the handle of a wooden spoon down through rice right to bottom of saucepan. Cover tightly; place over very low heat for 15 to 20 minutes, until rice is fluffy and tender.

CARIBBEAN RICE AND PEAS

Visitors to the Caribbean and Toronto's Caribana festival will be familiar with the ubiquitous peas and rice, the island staple that goes so well with most tropical main dishes. Each island has its own version of this dish: in the Dominican Republic red kidney beans and ham season the rice, Jamaicans favour dried red peas and bacon, while Cuban recipes feature fresh green peas. This is how it's prepared in the Bahamas, where it often accompanies fried grouper or conch.

2 tbsp	canola or corn oil	25 mL
3	medium tomatoes, chopped	3
1	medium onion, chopped	1
1	small sweet green pepper, seeded and chopped	1
2 cups	water	500 mL
1	can (16 oz/454 mL) green pigeon peas or black-eyed peas, undrained	1
1½ cups	long-grain rice	375 mL
⅓ cup	tomato paste	75 mL
2 tsp	dried thyme	10 mL
½ tsp	each salt and black pepper	2 mL

In large saucepan, heat oil over medium-high heat. Add tomatoes; stir well. Reduce heat to medium-low; cook, covered, for 10 minutes, stirring occasionally, until tomatoes are very soft. Stir in onion and green pepper; cook, covered, for 10 minutes, until onion is soft and tomatoes are reduced to a pulp.

Stir in water, pigeon peas, rice, tomato paste, thyme, salt and pepper; bring to boil over high heat. Reduce heat to low; simmer, covered, for 25 minutes, until rice is tender and has absorbed most of the liquid. If mixture seems too moist, cook, stirring, over medium-high heat for 3 to 5 minutes, until some of liquid has evaporated. Season with salt and pepper to taste.

Makes **6 servings**

Preparation time: **20 minutes**

Cooking time: **45 to 50 minutes**

*B*uttermilk, the old-fashioned sort that is thick and rich and tangy, is almost a thing of the past. Fortunately, M-C Dairy buttermilk is still handmade with care. Old-fashioned thick cream cheese, the kind that cries for a bagel, thick sour cream, pressed cottage cheese (for perogies) and creamy cottage cheese are sold at Future Bakeries in Toronto and at a handful of farmers' markets across Ontario.

Makes **24 biscotti**

Preparation time: **20 minutes**

Cooking time: **45 to 50 minutes**

$\mathcal{S}$caramouche has served *consistently* excellent food since the day it opened more than a decade ago. From the founding chefs, Jamie Kennedy and Michael Stadtländer, to today's brilliant man-at-the-stoves, Keith Froggett, who now is a partner in the restaurant, their mission has been to provide the best with the most local ingredients possible. Certainly you'll find imported products on the menu, but only when they are not available at home. From pan-roasted Riesling-marinated quail with fresh herbs to the caramelized apple and watercress soup, the menu celebrates the seasons and the talent of the folks in the kitchen. When you want to learn how to make such amazing dishes at home, join the classes in the Scaramouche Kitchen Studio.

PINE-NUT BISCOTTI

Scaramouche has enjoyed the reputation of being one of Toronto's premier restaurants for more than fifteen years. For eleven of those years pastry chef Joanne Yolles worked dessert magic in the kitchen creating divine sweet treats like these crisp, light biscotti. Serve them alongside ice cream or with a cup of coffee.

1¾ cups	all-purpose flour	425 mL
¾ cup	granulated sugar	175 mL
½ cup	pine nuts	125 mL
1 tbsp	baking powder	15 mL
	Grated rind of 2 lemons	
2	eggs	2
⅓ cup	light-tasting olive oil	75 mL
1 tsp	vanilla	5 mL
	Additional granulated sugar	

Preheat oven to 325°F (160°C). Line 2 baking sheets with parchment paper.

In medium bowl, stir together flour, sugar, pine nuts, baking powder and lemon rind. In separate bowl, whisk together eggs, olive oil and vanilla. Make a well in centre of dry ingredients; add egg mixture. Stir until ingredients are well combined and a smooth, slightly sticky dough forms. Divide dough in half; place each piece on a separate baking sheet. With floured hands, shape each piece of dough into a 12-inch (30 cm) long log. (Dough will spread dramatically during baking.)

Sprinkle logs evenly with additional sugar. Bake for 30 minutes, until logs are lightly browned and still feel slightly soft when pressed lightly. Remove from oven; let cool on baking sheets for 5 minutes.

Carefully remove one log from baking sheet; place on cutting board. With sharp knife, cut log into ¾-inch (2 cm) slices. Separate slices on baking sheet, arranging cut sides down. Repeat with other log. Return baking sheets to oven; bake for 15 to 20 minutes, until biscotti are lightly browned. Let cool completely on wire racks; store in airtight container.

*T*he Redpath Sugar Museum provides a glimpse into the early days of the sugar trade. The first sugar-processing facility was built by John Redpath in Montreal. With the advent of the St. Lawrence Seaway in the 1950s, Redpath Sugar relocated to Toronto, where the huge silos on the waterfront became instant landmarks. The museum is open from Monday through Friday (10 a.m. till noon and 1 p.m. till 3:30 p.m.). However, it is advisable to call ahead to ensure that it is not being used for seminars and that the curator is on site.

Makes **12 muffins**

Preparation time: **20 minutes**

Cooking time: **20 to 25 minutes**

*T*he Kortright Centre for Conservation is one of the jewels in Metro Toronto's conservation-area crown. As you turn south off Metro's busy Major Mackenzie Drive onto leafy Pine Valley Drive, it's hard to believe you're so close to the city. The Kortright Centre comprises 325 hectares in the Humber River Valley and features educational nature trails and hosts a wide variety of activities throughout the year. One of the most intriguing events held at Kortright is the annual honey festival in September. Kortright's bee house is open to the public, and from safely inside you can watch the intrepid bee-keepers outside deftly handling thousands of bees. The centre's honey is available for tasting, and a number of Metro-area beekeepers are on hand to sell their wares, including beeswax candles and hand cream and yummy treats, such as cinnamon-flavoured honey. The more athletic can join in the bee dance, and there are cooking demonstrations and competitions.

HONEY-DATE MUFFINS

Each September the Kortright Centre for Conservation celebrates the beginning of fall with a honey festival. Included in the festivities is a baking-with-honey contest. One of the lucky winners in 1995 was Marianne Crawford from Bramalea who was kind enough to share her recipe with us. We love honey so much we changed Marianne's recipe a little just so we could add more honey!

1½ cups	all-purpose flour	375 mL
1 cup	natural bran	250 mL
1 tsp	each baking powder and baking soda	5 mL
½ tsp	salt	2 mL
¼ tsp	cinnamon	1 mL
1½ cups	sour milk*	375 mL
½ cup	liquid honey	125 mL
⅓ cup	shortening, melted	75 mL
1	egg	1
¾ cup	chopped pitted dates	175 mL
¼ cup	walnut pieces	50 mL

Preheat oven to 375°F (190°C). In medium bowl, stir together flour, bran, baking powder, baking soda, salt and cinnamon.

In separate bowl, whisk together milk, honey, shortening and egg. Add milk mixture all at once to flour mixture; stir just until dry ingredients are moistened. Fold in ½ cup (125 mL) dates and the walnuts. Divide batter evenly among 12 buttered or paper-lined muffin cups. Top muffins with remaining dates, dividing evenly. Bake for 20 to 25 minutes, until toothpick inserted into centre muffin comes out clean. Remove muffins from pan; let cool completely on wire rack.

* To sour milk, place 2 tbsp (25 mL) lemon juice or white vinegar in glass measure; add milk to measure 1½ cups (375 mL). Stir; let stand for 5 minutes.

*C*anoe is a restaurant that honours the ingredients of all our national regions, from the wonderful Ermite cheese, caviar and foie gras of Quebec to the finest Alberta beef, Shediac lobster and succulent Digby scallops. There are salad greens from Ontario and in-house-smoked Atlantic salmon. Executive chef Michael Bonacini and dream-meister Peter Oliver have fashioned an upscale Canadian dining experience that smacks of nationalistic pride. Their wine list offers a huge VQA selection from both Ontario and British Columbia. Canada's reality is her ultimate regionality— Canoe judges the quality of its cuisine not by how much they can import, but rather how much of it *we grow*. Located on the 54th floor of the Toronto Dominion Centre; reservations strongly recommended.

Makes **12 tarts**

Preparation time: **20 minutes**

Cooking time: **20 to 25 minutes**

*H*ow about a slice of green tea cheese-cake? Want to try doing a bit of moon cake quality control by sampling the traditional sweet at a variety of Asian bakeries? Ever had Arabic coffee in a Chinese teacup in an Ethiopian restaurant that has no menu? Tasting TO has rarely been so healthy or rich in the cultural history of the city! Shirley Lum, a self-confessed foodie, leads bike and walking tours with the tummy in mind. She loves this city and its markets and, most importantly, its people. Meeting as a group or singly by appointment, she guides and chats and samples through the nooks and crannies of Little Italy, Greektown, two Chinatowns and Kensington with all their colourful ethnic markets.

DIM-SUM CUSTARD TARTS

These crumbly little mouthfuls are traditionally served warm for dim sum, China's—and now Toronto's—very civilized answer to brunch.

Crust:

½ cup	shortening	125 mL
2 tbsp	granulated sugar	25 mL
1	egg	1
1½ cups	all-purpose flour	375 mL
2 tbsp	cold water	25 mL

Filling:

½ cup	water	125 mL
¼ cup	granulated sugar	50 mL
3	eggs	3
½ tsp	vanilla	2 mL

Crust: In medium bowl, using electric mixer, beat shortening and sugar until light and fluffy. Beat in egg until well combined. Gradually stir in flour until well combined. Stir in water to make a soft dough. Turn out onto lightly floured surface; knead lightly until smooth.

Divide dough into 12 equal portions. Place each portion of dough in lightly greased 3-inch (8 cm) tartlet pan. Press dough evenly over bottom and 1 inch (2.5 cm) up sides of each tartlet pan. Refrigerate while you make the filling.

Filling: In small saucepan, combine water and sugar. Heat over medium-high heat, stirring occasionally, until sugar has dissolved. Remove from heat; let cool completely.

Preheat oven to 350°F (180°C). In medium bowl, beat eggs and vanilla until well combined. Gradually stir in cooled sugar mixture. Carefully pour egg mixture evenly into lined tartlet pans. Bake for 20 to 25 minutes or until filling is just set and pastry is golden brown. Serve warm or cold.

*Y*ou've heard of pick-your-own strawberry farms, but how about a pick-your-own flower farm? Cathy Bartolic has operated Perennial Petals in Stouffville for four years, and until recently she specialized only in flowers suitable for drying. In 1995, however, Cathy started to grow edible flowers, such as nasturtiums, calendula, marigolds and pansies. In addition to picking your own salad you can pick up some of Cathy's recipes for such yummy creations as corn bread muffins with calendula, or nasturtiums stuffed with guacamole. Future crops will include scarlet runner beans and begonias, which have a surprising lemony flavour, says Cathy. Perennial Petals is open weekends from mid-July to mid-September.

Makes **6 servings**

Preparation time: **20 minutes**

Cooking time: **3 to 4 minutes**

Chilling time: **2 hours**

*B*ill and Marilyn Redelmeier started their winery in a dairy barn on Major MacKenzie Drive north of Toronto in 1991 and since then have produced award-winning wines using grapes grown for them in the Niagara region. Their ambrosial raspberry dessert wine, Framboise, was developed in 1992 when they needed to use up a glut of raspberries during what Bill Redelmeier describes as "a real Scottish summer—cold and wet." Southbrook Farms is open from Mother's Day through Christmas. There's a lot going on all year, including a wine festival complete with tastings in July and wagon rides to the pick-your-own pumpkin fields at Halloween.

ROSEMARY-SCENTED BERRY COMPOTE

Summer berries are in season for such a short time it's often best to enjoy them relatively unadorned, as in this delicately flavoured compote. Use any combination of berries but only add strawberries, raspberries, loganberries or Tay berries 30 minutes before serving. Southbrook Farms Cassis is a dessert wine made from black currants produced at a winery in Maple, north of Toronto; you can buy it at the winery (on Major Mackenzie Drive between Bathurst and Dufferin) or at selected liquor stores. If you can't find it, substitute a berry-flavoured liqueur or use a nonalcoholic black currant nectar, such as Gabriele's Black Currant Nectar, produced by Gabriele Trenn on his farm near Colborne. Gabriele's nectar is available at the farm or at grocery stores in the Colborne area. We serve the compote with crème fraîche, but it's just as good with ice cream, over pound cake and even on its own for breakfast!

Crème Fraîche:

⅓ cup	whipping cream	75 mL
⅔ cup	sour cream	150 mL

Berry Compote:

6 cups	assorted prepared summer berries (red or black currants, blueberries, raspberries, Tay berries, loganberries, blackberries, strawberries; about 2 lb/1 kg)	1.5 L
¾ cup	granulated sugar*	175 mL
½ cup	water	125 mL
3	sprigs fresh rosemary	3
⅓ cup	Southbrook Farms Cassis, black currant nectar or a fruit-flavoured liqueur*	75 mL

Crème Fraîche: In medium bowl, whip whipping cream just until it thickens and is the consistency of yogurt. Gently stir in sour cream until well combined. Refrigerate, covered, until ready to serve.

Berry Compote: Prepare all the fruits by rinsing lightly (except for the delicate berries, such as raspberries; just wipe these with a damp cloth). Remove red and black currants from stalks by running the tines of a fork down each stalk. Slice any large strawberries. In large pretty glass serving bowl, combine all fruits, except delicate ones, such as strawberries, raspberries, loganberries and Tay berries.

In small saucepan, combine sugar, water and rosemary sprigs. Heat over medium heat, stirring occasionally, for 2 to 3 minutes, until sugar has dissolved. Increase heat to high; bring to boil. Pour hot syrup and rosemary over fruit. Add Cassis; stir gently. Refrigerate, covered, 2 hours or until chilled. Thirty minutes before serving, remove from fridge; stir in remaining fruit. Let stand at room temperature 30 minutes before serving. Serve compote in individual glasses or bowls; topped with crème fraîche.

* If using black currant nectar or liqueur, reduce sugar to ½ cup (125 mL).

*B*lack River Juice Company of Mississauga has been pressing a variety of pure Ontario fruit juices since 1988. When we talked, quality control manager Keith Wallace had just returned from inspecting Bartlett pears in Niagara. Keith met his partner, Grant Keane, in the early 1980s while working at the Ontario Federation of Food Cooperatives. They founded Black River, naming it after a small village near Picton where their fruit was purchased. Today they shop all over southwestern Ontario. They bottle cranberry (Johnston's p.174), peach, Bartlett pear, raspberry, Montmorency cherry, apple and currant juices, in addition to a new product, cranberry juice that has been frozen tart and fresh from the press.

Makes **6 to 8 servings**

Preparation time: **25 minutes**

Cooking time: **25 to 35 minutes**

*B*ruce's Mill Conservation Area, just north of Metro Toronto off County Road 14 west of Stouffville, boasts five hectares of working sugar bush, which produces enough maple syrup each season to supply the on-site store and refreshment room and to make taffy. A short self-guided trail meanders through the sugar bush, and rustic displays tell the story of maple syrup, including examples of old-fashioned methods of maple-syrup production. For example, the aboriginal peoples of Canada at one time poured the maple sap into a hollowed-out log then added hot stones until the sap boiled. After you've worked up an appetite, don't miss the refreshment room, where for around $4 you can buy a gargantuan portion of dinner-plate-size pancakes with a generous drizzle of Bruce's Mill's own maple syrup; add a helping of sausages and you won't need to eat for the rest of the week!

MAPLE-PECAN PIE WITH MAPLE-WHISKY CREAM

This luscious dessert packs a double hit of maple syrup. The maple-whisky cream is also perfect dolloped on fresh berries, baked apples, fruit crisp, black coffee or just about anything!

Maple-Pecan Pie:
Pastry for 9-inch (23 cm) single-crust pie (see recipe on page 112)

½ cup	packed brown sugar	125 mL
½ cup	maple syrup	125 mL
⅓ cup	corn syrup	75 mL
¼ cup	butter	50 mL
¼ tsp	salt	1 mL
3	eggs	3
1 cup	pecan halves	250 mL

Maple-Whisky Cream:

¼ cup	Canadian whisky	50 mL
3 tbsp	maple syrup	45 mL
1 cup	whipping cream	250 mL

Maple-Pecan Pie: Preheat oven to 375°F (190°C). On lightly floured clean tea towel, roll out pastry and use to line a 9-inch (23 cm) pie plate; set aside.

In medium saucepan, combine sugar, maple syrup, corn syrup, butter and salt; heat over medium heat for 3 to 5 minutes, stirring occasionally, until butter melts. Remove from heat; let cool to room temperature.

In medium bowl, beat eggs; beat in sugar mixture until well combined. Reserve 10 pecan halves; chop remainder. Stir chopped pecans into sugar mixture. Pour filling into pie crust; arrange reserved pecan halves decoratively on top. Bake for 25 to 30 minutes, until pastry is golden brown and filling is puffy and set around edges but centre still jiggles slightly. Let cool completely before serving.

Maple-Whisky Cream: In small bowl, combine whisky and maple syrup; set aside. In medium bowl, whip cream until it is the consistency of yogurt. Gradually add whisky mixture to cream, whipping just until soft peaks form and all whisky mixture is incorporated. Do not overwhip; cream should still be soft enough to drop from a spoon.

*T*he largest VQA wine list in the world has been assembled at the venerable Royal York Hotel. Selections are made prior to the various wine competitions, and since post-competition stocks of the award-winning wines are often extremely limited even at the wineries themselves, this list often includes hard-to-find champions.

Makes **6 to 8 servings**

Preparation time: **1 hour**

Chilling time: **20 minutes**

Cooking time: **55 to 60 minutes**

*T*he cliffs of the Escarpment near Kelso Conservation Area run through Springridge Farm. In the mid-seventies it was a cherry orchard, but the falling price of cherries meant that everyone had to get a job somewhere else. But what to do with the trees hanging with fruit? That was when the present-day pick-your-own operation began. A pitting machine was added and made available at no extra cost to customers. Over the ensuing decades more crops were added to the PYO list (strawberries, raspberries, pumpkins); the nineteenth-century barn has been restored and a full "from scratch" bakery has been added. Deep-dish cherry and summer berry pies are the favourites. In strawberry season it takes eight bakers to keep up with the demand for the strawberry custard tarts. Country lunches are served and may be washed down with Longlane Orchards apple cider. In the wintertime the season's harvest is made into thirty-five different jams, jellies and condiments, including a honey-garlic sauce made with honey harvested from hives in their own orchards.

PEAR AND CRANBERRY DEEP-DISH PIE

When we asked Dufflet Rosenberg, owner of Toronto's renowned Dufflet Pastries, to share an Ontario-style dessert recipe with us, she said, "You can't get much more Ontario than pears and cranberries." Here she's teamed them in a pretty pie that has both a streusel and a lattice topping. While the preparation time may seem lengthy, the pie can be prepared ahead in easy stages.

Pastry:

2 cups	sifted cake-and-pastry flour	500 mL
⅔ cup	cold unsalted butter, cut into small pieces	150 mL
Pinch	salt	Pinch
¼ cup	cold water	50 mL
1	egg yolk	1

Filling:

8	ripe pears, peeled, cored and sliced (about 3 lb/1.5 kg)	8
2 cups	cranberries (½ lb/250 g)	500 mL
⅔ cup	sour cream	150 mL
⅓ cup	granulated sugar	75 mL
¼ cup	all-purpose flour	50 mL
1	egg	1
1 tsp	each grated lemon rind and vanilla	5 mL

Streusel:

½ cup	each granulated and packed brown sugar	125 mL
½ cup	cold unsalted butter, cut into small pieces	125 mL
¼ cup	all-purpose flour	50 mL
¼ tsp	cinnamon	1 mL
Pinch	salt	Pinch
1	egg	1
1 tbsp	water	15 mL
	Additional sugar	

Pastry: In food processor, combine flour, butter and salt; process with on/off pulses until well combined and mixture resembles oatmeal. Transfer mixture to large bowl.

In glass measure beat together water and egg yolk. Make well in centre of flour mixture; pour egg-yolk mixture into well. With fork, stir just until dry ingredients are moistened. Gather dough into a ball; wrap in plastic wrap. Chill in the fridge for 20 minutes before rolling out.

Roll out two-thirds of pastry; use to line a 10-inch (25 cm) deep-dish pie plate, reserving pastry trimmings.

Filling: In large bowl, combine pears and cranberries. In small bowl, whisk together sour cream, sugar, flour, egg, lemon rind and vanilla. Add sour-cream mixture to fruit; stir gently to combine. Spoon filling into pie plate; set aside.

Streusel: In food processor, combine granulated and brown sugar, butter, flour, cinnamon and salt; process with on/off pulses until well combined and crumbly. Sprinkle streusel evenly over filling.

Preheat oven to 400°F (200°C). Roll out remaining pastry to ⅛-inch (3 mm) thickness; cut into ½-inch (1 cm) wide strips. Arrange strips in a lattice fashion over streusel, sealing edges well. In small bowl, beat together egg and water; brush over edges of pie. Cut leaf shapes out of pastry trimmings; arrange around edge of pie. Brush lattice and leaf shapes with egg mixture; sprinkle lightly with sugar. Place pie on baking sheet; bake for 15 minutes. Reduce temperature to 350°F (180°C); bake for 40 to 45 minutes, until pastry is golden brown and fruit is tender. Serve warm.

*D*ufflet's is *the* Toronto pastry shop. It was founded twenty years ago by Dufflet Rosenberg, and few places in Ontario have such glorious sweets. Cakes are crowned with great heaps of white chocolate curls, fluffy fillings spill out from between layers of delicate tortes, and tarts are mounded with streusel and fruit. Her decadent chocolate dessert sauce is laced with cognac, and her raspberry sauce is blended with cassis. And if eating isn't enough, clients have the opportunity to learn how to bake with Dufflet at Great Cooks, a "cooking forum for Toronto's culinary stars."

Great Cooks, a collaboration between Dufflet and her sister-in-law, Esther Rosenberg, operates in an intimate kitchen-theatre setting behind the pastry shop. Most of Toronto's top chefs cook there from time to time, and one evening is devoted to "chefs on the rise," showcasing the new talent that is so evident on this vital local scene.

Makes 4 half-pint (250 mL) jars

Preparation time: 30 minutes

Cooking time: about 25 minutes

Processing time: 5 minutes

*E*very November, the country comes to the city when the Royal Agricultural Winter Fair opens at Exhibition Place in Toronto to stylishly celebrate the harvest and welcome our great northern winter. Cows, pigs and sheep; horse jumping and athletic dogs; jam- and pickle-making; butter carving and championship cheese: the sights, sounds—and smells—of the farmyard have been a part of the Royal for more than sixty-five years. Tuxedos and ball gowns grace the gala evening events while denim is *de rigueur* the rest of the time. The Royal is the largest indoor agricultural show in the world, and its statistics are staggering. Throughout the twelve days of the fair, Exhibition Place is home to more than 3,000 cattle, 1,300 horses, 1,600 birds, 500 sheep, 300 goats and 300 pigs; that's quite an ark! Along with the livestock come the foods of rural Ontario: fabulous back bacon on a bun, barbecued lamb sandwiches, baked potatoes, maple syrup, honeycomb, jams, jellies and pickles galore. You can eat your way around the province without leaving Toronto!

PRIZEWINNING ROSEMARY APPLE CIDER JELLY

In 1994 Yvonne Tremblay won first prize in the jams and jellies competition at Toronto's Royal Agricultural Winter Fair with this crystal-clear aromatic jelly. It's the perfect condiment to serve with roast chicken or lamb; we also like it in sandwiches made with the leftover roast. Yvonne sometimes substitutes grape juice and sage for the apple cider and rosemary. Don't be tempted to reduce the sugar in this recipe; it's needed for a good set.

2 tbsp	fresh rosemary leaves	25 mL
	Sweet apple cider (about 2 cups/500 mL)	
3½ cups	granulated sugar	875 mL
½ cup	liquid fruit pectin	125 mL

Tie rosemary leaves in double thickness of cheesecloth. In very large stainless steel or enamel saucepan, combine rosemary and 2 cups (500 mL) apple cider; bring to boil over high heat (saucepan may seem too large but when jelly boils the foam may reach right to top of saucepan). Reduce heat to low; simmer, covered, for 20 minutes. Remove and discard rosemary.

Pour cooked cider into glass measure; add more cider if necessary to make 2 cups (500 mL). Pour cider back into saucepan; stir in sugar. Bring to full rolling boil over high heat. Add pectin. Bring to full rolling boil; boil for 30 seconds. Remove saucepan from heat; skim off any foam.

Immediately ladle into 4 hot, sterilized ½-pint (250 mL) jars, leaving ¼ inch (5 mm) headspace. Wipe jar rims to remove any excess jelly; seal with two-piece lids, tightening screw bands until just fingertip tight. Process in hot-water bath for 5 minutes. Remove jars from canner; let cool for 24 hours. Check jar seals (sealed lids curve downwards). Remove screw bands; label jars. Store jelly in cool, dark place.

Lake Ontario's Heartland

Stretching northwards from the rolling wooded hills that hug the shores of Lake Ontario, this heartland is a microcosm of the geography of the rest of the province. The fertile agricultural areas close to the lake soon give way to wilder scenery as the Shield begins to thrust up through the earth. Dotted with lakes and sparsely inhabited, the more northerly parts of the region offer rich pickings for hunters and fishers alike. The region supports almost every crop that grows throughout the rest of the province and even welcomed its first winery —Ocala, near Port Perry—in 1995. There's a cidery in Prince Edward County, where there's also a thriving tender-fruit industry.

The region has a flourishing and rich native heritage with at least two major pow wows taking place each year. At the Curve Lake Reserve, north of Peterborough, you can sample native foods during the warmer months in the Summer Tea Room.

The winding roads beg to be explored, and with orchards and herb farms to visit, fish to catch and fry, cheeses to be sampled and wine sipped, Lake Ontario's Heartland is a peregrinating food lover's paradise.

Makes **6 servings**

Preparation time: **20 minutes**

Cooking time: **60 to 70 minutes**

$\mathcal{S}$ince garlic is native to cold, northern climates, it's appropriate that Ontario has the potential to be a major producer. Indeed, Ontario garlic does have larger cloves. Few know the plant better than Ted Macska, known across the province as the Fish Lake Garlic Man. Garlic is his life. He eats it and sometimes even drinks it in his Fish Lake Fire Water, a potent brew of vodka and crushed garlic cloves.

ROASTED GARLIC WITH HERBED GOAT CHEESE

If the thought of eating a whole head of garlic alarms you, remember that long, slow roasting renders the garlic sweet and mellow.

Herbed Goat Cheese:

¼ lb	goat cheese	125 g
1 tbsp	finely chopped fresh parsley	15 mL
1 tbsp	milk	15 mL
½ tsp	minced fresh rosemary leaves	2 mL
¼ tsp	black pepper	1 mL

Roast Garlic:

6	large heads garlic	6
2 tbsp	canola or corn oil	25 mL
1 tbsp	fresh rosemary leaves	15 mL
	Black pepper to taste	
1	narrow baguette	1
6	sprigs fresh rosemary	6

Herbed Goat Cheese: In small bowl, stir together goat cheese, parsley, milk, rosemary and black pepper until well combined. Pack into small serving dish; refrigerate, covered, until ready to serve.

Roast Garlic: Preheat oven to 400°F (200°C). With large sharp knife, slice off tops of heads of garlic to expose tops of cloves. Place garlic on sheet of foil large enough to enclose all six heads. Drizzle 1 tsp (5 mL) of the oil over each head of garlic; sprinkle evenly with rosemary and pepper. Enclose garlic loosely in foil, sealing edges tightly. Place on baking sheet; bake for 50 to 60 minutes, until garlic feels tender when a sharp knife is inserted into one of the cloves.

Cut baguette into ½-inch (1 cm) slices; arrange on baking sheet. Place in oven alongside garlic; bake 7 to 10 minutes, turning occasionally, until golden brown.

Place each head of garlic on individual plate; surround with toasted baguette slices and garnish with rosemary. Serve with goat cheese. To eat, scoop out garlic cloves with a knife; spread on baguette slices, along with goat cheese.

*T*he British Empire Cheese Show is held annually in Belleville at the end of November. It is the largest cheese exposition in Canada with the largest display of both Canadian and international cheeses and butter in competition. The Central Ontario Cheesemakers' Association, the show's sponsor, demonstrates the making of Cheddar. The entire show is open to the public, from the luncheon and speakers to the awards ceremony. Entries, from an Australian Cheddar to a Toronto-made Romano, are assembled and displayed before being sliced and wrapped for sale. However, they are snapped up quickly—some as soon as they are displayed. According to organizer and dairy farmer Norm McWaters, the Italian barbers down the street clean out almost all of the Romano.

*Makes **4** servings*

Preparation time: **15 minutes**

Standing time: **30 minutes**

*A*dventurous trips don't necessarily have to involve white-water rafting or clinging by your fingernails to a sheer cliff face. Organized forays into the Ontario countryside are just as fun and not nearly as dangerous. One of the first people in the province to recognize the untapped pleasures of such a trip is Kristin McCrea, who in 1993 instigated the Great Ganaraska Countryside Adventure around the Ganaraska Forest area, which straddles Durham and Northumberland counties. For a small fee participants are provided with a button (their entry to various stops along the way) and a map, and for a weekend in August they intrepidly explore the region, stopping at local farms, church halls and museums. In 1995, participants in the Great Ganaraska Countryside Adventure had a choice of sixty-eight locations to visit, including the hundred-year-old Tyrone Mill, a trout hatchery, a mushroom farm and an operating blacksmith's forge. Various church halls supplied refreshments, which ranged from burgers and beans to a magnificent pig roast.

CHILLED STRAWBERRY SOUP WITH PEPPER CREAM

Black pepper may seem an unusual seasoning for this gorgeous deep-pink soup, but the flavours of strawberries and pepper go beautifully together. Try a light sprinkling of black pepper on your next bowl of strawberries and cream. Trust us; it's wonderful!

Pepper Cream:

⅓ cup	sour cream	75 mL
½ tsp	finely ground black pepper	2 mL

Soup:

4 cups	sliced strawberries (about 1½ lb/750 g)	1 L
½ cup	granulated sugar	125 mL
1 cup	Ontario red wine, such as Cabernet Sauvignon	250 mL
½ cup	sour cream	125 mL
4	small strawberries for garnish	4

Pepper Cream: In small bowl, combine sour cream and pepper. Refrigerate, covered, until ready to serve.

Soup: Place strawberries in medium bowl; sprinkle with sugar. Let stand for 30 minutes, stirring occasionally, until sugar has dissolved.

In blender, blend strawberry mixture in batches until smooth. Transfer to bowl or pitcher. Whisk in wine and sour cream until smooth. Refrigerate, covered, until well chilled. Ladle into chilled soup bowls; garnish each serving with a spoonful of pepper cream and a strawberry.

FRESH CORN AND ROASTED RED PEPPER SALSA

This colourful salsa is great alongside all kinds of grilled meats and fish. Towards the end of August, just when our wonderful local corn is at its best, Sheppard peppers appear in the stores. These long, skinny peppers are deliciously sweet and tend to be cheaper than the earlier hothouse bell peppers.

1	large sweet red pepper	1
2	ears corn, shucked	2
4	green onions, chopped	4
1 tbsp	each white wine vinegar and canola, corn or nut oil	15 mL
1	clove garlic, minced	1
1 tsp	finely minced hot pepper	5 mL
1 tsp	fresh thyme leaves	5 mL
¼ tsp	each salt and black pepper	1 mL

Preheat barbecue grill to high. Grill pepper for 15 to 20 minutes, turning often, until blackened all over. Remove from grill; place in brown paper bag. Let stand for 10 minutes.

Meanwhile, in large pot of boiling salted water, cook corn for 10 minutes, until kernels are tender. Drain well; cool under cold running water. Remove kernels from ear of corn by standing ear on one end and running a sharp knife down between kernels and ear. Place kernels in serving bowl, breaking up any clumps of kernels with your fingers.

Remove pepper from bag; peel off skin. Cut into 1-inch (2.5 cm) pieces, discarding seeds and stem. Add pepper to corn, along with onions, vinegar, oil, garlic, hot pepper, thyme, salt and pepper; stir gently. Serve at room temperature for best flavour.

*Makes **4 servings***

*Preparation time: **20 minutes***

*Cooking time: **25 to 30 minutes***

*M*ike and Carole Plunkett, who grow organic herbs and vegetables just north of Port Hope, are at the Cobourg Farmers' Market most Saturdays, and their stall is a great place to buy trendy greens such as arugula at non-city prices. Among the other unusual crops the Plunketts grow are ground cherries, which are the same as cape gooseberries and which make a fabulous wine; tomatilloes, native to Central and South America and used in salsas; and Oriental spinach. During the week in the summer months, Carole also has a farm stand at the end of their driveway at Highway 28 and the 7th Concession in Bewdley. From there she sells her cornucopia of vegetables and herbs, including potato squash that really does taste like potato, and tiny squash she calls fruit-dumpling, packaged in individual portions by Mother Nature.

Handle all hot peppers with care. Always wear plastic or rubber gloves, and never touch your face with your hands while you prepare them.

Makes **8 servings**

Preparation time: **25 minutes**

Cooking time: **about 3¾ hours**

*J*ust south of the picturesque town of Port Perry and far from Ontario's traditional wine country lies Ocala Orchards Farm Winery. In 1995, owner Irwin Smith and his wife, Alissa, decided to turn their winemaking hobby into a business and opened a winery in a converted cow barn on the former dairy farm. The fields of vines you pass as you drive up to the farm are a surprise. Since windswept Durham region is too cold for the traditional trellis system of growing vines used in the Niagara region, the Smiths follow the example of Quebec vineyards, growing their vines close to the ground and burying the main shoots, or canes, in the winter. In addition to a Riesling and a good barrel-aged Chardonnay, the Smiths produce a range of fruit wines, including McIntosh and Spartan apple wines. Tours of the orchard, vineyard and winery are available year round, and the full range of wines is for sale in the tasting room, along with wine-related gifts, local cheeses, preserves and maple syrup.

ROAST CAPON WITH SHIITAKE MUSHROOM AND WILD RICE STUFFING

This recipe is a happy marriage of two of Peterborough farmers' market's specialties—organic capon and shiitake mushrooms—and wild rice, which used to be harvested at nearby Rice Lake. A capon is a neutered male chicken; it has very moist, tender flesh and a mild flavour. You can substitute a 10-lb (4.5 kg) turkey for the capon, if you prefer.

Stuffing:

4	slices bacon, chopped	4
1	onion, chopped	1
2	stalks celery, sliced	2
2	cloves garlic, minced	2
¼ lb	shiitake mushrooms, sliced (2 cups/500 mL)	125 g
1½ cups	chicken stock	375 mL
⅓ cup	wild rice, rinsed and drained	75 mL
1	bay leaf	1
¼ tsp	each salt and black pepper	1 mL
⅓ cup	long-grain rice	75 mL
½ cup	chopped fresh parsley	125 mL
2 tbsp	shredded fresh sage leaves or ½ tsp/2 mL ground sage	25 mL

Capon:

1	capon (10 lb/4.5 kg)	1
1 tbsp	canola or corn oil	15 mL
1 tsp	minced fresh sage leaves or ¼ tsp/1 mL ground sage	5 mL
¼ tsp	black pepper	1 mL
½ cup	each maple syrup and apple cider	125 mL

Stuffing: In medium saucepan, cook bacon over medium-high heat for 3 to 5 minutes, stirring occasionally, until browned and just starting to crisp. Remove with slotted spoon; place on paper-towel-lined plate. Drain off all but 1 tbsp (15 mL) fat.

Add onion, celery and garlic to saucepan; cook, stirring, over medium heat for 3 to 5 minutes, until onion is softened. Add mushrooms; cook, stirring, for 2 minutes, until mushrooms start to soften.

Add stock, wild rice, bay leaf, salt and pepper. Bring to boil over high heat, stirring to scrape up any brown bits from bottom of saucepan. Reduce heat to medium-low; simmer, covered, for 15 minutes.

Add long-grain rice; simmer, covered, for 15 minutes, until most of liquid has been absorbed (mixture should still be moist) and rice is almost tender. Stir in bacon, parsley and sage; let cool completely before stuffing capon.

Capon: Preheat oven to 325°F (160°C). Pat capon dry inside and out with paper towels. Spoon stuffing into body cavity. Place capon on oiled rack in roasting pan, tucking wing tips under body. Rub capon all over with oil; sprinkle evenly with minced sage and pepper. Roast for 2½ hours, basting occasionally with juices in roasting pan.

In small saucepan, combine maple syrup and apple cider. Bring to boil; boil over high heat for 5 to 7 minutes, until reduced to ½ cup (125 mL). Pour half of maple-syrup mixture over capon; roast for 15 minutes. Pour remaining maple-syrup mixture over capon; roast for 15 minutes, or until meat thermometer inserted into thickest part of thigh registers 185°F (85°C) and juices that run out are no longer pink.

Transfer capon to warmed platter. Tent loosely with foil; let stand 20 minutes before carving.

Makes **4 to 6 servings**

Preparation time: **30 minutes**

Cooking time: **50 to 60 minutes**

*R*abbit yields a low-fat healthful meat that's fast gaining in popularity in Canada, though we'd have to eat a lot more than our present annual two ounces per capita to compete with the world's leading rabbit-loving nation, Malta, where rabbit is consumed at a rate of thirteen pounds per person each year. At their farm All Rabbits Inc. just north of Cobourg, Harry Kuehn and his wife, Christa, sell 2½ to 3½ pound fryers and larger 5 to 6 pound roasters from the freezer, as well as Christa's tasty rabbit burgers, all ready to pop on the grill. There's fresh meat available on Tuesdays and Thursdays, but you must call ahead to order it.

HOT AND SPICY GARLIC RABBIT

Rabbits are usually sold whole, so we have given instructions for cutting the rabbit into portions; it's really quite easy. If you do find a supplier or butcher who sells rabbit pieces, the back legs are the meatiest part (all that hopping!). Cooking rabbit slowly in this wonderfully tangy sauce makes it extra juicy and tender. We like the dish fairly spicy, but for a milder flavour simply reduce the cayenne to ¼ tsp (1 mL). Skinned chicken drumsticks can be substituted for the rabbit if you prefer.

1	2- to 3-lb (1 to 1.5 kg) rabbit	1
⅓ cup	all-purpose flour	75 mL
2 tbsp	canola or corn oil	25 mL
½ cup	each maple syrup and rabbit or chicken stock	125 mL
2 tbsp	each cider vinegar and soy sauce	25 mL
2	cloves garlic, minced	2
2 tsp	ground ginger	10 mL
½ tsp	cayenne	2 mL
¼ tsp	salt	1 mL
2	green onions, chopped	2

If any offal (liver, kidneys, etc.) remains in rabbit, remove and reserve for making stock. Place rabbit on its back on a cutting board. With sharp heavy knife, cut the back legs off where they join the body; cut the front legs off by cutting close to the rib cage and behind the shoulder blades. Cut the rib cage from the body (reserve for making stock); cut the remaining body crosswise into two pieces.

In medium bowl, toss rabbit portions one at a time in flour, shaking off any excess. In large skillet, heat oil over medium-high heat. Cook rabbit pieces in batches for 4 to 6 minutes, turning often, until browned on all sides. Remove rabbit from skillet; pour off any excess fat from skillet. If necessary, lightly wipe out skillet to remove any burned flour.

In medium bowl, whisk together maple syrup, stock, vinegar, soy sauce, garlic, ginger, cayenne and salt. Pour maple-syrup mixture into skillet; bring to boil, scraping up any browned bits from bottom of skillet. Return rabbit to skillet, spooning sauce over rabbit. Reduce heat to medium-low; simmer, covered, for 40 to 45 minutes, turning rabbit occasionally, until rabbit is tender. Remove rabbit from skillet; arrange on serving platter. Keep warm.

Place skillet over medium-high heat; bring to boil. Boil for 3 to 5 minutes, until sauce is thickened and reduced; pour evenly over rabbit. Sprinkle with green onions.

Makes **6 to 8 servings**

Preparation time: **25 minutes**

Cooking time: **1½ to 2 hours**

*H*igh on a ridge overlooking Waupoos Island and Prince Edward Bay you'll find one of the province's newest cideries. County Cider was founded on Grant Howe's family farm. Fifty acres of orchards bearing Winesap, Golden Russet and Northern Spys provided the apples to press his first hard ciders. The tasting room is in the 1837 farmhouse. Since obtaining his license, Howe has grafted an additional 1,500 trees of small, tannin-loaded English cider apples. His first cider, fermented in an English style, is unique to Ontario because it contains only late-harvest apples. Some of the juice he ferments with Champagne yeast to produce a French-style cider, and he's experimenting with a low-alcohol product made strictly from McIntosh apples. Two varietal wines, Ida Red and Empire, will be marketed shortly.

CIDER-ROASTED PORK WITH BRAISED FENNEL

Ontario-grown fennel—a traditional Italian winter vegetable—appears briefly in the Holland Marsh area in September and October. Also called anise, it imparts a mellow aniseed flavour to this roast of pork. The recipe comes from Margaret Browne, an excellent cook who just happens to be Julia's mum and who has provided us with many a good recipe in the past.

1	1-lb (500 g) bulb fennel (anise)	1
3 lb	boneless centre-cut pork loin roast	1.5 kg
12	fresh sage leaves	12
1	clove garlic, minced	1
½ tsp	each salt and black pepper	2 mL
1	bottle (341 mL) Ontario hard (alcoholic) cider or 1⅓ cups (325 mL) sweet apple cider	1
½ cup	each chicken stock and whipping cream	125 mL

Preheat oven to 325°F (160°C). Trim feathery tops from fennel; chop finely to make ¼ cup (50 mL), discarding remaining tops. Set aside. Slice fennel bulb lengthwise into thin slices; cut each slice lengthwise into 1-inch (2.5 cm) strips. Arrange sliced fennel in a shallow roasting pan; set aside.

Untie roast and open up like a book. Cut 6 sage leaves into thin slivers. Sprinkle slivered sage, chopped fennel tops, garlic and ¼ tsp (1 mL) each salt and pepper over one side of pork. Re-form roast; tie securely with string.

Sprinkle remaining sage leaves, salt and pepper over fennel in roasting pan. Place pork on top of fennel; pour cider into pan. Roast for 1½ to 2 hours or until meat thermometer inserted into pork registers 160°F (70°C). Remove pork to serving platter. With slotted spoon, remove fennel from roasting pan; arrange around pork. Let pork stand, loosely tented with foil, in a warm place for 15 minutes to rest.

Add stock to juices in roasting pan; place pan over high heat. Bring to boil, scraping up any brown bits from bottom of pan. Add cream to roasting pan; boil over high heat for 2 to 3 minutes, until reduced and thickened slightly. Add any juices to roasting pan that have accumulated under pork on platter; season gravy with salt and pepper to taste. Slice pork; serve with fennel. Pass gravy separately.

Makes **6 servings**

Preparation time: **15 minutes**

Cooking time: **15 to 20 minutes**

*T*he end of March through the middle of April is pickerel-spawning time near Gamebridge. For the best view of the schools of majestic fish as they battle their way upstream from Lake Simcoe to the foot of the Talbot River Dam, turn east off Highway 11 onto Durham Road 50 (it's the Gamebridge turn-off, one road north of the Trent-Severn Canal). Follow Durham Road 50 where it turns right at the general store in Gamebridge and continue on to the bridge just before the dam. On a good pickerel-spotting day—bright and sunny with few clouds—it may seem as if every sports fisher in Ontario has turned out, perhaps to eyeball a future trophy. Be sure to treat yourself to a sausage on a bun from the enterprising hot-dog seller (his homemade sauerkraut is awesome). If you ask, he'll tell you everything you need to know about pickerel. For instance, the fish puts on a pound of weight for every year of its life, and it's just about the best eating fish there is.

CRISPY CORNMEAL-COATED PICKEREL FILLETS

Pickerel (a.k.a. walleye) is widely held to be the very best eating fish there is in Ontario. We both love it and think that the simplest of preparations is often the best. Our Apple Cider Mayonnaise (see recipe on page 222), with some finely chopped chives and parsley stirred into it, is wonderful with the fish.

6	6-oz (175 g) pickerel fillets	6
¼ cup	milk	50 mL
1	egg	1
⅔ cup	cornmeal	150 mL
⅓ cup	all-purpose flour	75 mL
¾ tsp	salt	4 mL
½ tsp	black pepper	2 mL
3 tbsp	unsalted butter	45 mL
1 tbsp	canola or corn oil	15 mL

Pat pickerel fillets dry on paper towels. In shallow bowl, beat milk and egg until well combined. On large plate, stir together cornmeal, flour, salt and pepper until well combined. Dip pickerel fillets in egg mixture to coat well; then dip in cornmeal mixture, turning to coat on all sides.

In large heavy skillet, heat 1 tbsp (15 mL) butter and the oil over medium heat, until butter melts and is sizzling. Add 2 pickerel fillets; fry for 5 to 7 minutes, turning once, until fish flakes easily with a fork and is deep golden brown and crisp on the outside. Remove from skillet; keep warm. Repeat with remaining butter and pickerel fillets, frying in 2 batches. Serve at once.

THE GREAT ONTARIO CHEESE FONDUE

Tradition dictates that anyone whose bread falls from the fondue fork into a cheese fondue is dispatched to fetch the next bottle of wine. If hard (alcoholic) cider is unavailable, substitute 1½ cups (375 mL) dry white wine or apple cider.

2½ cups	each shredded old Ontario Cheddar and Monterey Jack (about ½ lb/250 g each)	625 mL
2 tbsp	cornstarch	25 mL
½ tsp	dry mustard	2 mL
¼ tsp	cayenne	1 mL
1	clove garlic, cut in half	1
1	bottle (341 mL) hard (alcoholic) cider	1

Accompaniments:
Cubes of rye bread; blanched broccoli or cauliflower florets; cubed, cooked potatoes; cooked sausage; cubed ham

In large bowl, combine cheeses, cornstarch, mustard and cayenne; toss well. Set aside. Rub cut sides of garlic around inside of fondue pot; leave garlic in pot. Add cider to fondue pot; bring to boil over high heat. Reduce heat to medium; simmer for 1 minute. Reduce heat to low.

Gradually whisk in cheese mixture. Simmer over medium heat, whisking constantly, for 2 to 3 minutes until thickened and smooth. Place fondue pot over fondue burner; light burner. Serve with suggested accompaniments for dipping.

Makes **4 servings**

Preparation time: **20 minutes**

Cooking time: **about 5 minutes**

*F*or seven years, Sharon and Bruce Vanden Berg have been making goat's milk cheese at the Mariposa Dairy in Oakwood. The Vanden Bergs raise more than three hundred goats on their farm west of Lindsay, and every day they milk about half of them to make their wonderful goat's milk cheeses. There are three varieties of cheese available under the Mariposa label: a feta, a soft chevre-style cheese and a Gouda-style goat's milk cheese. Mariposa cheese is popular with both vegetarians and orthodox Jews, as no rennet is used in the manufacturing process; all that's added to the milk is sea salt and a vegetable-based microbial enzyme (in place of rennet). The chevre is available plain or flavoured with additive-free dried vegetables; the Gouda-style comes in a mild version, called Belfair, or an aged variety. In 1995 the Vanden Bergs' Belfair Gouda won an award of excellence at the Canadian Fine Food Show.

Makes **4 servings**

Preparation time: **20 minutes**

Cooking time: **1 hour, 5 minutes**

*F*or more than twenty-five years, foodies-in-the-know have flocked to the small village of Goodwood, northeast of Stouffville, to visit an ordinary-looking farm on the south side of Highway 47, just east of town. The only hint of its purpose is the sign "Herbs" in faded paint on the barn roof, but adjacent to the barn is a greenhouse complex that is home to every fresh herb you can think of, from agrimony to yucca and more besides. Otto Richter and his wife, Waltraut, started the herb farm in 1969, and although Otto passed away in 1991, the farm has remained a family affair and now boasts an inventory of more than 750 culinary and medicinal herbs. In addition to herbs, Richter's sells wild-flower seeds and rootstocks, seeds or tubers for gourmet vegetables such as artichoke, jicama and tomatillo. There's a small gift store, which stocks a good selection of books, plus dried herbs, herbal teas and gardening equipment, and the company also publishes an excellent annual brochure, which reads like a mini herbal encyclopedia. Richter's is open seven days a week; throughout the year there are informal free lectures on occasional Sundays, which cover all kinds of herb-related topics, from natural pest control to making herbal teas.

ROASTED BEETS ON SPRING GREENS WITH HONEY VINAIGRETTE

Roasting beets brings out their sweet, earthy flavour, and serving them on a bed of greens emphasizes their jewel-like colour.

4	medium beets (about 1 lb/500 g trimmed)	4
1 cup	water	250 mL
6	slices bacon	6
¼ cup	canola, corn or nut oil	50 mL
2 tbsp	cider vinegar	25 mL
1 tbsp	liquid honey	15 mL
1	clove garlic, minced	1
¼ tsp	each salt and black pepper	1 mL
6 cups	washed and torn mixed salad greens	1.5 L

Preheat oven to 400°F (200°C).

Scrub beets; trim stalks so that they're 1 inch (5 cm) long, leaving root end on. In 8-inch (2 L) square baking dish, combine beets and water. Cover dish with lid or foil; cook for about 1 hour or until beets feel tender when pierced with a skewer. Let cool.

When beets are cool enough to handle, cut off stems with knife; peel off skins with your fingers. Cut beets into ½-inch (1 cm) pieces; set aside.

In small heavy skillet, cook bacon over medium-high heat for 3 to 4 minutes, until crisp. Drain on paper towels; crumble into small pieces. Set aside.

In small bowl, whisk together oil, vinegar, honey, garlic, salt and pepper.

Just before serving, place greens in large shallow salad bowl. Add all but 2 tbsp (25 mL) dressing; toss well. Arrange beets on top of greens; drizzle with remaining dressing. Sprinkle with bacon; serve at once.

ROASTED ONTARIO SUMMER RATATOUILLE WITH FRESH HERBS

Roasting vegetables seems to intensify their flavour. Feel free to vary the vegetables according to what's in season and what you happen to have on hand.

1	small eggplant (about ½ lb/250 g)	1
1	large sweet red pepper	1
1	yellow or green zucchini	1
1	small red onion	1
4	plum tomatoes, cut in half lengthwise	4
2	cloves garlic, sliced	2
2	bay leaves	2
¼ tsp	each salt and black pepper	1 mL
¼ cup	canola or corn oil	50 mL
⅓ cup	slivered fresh basil leaves	75 mL

Preheat oven to 400°F (200°C). Remove stem from eggplant; cut eggplant into 1-inch (2.5 cm) cubes. Cut red pepper into 1-inch (2.5 cm) pieces, removing seeds and stem. Cut zucchini into ½-inch (1 cm) slices. Peel onion; cut into thick wedges.

In 13- by 9-inch (3 L) baking dish, combine vegetables with tomatoes, garlic, bay leaves, salt and pepper. Drizzle with oil. Bake for 40 to 50 minutes, until vegetables are tender, stirring every 10 minutes. Discard bay leaves; gently stir in basil. Taste and adjust seasoning.

Makes **4 to 6 servings**

Preparation time: **20 minutes**

Cooking time: **40 to 50 minutes**

*A*t Stickling's Landhaus Bakery in Peterborough, Hans Stickling maintains his purist philosophy by using only organic grains, many of which are grown for him in the Peterborough area. Fresh *spaetzle* (egg noodles), dense multiseed breads and wonderfully buttery German-style pastries fill his two stores. Every Saturday, he makes the trek into Toronto to the Knives and Forks organic market, but to appreciate the depth and variety of his full-flavoured product, one has to head into the countryside for a personal visit to his bakeries.

Makes **6 servings**

Preparation time: **15 minutes**

Cooking time: **25 to 30 minutes**

*D*own a winding country road outside Warkworth, hidden in its own leafy wooded valley, lies the idyllic Schoolhouse Gardens herb farm. In 1987 Dennis Gebhardt and Tom Harris bought the nineteenth-century stone schoolhouse that gives the farm its name, along with ten acres of bush. Since then they've created a picture-perfect three-acre herb and perennial garden adjacent to the schoolhouse. The garden is open every Sunday throughout the summer, and it's well worth taking the reasonably priced tour as both Dennis and Tom are experts on all things herbal, from how to remove a sliver (apply comfrey leaves) to a gas-free alternative to cucumber salad (burnet leaves). They'll also treat you to a fresh herbal tea (hyssop, lemon balm and peppermint is a favourite concoction). There's a gift store located in the wood-shed where you can buy Dennis and Tom's own homemade vinegars and salad dressings, and their awesome mixed vegetable chutney.

MAPLE-GLAZED ACORN SQUASH

Acorn squash are small with deeply ridged dark-green skins, sometimes mottled with orange. Their nutty flavour makes them a good choice for baking, and in this recipe a spicy maple glaze adds extra sweetness.

1	large acorn squash (2 lb/1 kg)	1
¼ cup	each maple syrup and packed brown sugar	50 mL
2 tbsp	butter	25 mL
½ tsp	ginger	2 mL
¼ tsp	grated nutmeg	1 mL
2 tbsp	chopped fresh parsley	25 mL

Preheat oven to 350°F (180°C). Cut squash in half lengthwise; scoop out seeds. Cut each half crosswise into 6 slices. Arrange squash slices in single layer on foil-lined baking sheet.

In small saucepan, combine maple syrup, brown sugar, butter, ginger and nutmeg. Cook over low heat, stirring often, for 2 minutes or until sugar has dissolved and butter has melted. Brush squash slices with half of maple mixture. Bake for 15 minutes. Turn squash slices over; brush with remaining maple mixture. Bake for 5 to 10 minutes or until squash is tender and maple mixture is bubbly. Arrange squash slices in serving dish; drizzle with any maple mixture remaining on baking sheet. Sprinkle with parsley.

PRINCE EDWARD COUNTY BLACK-CHERRY MUFFINS

Although the majority of Ontario's sweet-cherry crop comes from the Niagara region, cherries also thrive in Essex and Kent counties, the Georgian Bay area and Prince Edward County. Their season is so short, we try to use cherries every way we can, including mixing them into these easy muffins. The muffins freeze well, so make a couple of batches when cherries are plentiful so that you can enjoy the fruits of your labours later in the season.

½ cup	granulated sugar	125 mL
⅓ cup	canola or corn oil	75 mL
1	egg	1
	Grated rind of 1 orange	
2 cups	all-purpose flour	500 mL
2 tsp	baking powder	10 mL
½ tsp	each baking soda and salt	2 mL
1 cup	buttermilk or sour milk	250 mL
1 cup	pitted and halved black cherries	250 mL

Preheat oven to 400°F (200°C). In medium bowl, beat together sugar, oil and egg until light in colour; stir in orange rind.

In separate bowl, stir together flour, baking powder, baking soda and salt. Stir into creamed mixture alternately with buttermilk just until dry ingredients are moistened. Fold in cherries until well combined.

Divide batter among 12 paper-lined or well-greased muffin cups. Bake for 20 to 25 minutes or until risen and golden, and toothpick inserted into centre of muffin comes out clean.

Makes **12 medium muffins**

Preparation time: **20 minutes**

Cooking time: **20 to 25 minutes**

"*J*ust about the most forgotten man that ever lived in Canada," said Senator J.J. Duffus in 1955. Senator Duffus was describing David Fife, who settled in Peterborough County in 1820. By 1842 Fife was farming two hundred acres and was disappointed in the lack of hardiness of the wheat he and his neighbours grew. In her book *David Fife and Red Fife Wheat*, historian Jean Murray Cole describes how a friend of Fife's in his native Scotland sent over some seeds of a hardy wheat that grew well in Poland. The first planting yielded three heads of what was to become Red Fife wheat. According to Jean Murray Cole, Red Fife wheat was the most important spring wheat in Canada for more than sixty years, from the 1850s to 1915.

To sour milk, place 2 tbsp (25 mL) lemon juice or white vinegar in glass measure; add milk to measure 1½ cups (375 mL). Stir; let stand for 5 minutes.

Makes **about 12 squares, depending on size**

Preparation time: **20 minutes**

Cooking time: **50 to 60 minutes**

*I*n 1992 Ruth Still decided it was time to put Eagle Lake on the map. The hamlet just north of Haliburton, while picturesque, wasn't particularly famous for anything. However, every garden in the village seemed to sport its own little patch of rhubarb, so after a meeting or two it was decided to launch the annual Eagle Lake Rhubarb Festival and attach the moniker Rhubarb Capital of Ontario to the town's name. Sounds simple, doesn't it? Except that Shedden, southwest of London, had already claimed that title in honour of the town's annual Rosy Rhubarb Days. For the next few years a fairly good-natured feud developed between the two communities. Finally, in 1995, the hatchet was buried at last with the twinning of the two towns. Now both can claim to be the Rhubarb Capital of Ontario. To avoid upsetting either party, be sure to attend both festivals. Shedden's takes place the second weekend in June. The festivities in Eagle Lake are on the third Saturday in July, at the end of blackfly season, and the celebration includes a watermelon-seed-spitting contest and a river race for wooden rhubarb leaves.

EAGLE LAKE RHUBARB SQUARES

You may need a fork to eat these super-moist squares, especially if they're still warm from the oven. The recipe is based on one from Ann McLeod, a cottager in Eagle Lake, whose version appears in the Eagle Lake Rhubarb Festival cookbook Rhubarb Recipes. *Ann, a self-professed rhubarb addict, says that children love these squares. We think grown-ups will, too. Frozen rhubarb can be used to prepare the squares. Thaw it partially (just until the frost disappears) then blot any excess moisture from the rhubarb with paper towels.*

Base:

2 cups	all-purpose flour	500 mL
½ cup	packed brown sugar	125 mL
½ cup	cold butter, cubed	125 mL
1	egg, beaten	1

Filling:

4 cups	sliced rhubarb (about 1 lb/500 g)	1 L
1½ cups	granulated sugar	375 mL
⅓ cup	all-purpose flour	75 mL
½ tsp	cinnamon	2 mL
2	eggs	2
1 tbsp	fresh lemon juice	15 mL

Base: Preheat oven to 375°F (190°C). In food processor, combine flour, sugar and butter; process until mixture resembles coarse crumbs. With motor running, add egg through feed tube; process just until mixture is crumbly and well combined, scraping down sides once or twice. Alternatively, in medium bowl, cut butter into flour until mixture resembles coarse crumbs; stir in sugar then egg until well combined. Measure ¾ cup (175 mL) mixture; set aside. Pat remaining mixture evenly into lightly buttered 9-inch (2.5 L) square pan.

Filling: In large bowl, combine rhubarb, sugar, flour and cinnamon. In small bowl, beat together eggs and lemon juice. Add egg mixture to rhubarb mixture; stir until well combined and dry ingredients are moistened. Spoon filling evenly over base; sprinkle evenly with reserved base mixture. Bake for 50 to 60 minutes, until golden brown and top is firm to touch. Let cool in pan; cut into squares.

*O*ne of Ontario's oldest operating water-powered mills can be found in the village of Tyrone, north of Bowmanville. Set in a picturesque hollow, nestled among willows by a fast-flowing creek, the imposing black and white building was erected in 1846 as a gristmill to serve local farmers. Since 1979, the present owner, Robert Shafer, has operated the business as a sawmill, but in the fall and winter the Tyrone mill becomes especially popular as families flock to sample Robert's famous freshly pressed apple cider. Up to three hundred gallons a day of preservative-free cider is produced in a press built in 1950 in Connecticut. The mill is open Monday through Saturday throughout the year, and seven days a week during cider-making season. There's a well-stocked store in the mill, which sells apple cider, cider vinegar and ambrosial freshly made cider doughnuts. There's also local maple syrup, organically grown herbs and, believe it or not, toy train sets.

Makes **15 pieces**

Preparation time: **20 minutes**

Cooking time: **about 20 minutes**

*V*enison farms are popping up all over the province as more and more people discover how lean and delicious venison is. One such is Ste. Anne's Deer Farm, located adjacent to the luxurious Ste. Anne's Country Inn and Spa in Grafton. Succulent roasts, steaks, chops and even pies are available and can be purchased at the farm Monday to Friday or by phone for pick-up at Grafton. The farm also houses a bottling plant for the inn's own spring water, which bubbles up from the lush hills of Northumberland County.

CURVE LAKE FRIED INDIAN BREAD

Ida Coppaway has been cooking up a storm at the Summer Tea Room on the Curve Lake Indian Reserve, north of Peterborough, ever since it opened more than 25 years ago. The tea room is adjacent to the fabulous Whetung Ojibwa Craft and Art Gallery and is open from the last weekend in April through Thanksgiving (the gallery is open all year round). The menu features traditional native foods, including chick-nee-as-gun *(corn soup),* p'quash-gun *(bush bread), buffalo burgers and this fried bread, called* sauce-gun. *Originally, the bread would have been fried in bear fat, or the dough would have been placed directly on a hot stone or wound around a stick over an open fire. At the tea room Ida fries the bread in lard, but we think it's almost as good cooked in vegetable oil. Serve the bread as soon as it's cooked, with soup or with butter and jam.*

1 cup	each milk and water	250 mL
4 cups	all-purpose flour	1 L
1 tbsp	baking powder	15 mL
1 tsp	salt	5 mL
	Canola or corn oil for frying	

In glass measure, combine milk and water; set aside.

In large bowl, stir together flour, baking powder and salt. Make a well in centre of dry ingredients; pour in milk mixture. Stir gently until a soft dough forms. Turn dough out onto well-floured surface; knead gently about 20 times just until dough is elastic; do not knead too much or bread will be tough (dough will still be sticky in places). Roll out to 1-inch (2.5 cm) thickness; cut out rounds with a floured 2-inch (5 cm) cutter.

In large heavy skillet, pour oil to depth of 1 inch
(2.5 cm); heat over medium-high heat until hot
but not smoking. Fry rounds of dough a few at a
time for 3 to 4 minutes on each side, until golden
brown and cooked through. With slotted spoon,
remove bread from skillet; let drain on paper-
towel-lined plate. Keep warm in oven while you
fry remaining dough. Serve at once.

Makes **6 servings**

Preparation time: **30 minutes**

Cooking time: **30 to 35 minutes**

*T*he Domain of Killien, with its rustic log lodge and pretty little cabins, has a dining room of international calibre. It's located in a five-thousand-acre private forested preserve, and guests fly-fish, canoe, hike, or cross-country ski and then return to the lodge for Chef Dante Lacarde's fine cuisine. From the morning's croissants to the final dessert of the evening, everything is inn-made.

*B*loomsbury Edible Flowers and Herbs is tucked away down a concession road off County Road 504 east of Apsley. Linda Fierheller and Carmel Morrison moved to the cottage-style home on a hundred acres in 1989 and proceeded to carve a garden out of the bush. They now grow every herb you can think of, and much more besides. They also grow edible flowers for many restaurants in the Peterborough/Lindsay area. Pop in by chance on weekends and Linda and Carmel will be happy to show you around and share some of their encyclopedic knowledge. Did you know, for instance, that anise hyssop flowers are a colourful and tasty garnish for chocolate cake? Linda and Carmel also make charming dried flower and herbal wreaths, herb vinegars and jellies, including a sparkling claret-coloured jelly flavoured with purple opal basil, which is divine with roast Ontario lamb.

AUTUMN PEARS POACHED IN LATE-HARVEST RIESLING WITH VANILLA CUSTARD SAUCE

Russet-coloured Bosc or golden-yellow Clapp's pears are both good varieties to choose for this elegant dessert. If you can find them, tiny Seckle pears are also good (you may need three extra since they're so small, and you'll need to cook them for only 8 to 10 minutes). For an extra-special treat, prepare the Niagara Wine-Berry Sauce (see recipe on page 49) and swirl a little into the custard sauce after spooning it onto the dessert plates.

Poached Pears:

2 cups	late-harvest Riesling	500 mL
1 cup	granulated sugar	250 mL
1 tsp	fennel seeds	5 mL
6	firm ripe pears	6
	Fresh mint sprigs	

Vanilla Custard Sauce:

4	egg yolks	4
¼ cup	granulated sugar	50 mL
1½ cups	hot whole milk	375 mL
1 tsp	vanilla	5 mL

Poached Pears: In large saucepan, combine wine, sugar and fennel seeds; bring to boil over medium-high heat, stirring to dissolve sugar. Boil over medium-high for 5 minutes.

Meanwhile, peel pears; cut in half. With a melon baller or teaspoon, scoop out cores. Add pears to saucepan. Reduce heat to medium-low; simmer, covered, for 10 to 12 minutes, until pears are tender. Remove saucepan from heat; let pears cool completely in liquid.

Remove pears from saucepan; refrigerate, covered, until ready to serve. Place saucepan containing cooking liquid over medium-high heat; bring to boil. Boil for 5 to 7 minutes until liquid is reduced to about ¾ cup (175 mL). Strain through sieve, reserving liquid and discarding fennel seeds; let cool completely.

Vanilla Custard Sauce: In medium stainless-steel bowl over saucepan of simmering (not boiling) water, whisk together egg yolks and sugar. Stir in hot milk. Cook, stirring, for 10 to 12 minutes or until sauce thickens and coats the back of a spoon. Remove from heat; stir in vanilla; let cool completely, stirring occasionally.

To serve, spoon a pool of custard sauce onto each of six dessert plates; place two pear halves cut-sides up on custard sauce. Drizzle pears with cooking liquid; garnish with mint.

*B*lack River Cheese has been in business since 1901 amidst the apple orchards of Prince Edward County. Owned as a cooperative by a group of Prince Edward County farmers, the rule is simple: shareholders must be milk producers. Cheesemaker John Kelly has been with the cooperative for more than ten years and specializes in Cheddar. However, he also makes a unique marble combining mozzarella and mild Cheddar, great for any melted cheese dish. They use no rennet in their products, so Black River cheeses are often found in whole food stores. At the dairy, on County Road 13 off Highway 62, their full line may be purchased, along with other local products like honey and jam. This is where you'll find cones filled with the best, and richest, soft ice cream in the region. Their shop is open 7 days a week, 9 a.m. to 5 p.m.

Refrigerate leftover egg whites, in covered container, for up to 2 weeks, or freeze them for up to 3 months.

Makes **6 to 8 servings**

Preparation time: **25 minutes**

Chilling time: **30 minutes**

Cooking time: **50 to 55 minutes**

*A*pple growers in the Colborne area are working hard to reintroduce historic varieties of apples, such as Gravenstein, Duchess, Cox's Orange Pippin, Athabasca and Wolf River, with whose evocative names our forebears would have been familiar. A celebration of apples old and new is held in nearby Brighton every September at the annual Applefest. Parades, hay rides to the orchards, a craft sale and a display of antique harvesting equipment at the Proctor House Museum are the order of the day with, of course, fabulous apple treats to enjoy, such as *oliebollen,* a Dutch apple fritter introduced by early settlers from Holland.

GOOD NEIGHBOURS' APPLE AND ELDERBERRY PIE

Ruth Mitchell, Julia's next-door neighbour in Brooklin, makes the best apple pie. She uses McIntosh or Northern Spy apples and little else in the filling so that the flavour is intensely "appley." One day, when fellow Brooklinites Neil and Hilary McPherson popped over with a pail of their homegrown elderberries, we thought, "Why not?" and added a handful to Ruth's apple-pie filling. The result was pretty, tangy and delicious. The pastry recipe makes enough for two double- or four single-crust pies. The leftover pastry can be refrigerated for up to 2 weeks or frozen for up to 3 months. If elderberries are unavailable, substitute an extra apple.

Pastry:

5½ cups	all-purpose flour	1.375 L
1 tbsp	granulated sugar	15 mL
1 tsp	each salt and baking powder	5 mL
1½ cups	cold shortening, cubed	375 mL
½ cup	cold butter, cubed	125 mL
1	egg	1
1 tbsp	white vinegar	15 mL
	Cold water	

Filling:

1½ lb	McIntosh or Northern Spy apples, peeled, cored and sliced (6 medium)	750 g
1 cup	elderberries	250 mL
¾ cup	granulated sugar	175 mL
¼ tsp	cinnamon	1 mL
	Milk and granulated sugar for glaze	

Pastry: In very large bowl, stir together flour, sugar, salt and baking powder. With pastry blender or two knives, cut in shortening and butter until mixture resembles coarse crumbs. In glass measure, beat egg and vinegar together; add enough cold water to measure ¾ cup (175 mL).

Add all at once to flour mixture; stir until soft but not sticky dough forms, adding up to 2 tbsp (25 mL) extra water if dough seems to be too dry. Turn out dough onto lightly floured surface; knead lightly just until dough holds together. Divide into four even-size pieces. Wrap in plastic wrap; refrigerate at least 30 minutes. Remove dough from refrigerator 10 minutes before rolling out.

Preheat oven to 425°F (220°C). On lightly floured clean tea towel, roll out one piece of pastry; use to line a 9-inch (23 cm) pie plate.

Filling: Place half of apples in pie plate, spreading evenly. Sprinkle with half of elderberries, then half of sugar and all of cinnamon. Arrange remaining apples on top. Sprinkle with remaining elderberries and sugar.

On lightly floured surface, roll out a second piece of pastry. Dampen edges of bottom crust; top pie with pastry, trimming off any excess pastry and crimping edges to seal. Cut vents into top of pie for steam to escape. Brush top with a little milk; sprinkle lightly with sugar. Place pie on baking sheet; bake for 20 minutes. Reduce heat to 375°F (190°C); bake for 30 to 35 minutes, until pastry is golden brown, apples are tender when a sharp knife is poked through one of the steam vents, and juices are bubbly. Let pie stand for 20 minutes before slicing.

*N*orthumberland County, sandwiched between Rice Lake to the north and Lake Ontario to the south, is a rural landscape of rolling drumlins and dense woodland. Along the banks of Lake Ontario between Colborne and Trenton lies one of the province's most prolific apple-producing areas, said by some experts to yield the best McIntosh apples in the world. The area is so popular that three years ago local growers established the province's first Apple Route. The self-guided tour winds past farms and through historic villages along Highway 2 from The Big Apple at Colborne through Brighton to Trenton. There's lots to explore along the way, including sandy beaches lapped by Lake Ontario, pick-your-own farms, antique stores, museums and much more.

Makes 8½ cups (2.1 L)

Preparation time: 10 minutes

*T*ake a stroll around Lang Pioneer Village and you really do feel as if you're walking back through time. There's lots to see and do at this reconstructed village ten miles southeast of Peterborough. Most of the buildings are restored to the style of the mid- to late-1800s, and as you visit each you'll find them inhabited by volunteers in period costume. For the food lover, it's a fascinating exploration. The girls in the kitchen at the Keene Hotel might be busily preparing the morning's batch of bread, while over at the Milburn family's log home, a tray of oatmeal cookies is being prepared. If you time it right, you may even be offered a taste, and the knowledgeable volunteers are happy to answer questions. The village is open daily from mid-May to mid-October, and special events, such as corn roasts, sheep shearing and cider making, are featured throughout the summer.

LANG PIONEER VILLAGE HAY-TIME SWITCHELL

Old cookbooks make reference to "switchel" and even "swizzle," but in all cases the cooling drink is based on a mixture of water, vinegar, molasses and spices. It's very refreshing, so it should come as no surprise that it was consumed by the gallon during harvest time. This recipe is adapted from one that appears in the Lang Pioneer Village recipe calendar.

1 cup	granulated sugar	250 mL
½ cup	molasses	125 mL
2 tbsp	cider vinegar	25 mL
½ tsp	ground ginger	2 mL
2 cups	boiling water	500 mL
6 cups	cold water	1.5 L

In large heatproof pitcher, combine sugar, molasses, vinegar and ginger. Add boiling water; stir until sugar has dissolved. Add cold water. Refrigerate, covered, until chilled. Stir well before serving.

SUN-DRIED TOMATO PESTO

This pesto-with-a-difference is adapted from a recipe from Carmel Morrison and Linda Fierheller of Bloomsbury Edible Flowers and Herbs in Apsley. Carmel cheerfully admits that the recipe started out (as all good recipes do) as an experiment, but it's so good they make it all the time now. Use oil-packed dried tomatoes, reserving the oil (making it up to 1 cup/250 mL with extra oil if necessary) to add to the pesto, or dry your own tomatoes (see recipe on page 142).

1½ cups	dried tomatoes, drained if packed in oil and sliced	375 mL
4	cloves garlic, minced	4
1 tsp	minced hot pepper	5 mL
1 cup	freshly grated Parmesan cheese	250 mL
⅓ cup	chopped toasted walnuts	75 mL
15	fresh basil leaves, slivered	15
1 cup	canola, corn or olive oil	250 mL

In food processor, combine tomatoes, garlic and hot pepper; process until very finely chopped. Add cheese, walnuts and basil; process with on/off pulses, scraping down sides of processor from time to time, until very finely chopped.

With motor running, slowly add oil in a thin steady stream, processing until pesto is the consistency of thick mayonnaise. Pour into a sterilized jar; cover with a thin layer of oil. Cover tightly; refrigerate for up to 2 months. Each time you use the pesto, add a thin layer of oil before replacing in refrigerator.

Makes **about 2 cups (500 mL)**

Preparation time: **20 minutes**

*T*here are dozens of ways to use homemade pesto. Here are just a few:

Toss hot cooked pasta with strips of grilled chicken breast, steamed sugar snap peas and pesto.

Grill portobello mushroom caps stem-side down for 3 minutes. Turn over and spoon ½ tsp (2 mL) Sun-Dried Tomato Pesto into cavities of mushrooms; grill for 3 minutes, until mushrooms are tender.

Toss freshly steamed vegetables with pesto; garnish with fresh basil leaves.

Handle all hot peppers with care. Always wear plastic or rubber gloves, and never touch your face with your hands while you prepare them.

Makes **3 half-pint (250 mL) jars**

Preparation time: **15 minutes**

Cooking time: **12½ to 16 hours**

*T*he picturesque town of Cobourg has hosted a farmers' market since 1856. The original market hall, an attractive blond brick building just behind historic Victoria Hall in the centre of town, now houses a seniors' day centre, but the market still takes place every Saturday morning, May through October, and on Tuesday evenings in the summer, in the parking lot that surrounds the building. Though small—there's just a dozen or so vendors—the market is home to some enthusiastic growers and producers, such as the Organic Grain Shop run by Roger and Janice MacLean. The MacLeans grind spelt, flax seed and other grains and bake wonderfully flavourful breads, like Ezekiel Bread, which contains a mixture of grains and legumes.

Cook's Tip

An oven thermometer for checking your oven's temperature is a good investment; at very high or very low temperatures many domestic ovens are inaccurate.

EASY DRIED TOMATOES

Drying your own tomatoes is so easy! And when you consider the price of dried tomatoes in the stores, you'll save a bundle. Many thanks to Toronto food writer Lucy Waverman, who allowed us to adapt her simple method for drying tomatoes, which first appeared in her Seasonal Canadian Cookbook. *The tomatoes take some time to dry, so we do ours overnight.*

4 lb	medium plum tomatoes (about 32)	2 kg
	Salt	
	Canola, corn or olive oil	

Preheat oven to 200°F (95°C). Wash and dry tomatoes; cut in half lengthwise. Place wire cake racks on baking sheets; arrange tomatoes cut sides up on wire racks. Sprinkle lightly with salt. Place in oven for 30 minutes. Reduce heat to 150°F (65°C); leave tomatoes to dry in oven for 12 to 16 hours (time will depend on size of tomatoes and how moist they are), until tomatoes are leathery and there's no trace of moist flesh. Don't overdry tomatoes or they will become brittle.

Remove tomatoes from oven and let cool completely. If some of them still seem a little moist once they are cooled, return them to the oven (preheated to 200°F/95°C) for an hour or so. Pack cooled tomatoes into clean, dry jars; add oil to cover tomatoes completely. Seal jars and label. Store in refrigerator for up to 6 months. If you pack the tomatoes with olive oil, the oil will solidify in the fridge; let them stand at room temperature to liquefy oil before using.

Eastern Ontario is a region in which one can celebrate all the culinary seasons, from the deepest winter right up to the flower-strewn summer. It's wild mushrooms and fiddleheads, apple cider and tulips.

Rocky pastureland is bounded on the south by the St. Lawrence River, the rapids-filled waterway that opened the continent. This is old Ontario, the region into which many of the first settlers trekked. It was here in 1811 that John McIntosh discovered the McIntosh apple tree, now the leading cultivar in the entire province. The islands that fill the river near Gananoque are a watery playground, full of yellow perch, small- and largemouth bass, pickerel, sunfish and northern pike. A traditional shore dinner was often the fitting finale of any day on the water. Small fish were filleted and fried in salty bacon drippings in huge metal pans specifically saved for these old-time rituals. Maple forests were tapped—there's one bush that has been in production since 1802—and numerous cheese factories were founded, establishing the excellence of eastern Ontario Cheddar around the globe. Many of the farmers' markets are among the oldest in the nation. During the nineteenth century, the Rideau Canal was constructed, linking Kingston to Ottawa. Today it's the oldest continuously operating canal in North America, with twenty-four locks and dozens of small historic towns scattered along the 125-mile length.

Ottawa is what one might expect from a national capital, multicultural and colourful. There are Highland Games in Glengarry, the Greek Summer Festival, Fête Caribe, the Lebanese Festival and both German and Italian weeks. But there's also a salute to regional foods—from the venerable By Ward Market to Le Café, the sophisticated restaurant at the National Arts Centre.

Eastern Ontario

Makes **4 servings**

Preparation time: **15 minutes**

Cooking time: **20 minutes**

Country-Style Croutons

These easy baked croutons are lower in fat than most and add terrific crunch to soups or salads. Spread 1 cup (250 mL) ½-in (1 cm) cubes of good quality whole-wheat or granary bread on a baking sheet. Bake in 350°F (180°C) oven for 5 minutes, until crisp. In bowl, combine bread cubes and 1 tbsp (15 mL) canola, corn or nut oil (walnut oil is particularly good). Spread on baking sheet again; bake for 3 to 5 minutes, until just starting to brown. Let cool.

SPRINGTIME SOUP

Sorrel is a perennial herb whose green, arrow-shaped leaves have a slightly bitter, almost lemony flavour that makes this a particularly refreshing soup. If sorrel is unavailable, watercress, with any tough stems discarded, is a good substitute.

1 tbsp	butter	15 mL
8	green onions, chopped	8
4 cups	chicken stock	1 L
3 cups	each washed and torn Boston lettuce and sorrel	750 mL
½ cup	whipping cream	125 mL
½ tsp	granulated sugar	2 mL
¼ tsp	each salt, black pepper and grated nutmeg	1 mL
	Country-Style Croutons (see margin)	

In medium saucepan, melt butter over medium heat. Add onions; cook, stirring, for 2 minutes, until softened.

Add stock, lettuce and sorrel. Bring to boil over high heat. Reduce heat to medium-low; simmer, covered, for 15 minutes, until lettuce is very tender. Remove from heat; let cool slightly.

In blender, blend soup in batches until smooth. Return soup to rinsed-out saucepan. Stir in cream, sugar, salt, pepper and nutmeg. Heat over medium-high heat until simmering. Ladle into soup bowls; serve sprinkled with croutons.

ONTARIO-STYLE ONION SOUP

Few ingredients taste more "Ontario" than apple cider and great cheese. Here they team up to give a Canadian twist to traditional onion soup.

¼ cup	butter	50 mL
2 lb	onions, sliced	1 kg
¼ cup	all-purpose flour	50 mL
	Beef or chicken stock (about 5 cups/1.25 L)	
1½ cups	apple cider	375 mL
	Salt and black pepper	
6	1-in (2.5 cm) slices crusty bread	6
1 lb	thinly sliced mild cheese, such as Havarti, brick or Gaisli	500 g

In large saucepan or Dutch oven, melt butter over medium heat. Add onions; cook, stirring occasionally, for 12 to 15 minutes until onions start to brown. Stir in flour; cook, stirring, for 1 minute. Gradually stir in 5 cups (1.25 L) stock and the cider. Bring to boil over high heat, stirring constantly, until soup is bubbly and thickened. Add more stock if soup seems too thick. Reduce heat to medium-low; simmer for 3 to 5 minutes, stirring occasionally. Season with salt and pepper to taste.

Ladle soup into 6 onion-soup bowls or small ovenproof casseroles; place bowls on baking sheet. Top each with slice of bread; divide cheese evenly among bowls, sprinkling it over bread. Broil under hot broiler for 2 to 3 minutes, until cheese is bubbly. Serve at once.

*Makes **6 servings***

Preparation time: **20 minutes**

Cooking time: **about 20 minutes**

*F*orfar Dairy, north of Kingston, has been producing cheese, most notably Cheddar, from the same location for more than 130 years. In 1963 a group of seventeen wise, and perhaps brave, dairy farmers bought the plant to ensure that the tradition continued. The milk still is collected from the region, and Forfar cheeses are distributed all over eastern Ontario. Made with heat-treated rather than pasteurized milk and aged longer than most, their Cheddars are among the finest produced in the province. Now they're making a feta, which is getting rave reviews from the Greek community they serve. Their dairy store in the village of Forfar sells their full line in addition to other local products such as honey, apple cider, fudge, freshly baked pies and cookies.

Makes **4 servings**

Preparation time: **20 minutes**

*A*quintessential city market, By Ward has been at the heart of culinary Ottawa for one and a half centuries. Founded in 1830, it's awash in colour in the warm months and, in the blustery, sub-zero Ottawa winter, it's where shoppers head to buy cheeses, eggs, lots 'n' lots of root vegetables and to eat a beavertail, a deep-fried confection spread with raspberry jam or simply dusted with sugar. Because the city has so many foreign embassies, ingredients are never dull—shoppers can find wonderful fish, great cheeses, spices from around the world and herbs from the Gatineau hills of Quebec.

CARROT AND ZUCCHINI RIBBON SALAD

This is a good make-ahead salad, which will keep for up to 2 days in the fridge. Use a good-quality sharp vegetable peeler to shave the carrots and zucchini into wafer-thin ribbons.

⅓ cup	canola or corn oil	75 mL
¼ cup	chopped fresh dill	50 mL
2 tbsp	cider vinegar	25 mL
1 tbsp	prepared mustard	15 mL
¼ tsp	each salt and black pepper	1 mL
4	medium carrots, scrubbed	4
1	medium zucchini, scrubbed	1

In serving bowl, whisk together oil, dill, vinegar, mustard, salt and pepper.

With vegetable peeler, shave carrots and zucchini into wafer-thin ribbons, dropping ribbons into oil mixture as you go and discarding thick cores of carrots and seeded part of zucchini (save for use in stock or soup). Toss well. Serve at once or refrigerate, covered, up to 48 hours.

MUSTARD-GLAZED ONTARIO LEG OF LAMB

Makes **6 servings**

Preparation time: **20 minutes**

Cooking time: **1¼ to 1½ hours**

Ontario lamb is so flavourful and succulent that we like to roast it simply, like this. The aroma of garlic and rosemary wafting from the oven as the lamb roasts will have everyone's mouth watering.

5 lb	bone-in leg of Ontario lamb	2.2 kg
12	1-inch (2.5 cm) sprigs fresh rosemary	12
2	cloves garlic, each cut into 6 slivers	2
⅓ cup	Sweet and Sour Mustard (see recipe on page 55)	75 mL
2 tbsp	chopped fresh parsley Black pepper	25 mL

Let lamb stand at room temperature for 30 minutes. Preheat oven to 450°F (230°C).

With small sharp knife, make 12 regularly spaced deep incisions through skin of lamb. Push a rosemary sprig and a garlic sliver into each slit. Place lamb on oiled rack in shallow roasting pan.

In small bowl, combine mustard and parsley; spread generously over lamb. Grind black pepper over lamb. Cook lamb in oven for 15 minutes. Reduce temperature to 350°F (180°C); cook for 1 hour to 1 hour, 20 minutes or until a meat thermometer inserted into lamb registers 140°F (60°C) for rare or 160°F (70°C) for medium. Remove lamb to warmed platter; cover loosely with foil. Let rest for 10 minutes before carving.

*T*he Arrow and the Loon is part of a small Ontario-created network of pubs that take pride in serving the province's finest micro-brews and using good local ingredients on their menus. You may find a buffalo-beef shepherd's pie or beer-braised pork, and there'll always be pub-made potato chips and good, verging on great, salads. Because draft beer is meant to be enjoyed fresh—without pasteurization, preservatives or excessive filtering—you'll have to ask what's on tap. The pub's blackboards list their current selections, and at this particular establishment, there's even a local root beer.

Makes **4 servings**

Preparation time: **25 minutes**

Cooking time: **about 50 minutes**

$\mathcal{T}$he Ottawa Food and Wine Show is one of the most prestigious events of its kind anywhere in the nation. There are master's classes and food-book signings by Canadian authors and international celebrity chefs. The convention hall is filled with Ontario's finest wineries and Ottawa's best purveyors of great foods, who offer samples of everything from late-harvest Riesling to wild mush-rooms. The wine competition plays a major role. Judging occurs before the show. The wineries set up their booths, proudly displaying their medals and allowing the public to sample their winners. The Liquor Control Board of Ontario opens a Vintages store right on site featuring only the wines of the show. Located at the Congress Centre next to the Westin Hotel, the show is held every year in late October or early November.

TENDERLOIN OF PORK WITH CABBAGE AND MUSTARD SAUCE

Winter cabbage becomes a special-occasion vegetable when it's teamed with tenderloin of pork and a piquant mustard sauce. Our Sweet and Sour Mustard on page 55 is perfect for the sauce, or use a mild mustard, such as Dijon.

1 tbsp	canola or corn oil	15 mL
1½ lb	pork tenderloin	750 g
¼ tsp	black pepper	1 mL
2 tbsp	butter	25 mL
6 cups	shredded cabbage (half a medium cabbage)	1.5 L

Mustard Sauce:

1	medium carrot, finely chopped	1
1	small stalk celery, finely chopped	1
1	shallot, minced	1
1	clove garlic, minced	1
1 cup	each red wine and beef stock	250 mL
½ tsp	dried thyme	2 mL
1	bay leaf	1
1 cup	table cream	250 mL
⅓ cup	prepared mustard	75 mL
¼ cup	chopped fresh parsley	50 mL
	Salt and black pepper	

In large skillet, heat oil over medium heat. Sprinkle pork tenderloin with pepper. Add pork to skillet; cook, for 25 to 30 minutes, turning often, until browned on all sides and no longer pink inside. Do not overcook. Transfer to heated plate; keep warm, loosely covered, while you prepare the sauce.

Meanwhile, in large heavy saucepan, melt butter over medium heat; stir in cabbage. Reduce heat to medium-low; cook, covered, for 10 to 12 minutes, stirring occasionally, until cabbage is tender. Set aside; keep warm.

Mustard Sauce: In same skillet used to cook pork, add carrot, celery, shallot and garlic to oil remaining in skillet. Cook for 2 to 3 minutes, stirring occasionally, until vegetables are almost tender.

Add wine, stock, thyme and bay leaf to skillet. Increase heat to high; bring to boil, scraping up any brown bits from bottom of skillet. Reduce heat to medium-high; boil for 5 to 7 minutes or until liquid is reduced by half and vegetables are tender.

Remove from heat; discard bay leaf. Whisk in cream, mustard and any juices that have accumulated under pork. Cook over low heat for 2 to 3 minutes until heated through; do not boil. Stir in parsley; season with salt and pepper to taste.

To serve, mound cabbage in centre of large heated serving platter. Slice pork tenderloin; arrange slices around edge of platter. Drizzle some of sauce over top; pass rest of sauce separately.

*A*griculture and Agri-Food Canada in Ottawa has had many success stories:

- Corn research was conducted at all Experimental Farms in the 1920s, concentrating on its use as silage. With the development of hybrid corn, the Research Branch was instrumental in pushing back the frontiers of the corn-growing area to the point where the majority of the acreage today is in places where corn could not be grown forty years ago. Grain corn is the most important cereal grown in Ontario and Quebec, where the value of production exceeds $500 million.

- Agriculture and Agri-Food Canada was the co-developer and leader in the transformation of canola as an industrial oil to the world's healthiest food oil with a 1993 value of $1.5 billion.

- The farm-gate receipts for beef and pork exceed $5 billion due in part to Agriculture and Agri-Food Canada's leadership in the production of lean meats. We are the second-largest exporter of pork in the world.

Makes **4 servings**

Preparation time: **15 minutes**

Standing time: **30 minutes**

Cooking time: **5 to 7 minutes**

*T*HE COOK NOT MAD; OR RATIONAL COOKERY: BEING A COLLECTION OF ORIGINAL AND SELECTED RECEIPTS, *Embracing not only the art of curing various kinds of Meats and Vegetables for future use, but of Cooking, in its general acceptation, to the taste, habits, and degrees of luxury, prevalent with the* CANADIAN PUBLIC . . . was published in 1831 in Kingston, Upper Canada (UC), by James Macfarlane. It has the distinction of being not only English Canada's first cookery book but also the first food book to be plagiarized in this country. From preserving eggs and making spruce beer to baking soft gingerbread or a "pumpion" (pumpkin) pudding, it offers an interesting glimpse of what life was like, or at least what it was supposed to be like, in that era. Reprinted by the Ministry of Agriculture and Food in 1984, a few copies of the tiny paperback are still hiding in out-of-the-way new and used bookstores.

STEAMED GINGER-LEMON PICKEREL

Cookbook authors come across interesting recipe ideas in the strangest of places. The inspiration for this dish came from a conversation with a tow-truck driver who one day rescued Julia and her car from Highway 401. The driver—who, alas, remains anonymous—was a keen fisherman, and said steaming pickerel fillets with Oriental flavourings was his favourite way of cooking them. If he's reading this, thanks—both for the tow and for the recipe idea!

1 lb	pickerel fillets, cut into 4 portions	500 g
	Salt	
1	lemon, sliced	1
1 tbsp	minced fresh gingerroot	15 mL
2	green onions, finely chopped	2
¼ tsp	black pepper	1 mL
1 tbsp	sesame oil*	15 mL

Arrange pickerel fillets on large platter; sprinkle lightly with salt. Refrigerate, covered, 30 minutes. (This removes excess moisture from fish.) Pat fillets dry with paper towels.

Line an Oriental bamboo steamer with cheesecloth. Arrange pickerel fillets in steamer in 2 layers, arranging lemon slices on each layer and sprinkling each layer evenly with gingerroot, green onions and pepper. Cover steamer with lid. In wok, bring 2 inches (5 cm) water to boil. Place steamer in wok; cover wok with lid. Steam over high heat for 5 to 7 minutes until fish is opaque and flakes easily with a fork.

If you don't have a steamer, arrange fish, lemon slices, gingerroot, green onions and pepper on lightly oiled plate. In large roasting pan, bring 2 inches (5 cm) water to boil. Place wire cooling rack in roasting pan; place plate on rack. Cover roasting pan with aluminum foil; steam over high heat for 5 to 7 minutes.

Discard lemon slices; drizzle fish lightly with sesame oil before serving.

* Available in Oriental section of most large supermarkets.

*A*griculture and Agri-Food Canada in Ottawa notes:

- Canada has a leading role in the world of value-added research not only as it pertains to its economic benefit, but as it relates to energy efficiency and waste reduction. Juice technology has increased cranberry juice yields in pressing by more than sixty percent, and improved the nutrition and quality of apple juice.

- A series of ten early-maturing soybean varieties has been developed starting with Mandarin in 1934, continuing with Maple Presto and culminating with Maple Glen. These have expanded the soybean-producing lands from a small area in southwestern Ontario to a national crop. Research Branch varieties are the leading early varieties in an industry valued at $300 million per year.

Makes **6 to 8 servings**

Preparation time: **30 minutes**

Rising time: **1 hour**

Cooking time: **55 to 60 minutes**

*I*n the rocky, lake-strewn region southwest of Ottawa is a cluster of natural
growers and producers that have created
a self-sustaining synergy. Allan and
Susan Brown use locally grown soybeans, delivered monthly by a Crysler
area farmer, to produce tempeh, a
particularly versatile high-protein food
sold under the brand name "Noble
Bean." The Browns crush the soybeans
before cooking them. The water is spun
off and the mashed beans are cultured,
sometimes with the addition of sea vegetables like dulse or a variety of organic
grains. Packed into porous bags and left
to incubate for twenty-four hours, the
beans solidify into the small, solid blocks
that are frozen before shipping to natural food stores across the province. After
freezing, tempeh is easy to slice and can
be used in all sorts of spice-laden dishes,
from Oriental-style stir-fry to ratatouille
to jambalaya.

GOAT CHEESE AND SPINACH TORTE

*Roslyn Levin-Gold and her husband, Jeffrey Gold,
own Maple Hill Farm and Gifts at the edge of the
Lanark Highlands near Perth, where goats and hens
range free, and Roslyn and Jeffrey grow organic vegetables. Roslyn prepares this rustic torte using their
own goat cheese. It's equally delicious served hot or
cold, and we like to take it on picnics as it's sturdy
enough not to crumble in transit.*

Dough:

1/4 cup	warm water (105°F/41°C)	50 mL
1 tbsp	honey	15 mL
1	pkg (8 g) active dry yeast	1
2 to 3 cups	all-purpose flour	500 to 750 mL
1/2 tsp	salt	2 mL
1/2 cup	butter, softened	125 mL
2	eggs	2

Filling:

1	pkg (10 oz/284 g) spinach	1
1 tbsp	canola or corn oil	15 mL
1	medium onion, chopped	1
2	cloves garlic, minced	2
6 oz	goat cheese, crumbled (1 cup/250 mL)	175 g
1	egg, beaten	1
1/4 tsp	each grated nutmeg, salt and black pepper	1 mL

Dough: In large bowl, whisk together water and
honey until honey dissolves. Sprinkle yeast over
top; set aside in warm place for 15 minutes until
puffy. Whisk in ½ cup (125 mL) flour and the salt.
Whisk in butter, then eggs. Stir in 1½ cups
(375 mL) flour until a soft dough forms, using
your hands when dough becomes too stiff to stir.
Turn out onto work surface; knead for 5 minutes,
working in additional flour to keep dough from
sticking. Form dough into ball; place in lightly
oiled bowl, turning dough to coat with oil.

Cover loosely with plastic wrap; let rise in warm, draft-free place for 1 hour or until doubled in size.

Filling: Rinse spinach; drain well, removing any tough stems. Place in large saucepan; cook, covered, over medium-low heat for 8 to 10 minutes, until wilted. Drain well. When spinach is cool enough to handle, squeeze out as much moisture as possible; set aside in large bowl.

In small skillet, heat oil over medium-high heat. Add onion and garlic; cook, stirring, for 3 to 5 minutes, until onion is soft but not brown. Add onion mixture to spinach, along with goat cheese, egg, nutmeg, salt and pepper.

Preheat oven to 350°F (180°C). Punch down dough; divide into two pieces, one slightly larger than the other. On lightly floured surface, roll out larger piece of dough to 10-inch (25 cm) circle. Press into base and partway up sides of greased 8-inch (2 L) springform pan. Spoon filling evenly over dough; fold any excess dough over edges of filling.

Roll out second piece of dough to 8-inch (20 cm) circle. Place dough over filling, sealing edges and tucking edges of dough down sides of pan. Cut slits in dough for steam to escape. Bake for 40 to 45 minutes, until torte is golden brown. Let stand for 10 minutes; release sides of pan. Slide torte onto serving plate; serve cut into wedges.

*J*ust down the road from Allan and Susan Brown's tempeh workshop is Maple Hill Farm, where Jeff Gold and Roslyn Levin-Gold raise British Alpine goats. Their ninety-eight-acre property is also the base for the creation of goat's milk yogurt, cream cheese and ice cream, each with a real difference. The light cream cheese may be used as a spread on your breakfast toast, but Roslyn really likes to gild the lily. She slathers it over hot waffles, pours on homemade strawberry sauce, dollops it with her own mild yogurt, then drizzles it with maple syrup that comes from their own bush or from a friend's. At the Saturday Ottawa Organic Market (Island Park Drive at the Queensway/ 10 a.m. to 2 p.m.) she sells feta, a plain hard cheese, sesame garlic cream cheese and one that's loaded with herbs. The ice cream is flavoured with raspberries, blackberries, strawberries, maple, honey, vanilla and one she calls Bee Bliss, which has energy-giving bee pollen added to the honey-vanilla base.

Makes **6 servings**

Preparation time: **20 minutes**

Cooking time: **4 to 6 minutes**

$\mathcal{S}$ome of the most important work ever to be done in Canadian agriculture has occurred at the Central Experimental Farm in Ottawa. Marquis wheat, first grown in Ottawa in 1904, revolutionized Prairie farming. By 1911 it had been commercially established, and by the early 1920s it made up ninety percent of the spring wheat crop in western Canada and sixty percent of the spring wheat in the United States. Today grain experiments continue. The Central Experimental Farm is located at the intersection of Prince of Wales Drive and National Capital Commission Driveway, and tours are available for groups of more than fifteen. Self-guided tour booklets are available for individual visitors. The Canadian Agricultural Museum is also on site with rotating exhibits that might include the history of the potato in Canada or barns of the 1920s. Hours of operation: 7 days a week 9 a.m. to 5 p.m. with shorter hours during the winter.

FRESH ASPARAGUS WITH STRAWBERRY VINAIGRETTE

Rosy pink vinaigrette made with the season's first strawberries and drizzled over bright green asparagus makes a dazzling dish. The vinaigrette can be stored in the fridge for three or four days, and there'll be enough left over to toss with a salad of Boston lettuce and watercress.

1 cup	sliced strawberries (about 6 oz/175 g)	250 mL
¼ cup	canola or corn oil	50 mL
2 tbsp	fresh mint leaves	25 mL
1 tbsp	red wine vinegar	15 mL
1 tsp	granulated sugar	5 mL
¼ tsp	each salt and black pepper	1 mL
1½ lb	asparagus	750 g
	Fresh mint sprigs for garnish	

In food processor, combine strawberries, oil, mint leaves, vinegar, sugar, salt and pepper; process until smooth. Pour into lidded container; refrigerate until needed.

Trim woody ends from asparagus by snapping each stalk where it breaks naturally. Rinse under cold running water. Pour water into large skillet to depth of 2 inch (5 cm); bring to boil over high heat. Add asparagus; return to boil. Reduce heat to medium-low; simmer, uncovered, for 3 to 5 minutes until asparagus is just tender. With large spatula or lifter, remove asparagus from skillet; place on paper-towel-lined plate to blot excess moisture. Arrange on serving platter; drizzle with strawberry vinaigrette. Garnish with mint.

GLAZED SWEET POTATOES WITH BACON AND ROSEMARY

Supermarket produce departments often mislabel Ontario sweet potatoes, calling them yams, but yams have a different taste and texture and grow only in subtropical regions. Our own sweet potatoes, with their colourful flesh and dense texture, are perfect for baking. Here they're layered with crisp bacon and rosemary and topped with a rich maple-syrup glaze.

1 cup	chicken stock	250 mL
½ cup	maple syrup	125 mL
1 tbsp	cider vinegar	15 mL
4	slices bacon	4
1	large onion, sliced	1
2	sweet potatoes (1½ lb/750 g), peeled and thinly sliced	2
1 tsp	minced fresh rosemary leaves	5 mL
½ tsp	black pepper	2 mL

Preheat oven to 400°F (200°C). In small saucepan, combine chicken stock, maple syrup and vinegar. Bring to boil over medium-high heat; boil for 10 to 12 minutes, until mixture is reduced by half. Set aside.

In large heavy skillet, cook bacon over medium-high heat for 5 minutes or until crisp. Drain on paper towels. Crumble into small pieces; set aside. Drain off all but 1 tbsp (15 mL) bacon fat from skillet. Add onion to skillet; cook over medium-high heat, stirring, for 3 to 5 minutes, until golden.

In greased 8-inch (2 L) baking dish, arrange one-third of sweet potatoes. Sprinkle with half of bacon, onion, rosemary and pepper. Arrange one-third of sweet potatoes over top; sprinkle with remaining bacon, onion, rosemary and pepper. Top with remaining sweet potatoes; drizzle chicken-stock mixture over top. Bake, covered, for 40 to 45 minutes, until sweet potatoes are tender and glazed.

Makes **4 servings**

Preparation time: **20 minutes**

Cooking time: **about 1 hour**

*O**ttawa's Repast: 150 Years of Food and Drink 1845–1995* was written by distinguished Canadian food writer Kathleen Walker. With her usual dedication to detail, Walker traces fifteen decades of culinary Ottawa from the early settlers and the life of a domestic servant to the illicit and legal booze trade. There's even a chapter on media—after all, Graham Kerr taped the *Galloping Gourmet* in Ottawa for a decade. Walker includes 166 historic and modern, thoroughly tested recipes. Printed as the 150th anniversary celebration of the *Ottawa Citizen*, the book may be purchased at Ottawa area bookstores or through the Promotions Department, *Ottawa Citizen*.

Makes **8 servings**

Preparation time: **20 minutes**

Cooking time: **about 45 minutes**

$\mathcal{M}$ost Polish settlement took place in western Canada after 1858. However, a small community in Renfrew County was the first of them all. The village of Wilno can rightfully claim to be the first Polish village in Canada. In 1858, some three hundred settlers from German-occupied Poland laboured up the Opeongo Road to establish a thriving agricultural community in a rough-and-ready wilderness.

WILNO RED CABBAGE WITH APPLES

In the 1860s, Polish immigrants began settling in the Wilno area, southeast of Algonquin Park, lured to Canada by government advertisements in the Polish press. In 1894, Ignancy Slominski bought the "stopping place" opposite the Wilno train station and opened the Exchange Hotel. The building has changed hands several times over the past hundred years but still operates as a hostelry. Present-day owners Miroslaw Lenc and his wife, Corinne Higgins, who advertise the Wilno Tavern as Canada's oldest Polish tavern, provide a menu of pub food combined with traditional Polish fare. Corinne agreed to share her excellent red cabbage recipe with us, and she says it's great served with roast pork.

3	slices bacon, chopped	3
2 lb	red cabbage, cored and shredded (half a medium cabbage)	1 kg
3	apples, peeled, cored and chopped	3
⅓ cup	water	75 mL
2	bay leaves	2
⅓ cup	red wine vinegar	75 mL
¼ cup	packed brown sugar	50 mL
1 tsp	salt	5 mL
½ tsp	black pepper	2 mL

In large heavy saucepan, cook bacon over medium-high heat for 3 to 4 minutes, until crisp. Stir in cabbage, apples, water and bay leaves; bring to boil. Reduce heat to medium-low; simmer, covered tightly, for 40 minutes, stirring often. Add a little more water if mixture seems too dry.

Stir in vinegar, sugar, salt and pepper; cook, stirring, until sugar melts. Adjust seasoning to taste; discard bay leaves and serve.

CHEDDAR BUNS WITH CIDER

Choose a good nippy Cheddar for these buns, and be sure to use a good Ontario-made cider, such as Brother John's or Southbrook Farms. The buns are best served as soon as they come out of the oven, but in a pinch, you can heat them up the next day.

2½ cups	all-purpose flour	625 mL
1½ cups	shredded old Cheddar (6 oz/175 g)	375 mL
⅓ cup	chopped fresh parsley	75 mL
1 tbsp	each baking powder and granulated sugar	15 mL
½ tsp	salt	2 mL
1⅓ cups	hard (alcoholic) cider, at room temperature	325 mL

Preheat oven to 375°F (190°C); grease 9 cups of a muffin pan.

In medium bowl, combine flour, cheese, parsley, baking powder, sugar and salt. Add cider; stir with a fork just until dry ingredients are moistened; do not overmix. (Dough will be sticky.)

Divide batter evenly among muffin cups. Bake for 20 to 25 minutes, until well risen and a toothpick inserted into centre bun comes out clean. Remove from pan; let cool slightly on wire rack.

Makes **9 buns**

Preparation time: **20 minutes**

Cooking time: **20 to 25 minutes**

Little Stream Bakery in Mississippi Station can only be characterized as a "craft bakery." The brick hearth is fired with wood from the Ottawa Valley's many lumber mills, the grain used in the dense sourdough breads is grown "as locally as possible," and the well water comes from deep within the Canadian Shield. Graham Beck is a purist, and his strong beliefs in the value of whole foods are reflected in his breads, from his spelt and raisin cinnamon buns to a great flax-speckled loaf, which we top with everything from Ernie Racz's Valencia peanut butter to extra-old Forfar Cheddar dabbed with Hellishly Hot Cherry Pepper Jelly (recipe on page 165). Graham has encouraged a friend to grow hard white wheat, a variety not widely known in Canada, and spelt, a grain that is gaining in popularity because few people have allergic reactions to it. Little Stream products show up all over Ontario in whole food stores but, if you call ahead—this is essential—Graham will be happy to share his understanding and love of the fine art of artisanal bread baking.

Makes **12 muffins**

Preparation time: **15 minutes**

Cooking time: **20 to 25 minutes**

WILD ELDERBERRY MUFFINS

You can pick wild elderberries in late summer, and they add a fresh tangy flavour to breakfast-time muffins. But, be warned, they take simply ages to strip off the stems, so we like to cheat and buy them at the farmers' market. If you can't find elderberries, blueberries (especially wild ones) are just as good in this recipe.

¾ cup	granulated sugar	175 mL
¼ cup	butter, melted	50 mL
1	egg	1
1 cup	buttermilk	250 mL
1 tbsp	cider vinegar	15 mL
½ tsp	vanilla	2 mL
2 cups	all-purpose flour	500 mL
1 tbsp	baking powder	15 mL
Pinch	salt	Pinch
1½ cups	elderberries or wild blueberries	375 mL

𝒜cross the province producers have opened their homes and created a network known as Ontario Farm and Country Accommodations. "Home-made" is the operative word in the kitchen from morning till evening. Take a weekend course in beekeeping, cross-country ski across snowy hills on private trails, walk through a cool forest in summer or just plain relax. OFCA was founded in 1967 and now has more than a hundred member hosts. The range of accommodation spans those who offer meals with the family to bed-and-breakfast homes to still others who offer housekeeping facilities in separate cottages or their second farm home.

Preheat oven to 400°F (200°C). In medium bowl, beat together sugar, butter and egg until light in colour. In glass measure, combine buttermilk, cider vinegar and vanilla. In separate medium bowl, combine flour, baking powder and salt.

Stir buttermilk mixture into sugar mixture until well combined. Add flour mixture all at once; stir just until dry ingredients are moistened (batter should be lumpy). Stir in elderberries.

Spoon batter into greased or paper-lined 12-cup muffin pan. Bake for 20 to 25 minutes, until muffins are well risen and golden brown and a toothpick inserted into centre muffin comes out clean. Remove muffins from pan; let cool on wire rack.

SOUR-CREAM HAZELNUT COFFEECAKE

Any of the province's nut varieties would be wonderful in this superb cake.

1 cup	toasted hazelnuts, coarsely chopped	250 mL
⅓ cup	packed brown sugar	75 mL
½ tsp	each cinnamon and nutmeg	2 mL
1 cup	granulated sugar	250 mL
½ cup	shortening, softened	125 mL
2	eggs	2
2 cups	all-purpose flour	500 mL
1 tsp	each baking powder and baking soda	5 mL
1 cup	light sour cream	500 mL

Preheat oven to 350°F (180°C). Grease and flour a 9-inch (3 L) tube pan.

In small bowl, combine hazelnuts, brown sugar, cinnamon and nutmeg; set aside.

In large bowl, cream together granulated sugar and shortening until light and fluffy. Add eggs, one at a time, beating well after each addition.

In medium bowl, stir together flour, baking powder and baking soda. Gradually add flour mixture to granulated-sugar mixture alternately with sour cream, beginning and ending with flour mixture.

Sprinkle half of nut mixture into base of prepared pan. Spoon half of batter into pan. Sprinkle remaining nut mixture over batter; top with remaining batter, spreading evenly. Bake for 45 to 50 minutes or until golden brown and toothpick inserted into centre of cake comes out clean. Let cake cool in pan for 10 minutes, then turn out and let cool completely on wire rack.

Makes **8 to 10 servings**

Preparation time: **20 minutes**

Cooking time: **45 to 50 minutes**

4-H: My Head to clearer thinking; my Heart to greater loyalty; my Hands to larger service; my Health to better living. This is the slogan that has been the underpinning for one of the most important clubs for young people in rural Ontario. Tracing its origins to Waterloo County in 1915, 4-H celebrated its eightieth anniversary in 1995. In the beginning there were two streams of programming, one "project-based" and the second designed for personal development. In 1982, they were merged into the dynamic organizational structure we see across today's province.

To toast hazelnuts, preheat oven to 350°F (180°C). Spread hazelnuts on baking sheet; bake for 5 to 7 minutes, until skins are dark brown and nuts are fragrant. Remove nuts from oven; wrap in clean tea towel. Let cool for 5 minutes, then rub vigorously in towel to remove loose skins.

Makes **4 to 6 servings**

Preparation time: **25 minutes**

Cooking time: **5 to 8 minutes**

Chilling time: **3 hours**

LANARK COUNTY MAPLE MOUSSE WITH CRANBERRY COULIS

At the historic Sam Jakes Inn in Merrickville, emphasis is placed on celebrating the region's food and heritage. The menu features local ingredients, and in keeping with the Scottish flavour of this part of the province a good selection of malt whiskies is available in the bar. Even better, the wine list features only Ontario wines and beers. This recipe from chef Erick Le Pors uses local maple syrup in a lovely light dessert topped with a pretty cranberry sauce.

Maple Mousse:

¼ cup	water	50 mL
1	envelope (7 g) unflavoured gelatin	1
1 cup	whipping cream	250 mL
½ cup	maple syrup	125 mL
4	egg whites	4
Pinch	salt	Pinch

Cranberry Coulis:

1½ cups	cranberries	375 mL
⅓ cup	granulated sugar	75 mL
¼ cup	water	50 mL
	Fresh mint sprigs	

Maple Mousse: Measure water into small bowl; sprinkle gelatin over top. Set aside until gelatin is puffy.

In medium bowl, whip cream until soft peaks form; set aside.

In small saucepan, bring maple syrup to boil over medium-high heat; boil for 3 minutes, until maple syrup is reduced to about ⅓ cup (75 mL). Remove from heat; stir in gelatin mixture until it is dissolved.

Meanwhile, in large bowl and with clean beaters, whisk egg whites and salt until stiff peaks form. Pour hot maple-syrup mixture into egg whites in thin steady stream, beating continuously; continue beating until meringue is glossy. Gradually fold in whipped cream. Divide among 4 or 6 individual glasses; refrigerate, covered, for 3 hours or until set.

Cranberry Coulis: In small saucepan, combine cranberries, sugar and water. Bring to boil over high heat. Reduce heat to medium; simmer, uncovered, for 2 to 3 minutes, stirring occasionally, until cranberries pop and mixture thickens. Remove from heat; rub through a sieve. Let cool completely. Serve mousse topped with cranberry coulis and garnished with a mint sprig.

The vegetarian community in Ottawa holds "Cornucopia, The Edible Utopia" yearly on World Vegetarian Day. It's a celebration of the ecology of eating. Lectures and demonstrations by stars like Bonnie Stern and Margaret Visser form the background for a huge sampling of great, all-vegetarian food and a "green bazaar," where you can taste and purchase treats like Don King's fiddlehead relish, Graham Beck's wood-fired-oven-baked breads and Maple Hill Farm goat's milk cheeses, yogurts and ice creams. Proceeds go to the Ottawa Food Bank and to CARE Canada for its overseas hunger relief work.

Refrigerate leftover egg yolks, with enough water to cover them, in a covered container for up to 2 days. Or freeze them —add ½ tsp (2 mL) salt or sugar for every six yolks —for up to 3 months.

Makes **6 to 8 servings**

Preparation time: **25 minutes**

Cooking time: **about 25 minutes**

Chilling time: **2 hours**

*T*he Cook Not Mad is the name of a small, brilliantly run restaurant in Gananoque. Chef/owner Mark Bussières is one of the gurus of regional cookery in Canada. For years his foods have been honest, locally based and very well prepared. Up early every morning, he begins the day by baking his seven-grain bread and signature corn bread, made with cornmeal ground at Kingston's Tara Natural Foods. Each Tuesday he shops at the Kingston Farmers' Market for such delicacies as morels, Flemish Beauty pears and Tydeman apples. From their own property Mark and his wife and partner, Nicole, harvest wild blackcaps and cultivated gold and red raspberries. His menus ebb and flow with the seasons, so it's rare to find the same dish on the menu for more than three to four weeks. For one brief "window" there'll be a soup of local sweet peas, tomato and fresh herbs from the garden overflowing with unusual flavours like cinnamon basil and Vietnamese coriander. Local shiitakes may find their way into a springtime tart, while in August Mark will roast guinea fowl and serve the tender birds with summer fruit salsa. Apples from the local growers of Prince Edward County play a large part year round. The Cook Not Mad is open for dinner from Wednesday till Sunday.

PUMPKIN-CARAMEL ICE CREAM

We think this is one of the most scrumptious ways to use pumpkin that we've ever tried, though it is undeniably rich. The recipe is adapted from one by chef Mark Bussières, who owns The Cook Not Mad restaurant in Gananoque. The restaurant is named for Canada's first cookbook, which was published in 1831. Appropriately, Mark specializes in preparing regional Canadian cuisine.

1 cup	granulated sugar	250 mL
3 cups	whipping cream	750 mL
6	egg yolks	6
1 tbsp	fresh lemon juice	15 mL
½ tsp	cinnamon	2 mL
¼ tsp	each ground cloves, ginger and grated nutmeg	1 mL
½ cup	pumpkin puree	125 mL

In medium heavy saucepan, heat sugar over medium heat for 5 to 7 minutes, stirring occasionally, until it is caramelized, lump-free and the colour of maple syrup (watch carefully; it burns easily). Meanwhile, in separate saucepan, heat cream over medium-high heat until cream boils.

Remove saucepan of caramelized sugar from heat. Using long-handled wooden spoon, gradually stir in hot cream ½ cup (125 mL) at a time. Be careful; the mixture will boil vigorously and may splatter at first. Cook caramel mixture over medium heat for 5 minutes, stirring constantly, until smooth and no lumps of caramel remain.

In medium bowl, whisk together egg yolks, lemon juice, cinnamon, cloves, ginger and nutmeg until light in colour. Gradually whisk in hot caramel mixture until well combined.

Place bowl over a saucepan of simmering water; cook, whisking constantly, for 10 minutes, until mixture thickens enough to coat the back of a spoon. Remove from heat; whisk in pumpkin puree. Place a piece of waxed paper or plastic wrap directly over surface of pumpkin mixture; refrigerate for 2 hours or until chilled. Freeze in ice-cream maker according to manufacturer's instructions.

Alternatively, pour mixture into shallow pan; freeze, covered, for 1 hour or until semifrozen. Scrape ice cream into food processor; process until smooth. Spoon ice cream into lidded container; freeze for 2 hours or until ice cream is firm. For best flavour, use within one week.

Thanks to Canada's work in genetic improvement, Canada is a world-leading country in the quantity and quality of milk produced per cow with farm level value of $3 billion.

Refrigerate leftover egg whites, in covered container, for up to 2 weeks, or freeze them for up to 3 months.

If using canned pumpkin puree, spoon remainder of can into freezer container; freeze for up to 6 months.

Makes **about 56 squares**

Preparation time: **20 minutes**

Cooking time: **about 20 minutes**

Cotton candy and blue ribbons, prize-winning pickles and Ferris wheels: the fairs in Ontario signal the changing seasons at their finest. From May until mid-October they are the spirit of many rural communities. The story of Ontario's fall fairs is a lengthy one. "The Agricultural Society of Upper Canada" was the first such organization created. It was founded in 1791 in Niagara. By 1878 there were more than 350 such societies across the province. The fall fairs they sponsored encouraged excellence, celebrated the local bounty and demonstrated to urban folk what agriculture was all about. The tradition still continues, to such a degree that we cannot list all the fairs in this publication.

SCOTTISH-STYLE FUDGE

The place names that dot a map of eastern Ontario are a clue to some of its original settlers. There's Perth, Forfar, Glen Nevis, St. Andrews and even a Loch Garry, all names to warm an expatriate Scot's heart! Along with the familiar names, Scottish immigrants brought their favourite foods, such as this simple candy, which is known as "tablet" in Scotland. The secret of good tablet is to beat the candy really well after boiling it to ensure that it's silky smooth; hard work but worth it! Don't be tempted to use an electric mixer for this step; it won't work. The original recipe would have included cream, but more modern versions use canned condensed milk.

4 cups	granulated sugar	1 L
1	can (300 mL) sweetened condensed milk	1
¾ cup	whole milk	175 mL
¼ cup	butter	50 mL
1 tsp	vanilla	5 mL

In large heavy saucepan, combine sugar, condensed milk, whole milk and butter. Heat over medium heat, stirring occasionally, for 15 minutes, until sugar has dissolved and butter is melted. Bring to boil over medium-high heat; boil for 5 minutes, stirring constantly, or until candy thermometer registers 240°F (116°C) and ½ tsp (2 mL) of the mixture dropped into very cold water forms a soft ball (brown spots may appear in mixture; don't worry, this is normal).

Remove saucepan from heat; stir in vanilla. With sturdy wooden spoon, beat mixture for 10 minutes until smooth, scraping down sides of saucepan if the mixture starts to solidify around edge. Spoon into an oiled 8-inch (2 L) square cake pan; let cool. Refrigerate, covered, until set. Cut into squares; refrigerate in airtight container with waxed paper between layers.

HELLISHLY HOT CHERRY PEPPER JELLY

Always wear plastic gloves when preparing hot peppers, and have ready a sink full of hot, soapy water to drop all your utensils into immediately you've finished preparing the peppers. Small, fleshy cherry peppers ripen in September and make a gorgeous jelly with a real kick. To speed up preparation, use a food processor to chop the peppers.

½ lb	cherry peppers (about 9 peppers)	250 g
¼ lb	jalapeño peppers (about 5 peppers)	125 g
6 cups	granulated sugar	1.5 L
1¼ cups	cider vinegar	300 mL
2	pouches (85 mL each) liquid pectin	2

Cut peppers into quarters; remove stems and seeds. In food processor, process peppers until finely chopped.

In large stainless steel or enamel saucepan, combine peppers, sugar and vinegar. Heat over medium heat, stirring often, until sugar is dissolved (mixture will no longer be gritty). Increase heat to high; add pectin. Bring to full, rolling boil. Boil hard for 1 minute, stirring constantly.

Remove from heat; let cool for 4 to 5 minutes, stirring occasionally and skimming off any scum. Ladle into 6 hot, sterilized ½-pint (250 mL) jars, leaving ¼ in (5 mm) headspace. Wipe jar rims to remove any excess jelly; seal with two-piece lids, tightening screw bands until just fingertip tight. Process in hot-water bath for 5 minutes. Remove jars from canner; let cool for 24 hours. Check jar seals (sealed lids curve downwards). Remove screw bands; label jars. Store jelly in cool, dark place.

Makes **6 half-pint (250 mL) jars**

Preparation time: **25 minutes**

Cooking time: **5 to 6 minutes**

Processing time: **5 minutes**

*I*f you love great bread, you simply must stop at Kingston's Pan Chancho Bakery for artisan breads, loaves that are built with organic ingredients, natural starters, spring water and loving care. Sometimes free-form, as in the French *levain*, or shaped in rectangular woven willow baskets, many of them are started as our pioneer ancestors did, with air-borne yeasts. Although the methodology is old-fashioned, the flavours are a taste of the 1990s: toasted tamari, sesame and pumpkin seed bread with cumin . . . walnut and currant . . . a true apple sourdough dusted with cornmeal. Pan Chancho's take-out menu may include seasonal treats like Wolf Island asparagus salad with shallots and veggie sushi, or the Abner, a sandwich made with Mennonite sausage from Waterloo County and extra-old Forfar Cheddar.

Lakelands

Drop off the main highways onto the two-lane country roads that meander through this part of rural Ontario. Mature elms and maple forests line the byways. Grocery stores, garages and Chamber of Commerce offices have Coming Events boards packed with local activities. Rivers with names like Maitland, Saugeen and Nottawasaga wind through the countryside, beside towns that once depended upon them for mill power. Today, they're used for paddling and fly-fishing. The rolling fields are filled with sweet-smelling canola and grains of every description. Pastures hold more cattle than anywhere else in the province. The dairy industry is flourishing. This is where Anita's grandfather's phrase "going for a joy ride" says it all. There is still a real connection to the earth. Buy the flour or grind the grain yourself; savour fine pastries and wholesome breads from any number of bakers; do a taste comparison of smoked fish or cheese or garlic. You'll be enjoying our land, its history and, most important, its future possibilities.

BRUCE COUNTY BEEF SOUP WITH BARLEY AND WINTER ROOT VEGETABLES

In the summer, cattle by the hundreds graze on the long grasses of the Bruce County peninsula from Owen Sound to Tobermory. For best flavour, use homemade beef stock for this easy soup. It may thicken if you make it ahead of time, so add extra stock when you reheat it.

1 lb	lean stewing beef	500 g
8 cups	beef stock	2 L
1	large onion, chopped	1
⅔ cup	pearl barley	150 mL
3	carrots, chopped	3
2	potatoes, peeled and cubed	2
2	stalks celery with leaves, sliced	2
1½ cups	chopped turnip	375 mL
1 tsp	dried rosemary or thyme	5 mL
	Salt and black pepper	

Trim any excess fat from the beef; cut into ½-inch (1 cm) cubes. In large pot or Dutch oven, combine stock, beef, onion and barley; bring to boil over high heat. Reduce heat to medium-low; simmer, covered, for 1 hour. Add carrots, potatoes, celery, turnip and rosemary. Simmer, covered, for 30 minutes or until vegetables are tender. Season with salt and pepper to taste; ladle into warm soup bowls.

Serves **8 to 10**

Preparation time: **25 minutes**

Cooking time: 1½ **hours**

*B*ruce County has combined its tourism and agriculture offices. The link is a natural one. It just makes sense, because when one travels through Bruce County, one is deep in the heart of the country.

Bruce County is the number-one beef producer in Ontario and ranks number two in its production of canola. On its 600,000 acres of agricultural area there are 3,750 farm operators, and a full sixty-three percent of them are on family farms. The diversity is particularly impressive. And there are bed-and-breakfast farms, and others that open their doors for an autumnal Explore the Country Tour.

Makes **about 1½ cups (375 mL);**
4 to 6 servings

Preparation time: **20 minutes**

*F*or many, the name Michael
Stadtländer conjures up fond culinary
memories. Stadtländer has been a
troubadour, exploring Canada with the
eye of a brilliant chef. His love of ingredients led him to settle with his wife and
partner, Nobuyo, on a farm north of
Singhampton. Eigensinn Farm is everything they are—experimental, colourful
and uncommon. In their wild meadows
and forests they harvest chanterelles,
morels and cêpes mushrooms. Wild
leeks grow in large patches in their bush,
where sometimes guests are able to dine.
The hedgerows yield apples of unknown
origin, and ground cherries flourish in at
least one pasture. They head to the fish-
ermen in nearby Collingwood for splake
and sometimes catfish, which they will
smoke. Michael raves about the quality
of Grey County lamb, which dine on
the wild herbs and grasses of the Niagara
Escarpment. From fallow deer to sturgeon, there's not much chance that
anyone who experiences the foods of
Eigensinn will have had such a deliciously esoteric meal before!

*To toast walnuts, preheat oven
to 350°F (180°C). Spread
walnuts on baking sheet; bake
for 5 to 7 minutes, until golden
and fragrant. Watch carefully;
they burn easily.*

SMOKED TROUT PÂTÉ WITH TOASTED WALNUTS

*Smoked fish pâtés are so easy to make but look very
special. This one is given added crunch by a handful
of toasted walnuts; serve it with crisp toast triangles,
crackers or good crusty bread.*

½ lb	smoked trout fillets, skin and bones removed	250 g
¼ lb	cream cheese, cut into pieces (half a 250-g pkg)	125 g
2 tbsp	cider vinegar	25 mL
1	large clove garlic, minced	1
1 tsp	dry mustard	5 mL
½ tsp	black pepper	2 mL
⅓ cup	chopped walnuts, toasted and cooled	75 mL
	Paprika and chopped fresh parsley	

In food processor or blender, combine trout,
cream cheese, vinegar, garlic, mustard and pepper;
process until fairly smooth. Spoon into a medium
bowl; stir in walnuts. Spoon pâté into 2-cup (500
mL) serving dish; smooth surface level. Chill well.
Sprinkle with paprika and parsley before serving.

BUTTER LETTUCE WITH LIGHT YOGURT-DILL DRESSING

Makes 6 servings

Preparation time: 15 minutes

The Idyll Bakery and Café in downtown Markdale is a foodie haven in the midst of farm country. Using only organically grown flour and every other good ingredient they can find, the bakers create everything from whole-wheat pita bread to bittersweet choco-late-glazed cream puffs filled with fresh whipped cream and gooey, dark, cinnamon sticky buns. For several of their salad dressings they use mild Saugeen Country yogurt from just down the road.

1	large head butter (Boston) lettuce	1
½ cup	plain yogurt	125 mL
¼ cup	well-packed finely minced dill	50 mL
2 tbsp	cider vinegar	25 mL
2 tsp	liquid honey	10 mL
¼ tsp	each salt and black pepper	1 mL
¼ cup	canola or corn oil	50 mL
3	green onions, finely chopped	3

Remove core from lettuce and run cold water through the leaves, maintaining the head intact. Dry well in kitchen towel; refrigerate wrapped in a damp towel until ready to serve.

In small bowl, whisk together yogurt, dill, vinegar, honey, salt and pepper until smooth. Whisk in oil until well combined. Refrigerate dressing in covered jar until ready to serve. Just before serving, arrange lettuce leaves on individual plates. Drizzle with dressing; sprinkle with green onions. Serve at once.

*I*n early June, with the Saugeen River flowing swiftly nearby, Durham holds its annual Herb Fair behind the old town hall. Go early! It seems that every year the event becomes more popular. Perhaps it's the signal that spring has really come to this part of the snow belt, but whatever the reason, you can buy woodruff and basil, silver thyme and old-fashioned iris. One of the local churches has a homemade pie and coffee booth—a particular joy of shopping in a small town where honest food is still not a luxury.

Makes **6 servings**

Preparation time: **20 minutes**

Cooking time: **10 to 12 minutes**

AUTUMN GREENS WITH MAPLE APPLES AND SPICED PINE NUTS

This is one of the prettiest salads we've ever seen and one of the most flavourful. The spiced pine nuts are delicious, and served by themselves they make a good accompaniment to drinks.

4 cups	washed, dried and torn young spinach leaves, stems removed (about half a bunch)	1 L
2 cups	washed, dried and torn radicchio (about 1 small head)	500 mL
1	small leek (white and light green parts only), cleaned and thinly sliced	1
½ cup	pine nuts	125 mL
1 tsp	chili powder	5 mL
¼ tsp	salt	1 mL
2	Spartan apples, peeled, cored and sliced	2
¼ cup	each maple syrup and apple cider	50 mL
¼ cup	canola or corn oil	50 mL
2 tbsp	cider vinegar	25 mL

With a fair bit of pomp and circumstance and of course the inevitable cake, the Owen Sound Farmers' Market celebrated its 150th anniversary in 1995. This venerable market is a class act, with forty-one vendors year round and many others who set up shop seasonally. They journey from all over Bruce and Grey counties to sell apples from Thornbury, fish from Wiarton, organic baking and yogurt from Durham and star thistle honey from Chatsworth. And after the market, cast a fishing line into the Sydenham River, which flows adjacent to the building, have a coffee or a great local lunch at the Marketside Café. Try their homemade pasta! Then finish the foodie tour by browsing your way through the Ginger Press Bookstore, one of Ontario's few seriously independent publishers, run by Maryann Hogbin, who loves great food and great food writing.

In salad bowl, combine spinach, radicchio and leek; refrigerate, loosely covered.

In heavy skillet, combine pine nuts, chili powder and salt; cook over medium heat for 5 to 7 minutes, stirring occasionally, until pine nuts are golden and fragrant (watch carefully; they burn easily). Remove pine nuts from skillet; set aside. Wipe out skillet with paper towels.

In same skillet, combine apples, maple syrup and apple cider; bring to boil over high heat. Reduce heat to medium-high; simmer, uncovered, for 2 to 3 minutes, until apple slices are tender but not broken up. With slotted spoon, remove apple slices from skillet; set aside.

Increase heat to high; boil maple-syrup mixture in skillet for 1 to 2 minutes, until reduced to about 2 tbsp (25 mL). Whisk in oil and vinegar; let boil for 1 minute. Immediately add dressing to spinach mixture; toss well. Top with apple slices and pine nuts; serve at once.

*R*einhart Vinegar in Stayner began as a cider mill in 1910. Apples were then, as they still are, harvested in the rich apple-growing areas that bound the southern shore of Georgian Bay. Today, a few extra tons are added from Norfolk County. For full-flavoured apple cider vinegar, the apple of preference is the wonderful old-fashioned Northern Spy. The juices are pressed and fermented to alcoholic cider, then a second "acetous" fermentation occurs, converting the alcohol to vinegar. Reinhart makes a number of other specialty vinegars, including white and red wine, which are sourced from Niagara. They also pack in bulk so, unless you own a restaurant, their Stayner plant may be the only place in Ontario you can buy true Ontario white wine vinegar in a 5-litre jug.

Makes **6 servings**

Preparation time: **20 minutes**

Marinating time: **at least 30 minutes**

Cooking time: **about 6 minutes**

*L*ook for Bruce Brand tomatoes . . . the heat that nurtures these hardy plants comes from the Bruce Nuclear Station. No, you won't glow in the dark! All year round, the cherry tomatoes produced there rival the finest summer grown.

*O*ne of the best foodie exhibitions in the province takes place in Owen Sound every April when a dynamic group of Bruce and Grey County producers called Market Grey Bruce set up their wares for a public tasting. It's hard to believe how rich this region is even at that time of year. From emu, shiitake and organic grains to maple syrup, pheasant and organic cheeses, it all comes from within a few hours of Owen Sound.

CHINESE-STYLE BEEF WITH CHERRY TOMATOES

Most small towns in Ontario boast a local Chinese restaurant, and this recipe pays homage to the hard work and enterprise of the new Canadians who make sure we can enjoy such delights as hot and sour soup in the farthest reaches of the province.

1 lb	sirloin steak	500 g
¼ cup	dark soy sauce	50 mL
2 tbsp	brown sugar	25 mL
1 tbsp	minced gingerroot	15 mL
2	cloves garlic, minced	2
1 tsp	minced hot pepper (optional)	5 mL
2 tsp	cornstarch	10 mL
2 tbsp	peanut oil	25 mL
1	sweet green pepper, seeded and cut into thin strips	1
3 cups	sliced assorted Ontario mushrooms (button, shiitake, portobello)	750 mL
2 cups	cherry tomatoes, cut in half	500 mL
4	green onions, cut diagonally into 1-in (2.5 cm) pieces	4
1 tsp	sesame oil (optional)*	5 mL

Wrap meat in plastic wrap; freeze for 30 minutes to make it easier to slice. Trim meat of any excess fat. With large, sharp knife, cut meat across the grain into thin strips; set aside.

In shallow nonmetallic dish, combine soy sauce, sugar, gingerroot, garlic and hot pepper, stirring to dissolve sugar. Add meat to soy-sauce mixture. Let stand, covered, at room temperature for 30 minutes or up to 4 hours in the refrigerator.

Strain meat and marinade through a sieve, reserving marinade; set meat and flavourings aside. Blend cornstarch into reserved marinade until well combined; set aside.

Heat wok or very large skillet over high heat. Add 1 tbsp (15 mL) peanut oil; heat over high heat. Add meat to wok; stir-fry for 2 minutes or until meat loses its red colour. With slotted spoon, remove meat from wok; set aside. Wipe out wok with paper towels.

Heat remaining peanut oil in wok over high heat. Add green pepper and mushrooms; stir-fry for 2 minutes, until pepper starts to soften. Add meat, tomatoes, green onions, reserved marinade and sesame oil to wok; cook, stirring, for 1 minute, until bubbly and sauce has thickened. Serve at once over steamed or boiled rice.

* Available in Oriental section of most large supermarkets.

*T*obermory has some serious culinary traditions, all centred around the harbour. First and foremost is Craigie's. Since 1932 this small grey restaurant at the head of the harbour has been serving whitefish and fries the way God intended. The fish is floured and fried, the potatoes are freshly cut and there's a bottle of malt vinegar on the table. The sign No Wetsuits Allowed attests to the area's booming scuba business. Shipwrecks litter the lake bottom; divers wander the town.

To buy whitefish or splake, the best place is at Wayne Raney's. His fishing boats are tied up outside. Freshwater herring, known to some as chub, are caught in schools at a depth of two hundred feet.

And if you are in the mood to overdose on fresh fish, try Shipwreck Lee's. Whitefish or any other catch of the day is served in seven different ways, from pan-fried in butter and garlic to blackened with heavy-duty Cajun spices.

Makes **4 servings**

Preparation time: **25 minutes**

Marinating time: **up to 1 hour**

Cooking time: **8 to 10 minutes**

$\mathcal{F}$loating in the marshy peat bogs of this region are cranberries (*Vaccinium macrocarpum*)—more than a million pounds of them. Cranberries need acid conditions, so they find peat bogs particularly acceptable. The berries are harvested throughout October. Johnston's Cranberry Marsh near Bala and the Iroquois Cranberry Marsh south of MacTier produce the entire provincial crop on a mere seventy-five acres.

Johnston's began growing cranberries in 1952. From the twenty acres they have in cultivation, they harvest two to three hundred thousand pounds of cranberries, much of it sold to wholesalers and to the Black River Juice Company in Mississauga. The rest they cook up into marvellous preserves, such as cranberry Niagara peach jam, cranberry chutney, cranberry apple relish and a cranberry mincemeat.

The process begins in late May, when the vines produce pretty pink blossoms. Johnston's rent bees to pollinate the berries. (They sell the cranberry blossom honey.) As the plants begin to fall dormant in September, the berries turn scarlet. The fields are then flooded, the staff pull on their hip waders and the harvest begins. From late September till the end of October, berries are collected. This is the best time to visit. The store brims with great gifts and edibles, and the clincher is back bacon smothered with cranberry chutney on a soft bun from Don's Bakery.

MAPLE-MARINATED GEORGIAN BAY SALMON WITH CRANBERRY SALSA

There's no commercial fishery for Great Lakes wild salmon, but if you're lucky enough to catch one yourself, here's a neat way to serve it. We use a food processor to chop the cranberries for this colourful salsa.

Maple-Marinated Salmon:

¼ cup	canola or corn oil	50 mL
¼ cup	apple cider	50 mL
2 tbsp	maple syrup	25 mL
4	6-oz (175 g) salmon steaks	4
	Fresh basil sprigs for garnish	

Cranberry Salsa:

1 cup	cranberries, coarsely chopped	250 mL
¼ cup	minced red onion	50 mL
2 tbsp	maple syrup	25 mL
2 tbsp	shredded fresh basil leaves	25 mL
1 tbsp	cider vinegar	15 mL
½ tsp	seeded and minced hot pepper	2 mL

Maple-Marinated Salmon: In shallow nonmetallic dish large enough to hold salmon steaks in single layer, whisk together oil, cider and maple syrup. Add salmon steaks to marinade, turning to coat on both sides. Refrigerate, covered, for up to 1 hour, turning occasionally. Remove salmon steaks from marinade; place on oiled barbecue grill. Grill over medium heat for 8 to 10 minutes per 1 inch (2.5 cm) of thickness, turning once, until salmon flakes easily with a fork. Garnish with basil sprigs; serve with salsa on the side.

Cranberry Salsa: In medium bowl, combine cranberries, onion, maple syrup, basil, cider vinegar and hot pepper. Let stand at room temperature for 1 hour for flavours to blend. Serve salsa alongside salmon.

FLASH-GRILLED LAKE HURON WHITEFISH

You'll need a gas barbecue and a good heavy cast-iron skillet for this recipe. It only has four ingredients, but it's the best way we've prepared fish in absolutely ages: seared on a piping-hot skillet. You'll have to cook the fish in two batches, but since it cooks so quickly, six portions take only a few minutes to prepare.

⅓ cup	butter, melted	75 mL
1½ lb	whitefish fillets (skin on), cut into 6 portions	750 g
	Salt and black pepper	

Remove rack from barbecue; heat barbecue to high. Place large heavy cast-iron skillet directly on coals or lava rocks; close lid of barbecue. Heat skillet on barbecue for 10 minutes or until very hot.

Meanwhile, pour butter into a shallow dish. Pat fish dry on paper towels; sprinkle with salt and pepper. Dip pieces of fish one at a time in melted butter to coat on both sides. Place three pieces of fish in skillet (stand back; there will be a lot of smoke and some flames). Cook with barbecue lid up for 1½ to 2 minutes on each side (wear oven mitts when turning fish), until fish starts to flake easily with a fork. Remove fish from skillet, leaving skillet on barbecue; keep warm while you cook remaining fish. Let skillet cool before removing from barbecue.

Makes **6 servings**

Preparation time: **5 minutes**

Cooking time: **6 to 8 minutes**

*T*he tradition of a fish boil is unique to the Bruce Peninsula. It is a marvellous way to feed a crowd. June Golden, who works in one of the local gift stores, explained the method to us.

Water is brought to a boil then onions are added—about two per person. When they bob, they're done. Potatoes, all the same size and allowing two to three per person, are tossed in and cooked for about ten minutes. One fillet of whitefish per serving is then added, with a handful of salt. The poaching only takes a few minutes longer. The custom was simply to drain the meal by tossing it onto a clean, flat boulder. Now it's drained atop a screen. It's served with bread and sometimes with homemade pickles. Everyone eats so much there's no need for dessert.

Makes **4 to 6 servings**

Preparation time: **20 minutes**

Cooking time: **35 to 40 minutes**

*P*ine River Cheese and Butter Co-operative near Ripley was founded in 1885. Now, five or so generations later, it is still producing fine aged Cheddars in its sparkling-clean plant on the Blue-water Highway (Highway 21) a few kilometres from Lake Huron. There's a small collection of antiques lent by Kincardine's Bruce County Museum, and from the viewing gallery visitors can look on modern cheesemaking in all its stainless-steel finery. Their factory store sells a full selection of their cheese, including random-weights at substan-tially reduced prices, Robinson's maple syrup, local honey and special area treats such as Sweet Rose Bud Butter.

BAKED PINE RIVER CHEESE AND PASTA

This rich macaroni and cheese is the best you'll ever taste. It's based on Anita's mother's recipe, but we've added some summer sausage to spice it up.

2 cups	elbow macaroni	500 mL
¼ cup	butter	50 mL
1	medium onion, finely chopped	1
3 tbsp	all-purpose flour	45 mL
½ tsp	each black pepper and dry mustard	2 mL
¼ tsp	salt	1 mL
2 cups	milk, heated	500 mL
1 cup	each shredded old Cheddar and Monterey Jack cheese, such as Pine River	250 mL
¼ lb	summer sausage, chopped	125 g
1 cup	soft bread crumbs (1½ slices of bread)	250 mL

Preheat oven to 400°F (200°C). In large pot of boiling, salted water, cook macaroni for 5 to 7 minutes until al dente (tender but still with a bite). Drain well; set aside.

Meanwhile, in large saucepan, melt 2 tbsp (25 mL) of the butter over medium heat. Add onion; cook, stirring, for 3 to 5 minutes, until onion is soft but not brown. Stir in flour, pepper, mustard and salt. Cook, stirring, for 1 minute. Remove saucepan from heat; gradually whisk in hot milk. Cook over medium-high heat, stirring constantly, for 2 minutes or until sauce is thick-ened and bubbly. Remove saucepan from heat; stir in cheese until melted and smooth. Stir in sum-mer sausage and macaroni. Spoon mixture into buttered 8-cup (2 L) casserole dish; set aside.

In small skillet, melt remaining butter over medium heat. Add bread crumbs; cook, stirring occasionally, for 3 to 5 minutes until bread crumbs are golden. Sprinkle crumbs evenly over macaroni mixture. Bake, uncovered, for 20 minutes, until bubbly and golden brown.

A cooler and a few ice packs are essential equipment if you stop by Bruce Packers in Paisley. It's one of those wonderful places that cottagers drop in to before their long weekends in Southampton or Sauble Beach or Port Elgin. Few butchers make better summer sausage (we've bought them by the half dozen for a winter supply) or smoked pork chops or bacon. Then head downtown to Floreal's bakery—anyone can direct you—to buy the buttery croissants and magnificent Basque pastries for which he's been famous for the past two decades.

Makes **4 to 6 servings**

Preparation time: **15 minutes**

Cooking time: **50 to 55 minutes**

$\mathcal{S}$ay "Alliston" and "potatoes" in the same sentence, and it invokes images of flat, rich loam fields stretching across many hundreds of acres and covered with neat rows of white flowered plants. Here in this, the historical centre of the potato-processing industry, you'll find one of Ontario's oldest festivals, the Alliston Potato Festival, now well into its third decade.

MARILYN'S MAKE-AHEAD MASH

We first enjoyed a version of these ambrosial mashed potatoes at the home of our good friends Marilyn Short and Jeff Weiss in Toronto. We've transformed the recipe into a make-ahead dish so it's a perfect choice for entertaining, especially if you're celebrating the Alliston Potato Festival!

6	medium potatoes (about 2 lb/1 kg), peeled	6
2	cloves garlic, peeled	2
¼ lb	goat cheese, crumbled	125 g
½ cup	half-and-half cream	125 mL
3 tbsp	butter	45 mL
¼ cup	chopped fresh parsley	50 mL
	Salt and black pepper	
2 tbsp	bread crumbs	25 mL

Cut potatoes into chunks. In large saucepan, combine potatoes, garlic and enough cold water to cover them. Bring to boil over high heat. Reduce heat to medium-low; cook, covered, for 20 minutes or until potatoes are very tender. Drain well; return potatoes and garlic to saucepan. Place over low heat to dry out slightly, shaking saucepan occasionally.

Meanwhile, in small saucepan, combine goat cheese, cream and 2 tbsp (25 mL) butter; heat over medium heat until mixture is hot but not boiling and goat cheese and butter are melted. Add goat-cheese mixture to potatoes; mash roughly with fork. With electric mixer, beat potatoes until smooth and creamy. Stir in parsley and salt and pepper to taste.

Serve immediately or if making ahead, spoon potatoes into a greased 6-cup (1.5 L) baking dish. Don't smooth top too much; leave the texture slightly rough. Let cool completely. Sprinkle with bread crumbs; dot with remaining butter. Refrigerate, covered, up to 24 hours. Remove dish from refrigerator 30 minutes before baking.

Preheat oven to 400°F (200°C). Bake for 20 minutes. Remove lid; bake for 10 to 15 minutes or until bubbly and golden brown on top.

*I*n early October, the town of Port Elgin on the Bluewater Highway (Highway 21) is the headquarters for the World Pumpkin Confederation Weigh-off and Pumpkinfest. But the fun doesn't stop with the giant pumpkins. There's a wild eastern turkey search, a scarecrow-making contest, hot air balloon rides, the Robin Hood Multifoods baking contest and an underwater pumpkin carving competition.

Makes one 9-in (23 cm) loaf

Preparation time: 20 minutes

Cooking time: 50 to 55 minutes

$\mathcal{B}$rewing in Formosa dates back to 1870, when the region of Grey–Bruce had fourteen breweries. Located in an area dotted with dozens of natural springs and a huge aquifer, the original brewery, which is still in use today, was built atop the source, 980 feet below. Its history is mottled by sales and sellouts, but today, the newly refurbished business is known as the Algonquin Brewing Company. The old spring still flows as pure as it did in the 1800s, and the brewery is still an integral part of community life. Although there is a brewery store, only group tours are welcomed (ten minimum) and are held Monday through Thursday evenings after the busy bottling line finishes for the day.

CHEDDAR BEER BREAD WITH ONIONS AND SESAME SEEDS

Use a good Ontario-brewed beer for this tasty loaf. Serve the bread hot from the oven, sliced and slathered with butter, or prepare it ahead of time; wrap in foil and reheat in 325°F (160°C) oven for 15 to 20 minutes.

2¾ cups	all-purpose flour	675 mL
1 tbsp	each baking powder and granulated sugar	15 mL
1½ tsp	dry mustard	7 mL
½ tsp	salt	2 mL
1¼ cups	shredded old Cheddar cheese	300 mL
2	green onions, finely chopped	2
2 tsp	dried basil	10 mL
1	bottle (341 mL) beer, at room temperature	1
1	small onion, thinly sliced and separated into rings	1
1 tbsp	sesame seeds	15 mL

Preheat oven to 350°F (180°C). In large bowl, stir together flour, baking powder, sugar, mustard and salt; stir in 1 cup (250 mL) cheese, the green onions and basil. Pour in beer, stirring just until dry ingredients are moistened (do not overmix).

Spread batter evenly in greased 9- by 5-inch (2 L) loaf pan. Arrange onion rings over top; sprinkle evenly with remaining cheese and with sesame seeds. Bake for 50 to 55 minutes until loaf is well risen and golden, and a toothpick inserted in centre comes out clean. Let stand for 5 minutes in pan on wire rack. Remove from pan and let cool for 10 minutes before slicing.

Pumpkin-Apricot Bread

*If you don't have dried apricots, try dried peaches,
apples or sultana raisins in this autumnal loaf, which
is perfect spread with butter and apricot preserves.
Use kitchen scissors to "chop" the apricots, or use a
food processor.*

1 cup	packed dark brown sugar	250 mL
½ cup	canola or corn oil	125 mL
2	eggs	2
1 cup	pumpkin puree	250 mL
	Grated rind of 1 orange	
1¾ cups	all-purpose flour	425 mL
1 tsp	each salt, baking powder and baking soda	5 mL
½ tsp	each ground cinnamon and grated nutmeg	2 mL
¼ tsp	ground cloves	1 mL
½ cup	buttermilk	125 mL
1½ cups	chopped dried apricots	375 mL
½ cup	chopped walnuts	125 mL

Preheat oven to 350°F (180°C). Lightly oil a 9- by
5-inch (2 L) loaf pan; line base of pan with parchment or waxed paper.

In large bowl, beat brown sugar, oil and eggs until
light in colour. Stir in pumpkin puree and orange
rind, until mixture is smooth. In separate bowl,
stir together flour, salt, baking powder, baking
soda, cinnamon, nutmeg and cloves. Add flour
mixture to sugar mixture alternately with buttermilk, stirring just until no dry spots remain. Fold
in apricots and walnuts.

Spoon batter into prepared pan. Bake for 55 to 60
minutes, until toothpick inserted into centre of
loaf comes out clean. Let loaf cool in pan for
5 minutes, then turn out and let cool completely
on wire rack.

Makes **one 9-in (23 cm) loaf**

Preparation time: **20 minutes**

Cooking time: **55 to 60 minutes**

*R*iversong Studios is a herb lover's
dream, located on the banks of the
Saugeen River, northeast of the town of
Mount Forest. Home economist Pat
Crocker has intermingled her passion
for herbs with seminars, walks in the
forest and fabulous, by-reservation-only
luncheons. Her log home is filled with
herbal fragrances of some sort at every
time of year, and guests are encouraged
to sniff, smell and browse their way
through her inspiring little shop.

Makes two round loaves

Preparation time: **25 minutes**

Rising time: **4 to 4½ hours**

Cooking time: **25 to 30 minutes**

$\mathcal{S}$pelt, an ancient grain with origins in the Middle East, is high in protein, minerals and vitamins. The tough outer hull must be split before milling into a nutty, delicate-tasting flour.

DURHAM SPELT SEED BREAD

The secret to any whole-grain bread is lots of mixing and kneading. If you have a beater with a dough hook, now is the time to use it. Otherwise, an electric mixer may be used to incorporate the first 6 cups (1.5 L) of flour. Spelt bread is never light and airy, rather it is dense and very flavourful. Look for spelt flour and flax seeds in health-food or bulk stores.

4½ to 5 cups	each spelt flour and unbleached hard white flour	1.125 to 1.25 L
3 cups	warm water (105°F/41°C)	750 mL
1 cup	Grey County Sourdough Starter (see recipe on page 192)	250 mL
2 tsp	each salt and active dry yeast	10 mL
1 cup	flax or shelled sunflower seeds	250 mL
	Additional flour for kneading	

Topping:

1	egg white, beaten	1
1 tbsp	water	15 mL
1 tbsp	flax seeds	15 mL

In large bowl, combine spelt and white flours. In separate large bowl, whisk together warm water and sourdough starter. With electric mixer, beat in 4 cups (1 L) of the flour, the salt and yeast until smooth. Continue to beat in 3 cups (750 mL) flour 1 cup (250 mL) at a time until a sticky batter forms. Knead in 2 cups (500 mL) flour and the seeds, until well combined.

Turn dough out onto a floured surface; knead for 10 to 12 minutes, until smooth and elastic, adding more flour as necessary (seeds will start popping out when dough is kneaded sufficiently). Form dough into ball; place in lightly oiled bowl, turning dough to coat with oil. Cover loosely with plastic wrap; let rise in warm, draft-free place for 1½ hours or until doubled in size.

Punch dough down. Return to bowl; let rise, covered, in warm place for 1 hour, until doubled in size.

Divide dough in half; shape into round loaves. Place on parchment-lined baking sheets. Let rise, covered, in warm place for 1½ to 2 hours, until doubled in size. Preheat oven to 400°F (200°C).

Topping: In small bowl, beat together egg white and water. With very sharp knife, make 3 or 4 slashes in tops of loaves. Brush egg-white mixture over loaves; sprinkle evenly with flax seeds. Bake for 5 minutes. Reduce temperature to 375°F (190°C); bake for 20 to 25 minutes, until golden brown and risen and loaves sound hollow when tapped on bases.

*S*prings bubble up from many a hill in the rocky regions south of Collingwood. It follows that it would be here that one of Ontario's oldest microbreweries was established. Creemore Springs is located on the main thoroughfare of Creemore, one of the prettiest little towns in this part of Ontario. Brewery tours and tastings are scheduled on most days. To join the Loyal Order of Frothquaffers, contact the brewery. "Froth Talk," their newsletter, and a T-shirt are the membership rewards.

Makes **16 squares**

Preparation time: **20 minutes**

Cooking time: **30 to 35 minutes**

*D*on's Bakery is a Bala tradition. It's one of the prettiest little bakeries in the province, and its wide picture window doesn't merely display the fresh loaves and rich pastries, it's decorated with them. Inside, rows of orders await pickup by cottagers and locals alike. Try their fruit buns and great butter tarts. The multi-grain bread is rough and wonderful. There are even Eccles cakes, the currant-filled pastry that goes so well with tea.

JUNE JOHNSTON'S YUMMY CRANBERRY SQUARES

Yummy doesn't even come close to describing how good these pretty squares are with their light meringue topping. The recipe comes from the Cranberry Cookbook *by June Johnston of Gravenhurst. In 1953, between their last exams and their university graduation ceremony, June and Orville Johnston "celebrated" by planting a cranberry bog near the village of Bala. More than forty years later, the cranberry bog is still going strong, and even after all this time June says she never tires of the bouncy red berries, adding, "I eat cranberries nearly every single day."*

Base:

½ cup	butter, softened	125 mL
¼ cup	packed brown sugar	50 mL
1 cup	all-purpose flour	250 mL
½ tsp	baking powder	2 mL

Filling:

1 cup	cranberries, coarsely chopped (¼ lb/125 g)	250 mL
2 tbsp	granulated sugar	25 mL

Topping:

2	egg whites	2
1 cup	packed brown sugar	250 mL
1 tsp	vanilla	5 mL
½ tsp	baking powder	2 mL

Base: Preheat oven to 350°F (180°C). In medium bowl, cream together butter and sugar until fluffy. In small bowl, stir together flour and baking powder. Stir flour mixture into butter mixture until well combined. Press mixture evenly into 8-inch (2 L) square baking pan. Bake 10 to 12 minutes, until pale golden brown. Remove pan from oven; increase oven temperature to 400°F (200°C).

Filling: In small bowl, combine cranberries and sugar; sprinkle evenly over base.

Topping: In medium bowl, whisk egg whites until stiff peaks form. Gradually whisk in sugar, vanilla and baking powder; continue whisking until stiff glossy peaks form. Spoon egg-white mixture evenly over cranberries to cover completely. Bake for 20 to 25 minutes until topping is golden. Let cool completely in pan. Run a sharp knife around inside edge of pan; cut into squares.

*T*he Bala Cranberry Festival is slotted into the middle of cranberry harvest time, the weekend after Thanksgiving. On Saturday and Sunday mornings, the local branch of the Royal Canadian Legion holds a cranberry pancake breakfast. There is a judged competition for cranberry preserving and baking. Local restaurants use cranberry condiments or serve specials that incorporate cranberries. Buy a slice of cranberry bread and a coffee, or a crepe filled with cranberry sauce and cream and chocolate from one of Bala's churches.

Refrigerate leftover egg yolks, with enough water to cover them, in a covered container for up to 2 days. Or freeze them, adding ½ tsp (2 mL) salt or sugar for every six yolks, for up to 3 months.

Makes **6 servings**

Preparation time: **30 minutes**

Cooking time: **about 20 minutes**

*N*estled into a valley in the beautiful, ultimately rural town of Teeswater is a small country dairy owned by Gay Lea Foods Cooperative. Once typically old-fashioned, the former Teeswater Cream-ery is now on the leading edge of the dairy industry. In days gone by, when cheese was made, the whey was uncere-moniously dumped . . . wherever. Today, the whey is used to create a highly con-centrated (ninety percent) protein that can be added to all sorts of food prod-ucts. Then what's left—milk sugar and water—is further refined to produce a browning agent for the baking industry. All natural . . . all Ontario!

ONTARIO NUT LACE COOKIES WITH BLACK CURRANT SABAYON AND SUMMER BERRIES

A sabayon is a fluffy wine-flavoured sauce, which we love to pour warm over fresh berries, then serve with a crisp nut cookie. Use the freshest nuts you can find for the delicate cookies. Bake them in batches on parch-ment-paper-lined baking sheets and allow lots of room for expansion because the cookies will spread to about three times their original size. This recipe makes about 24 cookies; any leftovers will keep well in an airtight container for up to 5 days. If the cookies should soften slightly during storage, arrange them on a parchment-paper-lined baking sheet and pop them in a 400°F (200°C) oven for 1 to 2 minutes to crisp.

Cookies:

1 cup	walnut or pecan halves (¼ lb/125 g)	250 mL
½ cup	granulated sugar	125 mL
2 tbsp	butter	25 mL
2 tbsp	each corn syrup, maple syrup and milk	25 mL
1 tbsp	all-purpose flour	15 mL

Sabayon:

5	egg yolks	5
⅔ cup	granulated sugar	150 mL
2 tbsp	Old-Fashioned Black-Currant Preserves (see recipe on page 17, or use ready-made preserves)	25 mL
1 tsp	finely grated lemon rind	5 mL
⅔ cup	medium-dry white wine, such as Riesling or Gewürztraminer	150 mL
½ cup	Southbrook Farms Cassis	125 mL
6 cups	fresh berries	1.5 L

Cookies: Preheat oven to 400°F (200°C). Lightly oil two large baking sheets; line them with baking parchment (the oil helps the parchment paper stick to the baking sheets).

In food processor, process nuts just until finely ground. You should have about 1 cup (250 mL). Set aside.

In small heavy saucepan, combine sugar, butter, corn syrup, maple syrup and milk. Heat over medium heat, stirring occasionally, until sugar and butter have melted. Remove from heat; stir in flour until mixture is smooth. Stir in nuts. Batter will be runny.

Drop small spoonfuls (1 tsp/5 mL) of batter 3 inches (8 cm) apart on each baking sheet. Bake for about 3 minutes, until edges are starting to colour (watch carefully; cookies burn easily). Remove from oven; let cookies cool on baking sheets for 2 to 3 minutes until pliable. With palette knife or lifter, loosen edges of each cookie; remove to wire rack to cool completely. If cookies become too crisp to remove easily from baking sheet, return baking sheet to oven for 1 minute to soften cookies. Repeat baking process with re- maining cookie batter. When cookies are cool, store in a tightly covered container for up to 5 days.

Sabayon: In a large metal bowl using electric mixer, beat egg yolks and sugar until light in colour. Stand bowl over saucepan of simmering water; beat in preserves and lemon rind. Beat in wine and Cassis; continue beating over simmering water for 6 to 8 minutes, until mixture is fluffy and thick.

To serve, divide berries among six individual glasses; spoon sabayon evenly over top. Serve with lace cookies.

*J*ohn Wiggins, the founder of Creemore Springs Brewery, and John Denbock of Apple Valley Cider Mill pooled their talents and came up with two wonderful local beverages. Brother John's is the brand name of their dry sparkling ciders—cold pressed, cold fer- mented and bottled in Clarksburg from small bittersweet English cider apples grown around Georgian Bay. Olde Traditional (6%) is an English-style cider and Prise de Mousse (7½%) is made with the addition of champagne yeast so is similar to the ciders of Normandy. For lovers of classical ciders, at this writing, they are available only through the LCBO and Vintages.

Refrigerate leftover egg whites, in covered container, for up to 2 weeks, or freeze for up to 3 months.

Makes **6 servings**

Preparation time: **30 minutes**

Cooking time: **about 35 minutes**

*T*here is hardly a product with more value added than a bushel of corn when it is made into beverage alcohol. Canadian Mist Distillers of Collingwood make one single product, Canadian Mist Whisky, using exclusively Ontario, mainly Huron County, corn. A full, sunny season is needed to bring the corn to maturity, dry and rustling in the field. Only if the crop fails do they bring in corn from any other region in Canada or North America. After the whisky is distilled, the spent grains are recovered and dried to make a high-protein supplement for animal feed.

JOSEPHINE VARTY'S BUTTERSCOTCH PIE

Food writer Rose Murray is a good friend of ours who grew up on a farm in Duntroon south of Collingwood where her mother, Josephine Varty, made wonderful pies. In her Comfortable Kitchen Cookbook, *Rose recalls that harvest time on the farm meant crowds of hungry men coming in from the fields to gather round the kitchen table for dinner. Dessert was always pie and the variety infinite—raisin, pear, grape, even green tomato, or old-fashioned butterscotch, like this one.*

Pastry for 9-inch (23 cm) single-crust pie (see recipe on page 112)

Filling:

2 tbsp	butter	25 mL
¾ cup	packed brown sugar	175 mL
2 cups	whole milk	500 mL
¼ cup	cornstarch	50 mL
Pinch	salt	Pinch
2	egg yolks	2
1 tsp	vanilla	5 mL

Meringue Topping:

2	egg whites	2
¼ tsp	cream of tartar	1 mL
¼ cup	granulated sugar	50 mL
2 tbsp	cold water	25 mL
½ tsp	vanilla	2 mL
Pinch	salt	Pinch

Preheat oven to 375°F (190°C). On lightly floured surface, roll out pastry and use to line a 9-inch (23 cm) pie plate. Line pastry crust with piece of foil or parchment paper; fill with ceramic baking beans or dried beans. Bake for 10 minutes, until pastry just starts to colour around edges. Remove beans and foil; bake for 3 to 5 minutes, until pastry is very light golden and looks dry in centre. Remove from oven; set aside.

Filling: In medium saucepan, melt butter over medium heat; stir in brown sugar. Cook, stirring, for 2 to 3 minutes until mixture is smooth, thick and starts to sizzle. Watch carefully; it burns easily. Remove saucepan from heat.

In medium bowl, combine ¼ cup (50 mL) milk, the cornstarch and salt until smooth; whisk in remaining milk. Gradually whisk milk mixture into sugar mixture (mixture will be lumpy). Cook over medium heat, whisking constantly, for 2 to 3 minutes, until mixture is smooth and starting to thicken.

In small bowl, beat egg yolks lightly. Stir a little of the hot-milk mixture into the egg yolks until well combined. Add egg-yolk mixture to saucepan. Cook, whisking constantly, for 2 to 3 minutes until thickened and bubbly. Remove from heat; stir in vanilla. Let cool completely, stirring occasionally to prevent a skin forming. Pour into pie shell, spreading evenly.

Meringue Topping: Preheat oven to 375°F (190°C). In medium bowl using electric mixer, beat egg whites and cream of tartar until soft peaks form. Gradually beat in sugar until all is combined and mixture no longer feels gritty when a little is rubbed between finger and thumb. Add water, vanilla and salt; beat until stiff shiny peaks form.

Spoon meringue evenly over filling, spreading right to edges of pie so that there are no gaps between meringue and pastry. With flat side of a knife, make decorative peaks in meringue. Place pie on baking sheet; bake for 12 to 15 minutes, until tips of meringue are golden brown. Let cool before serving (do not refrigerate).

*R*hubarb grows by the field full in Dufferin County south of Collingwood, an area still renowned for its potatoes. According to Diane French, who with her husband, Bill, processes 1.2 million pounds of rhubarb annually, this region's growing conditions are ideal. There's lots of snow cover in the wintertime, and in the summer the "Honeywood loam" soil allows the plants to thrive. For pies her favourite variety is Sutton, which is red/green, full-flavoured and very tart. Valentine or "strawberry rhubarb" is great for jelly or juice. Throughout the winter a few growers maintain hothouse "forcing" businesses. From late January until spring, rosy stalks are sold at farmers' markets and in smaller, independent grocery stores and fruit markets.

Makes **8 to 10 servings**

Preparation time: **25 minutes**

Cooking time: **50 to 60 minutes**

*T*here are few things tastier or more versatile than applesauce, and it's simplicity itself to prepare. Peel and core 1½ lb (750 g) apples (Cortland, Empire, Golden Delicious, McIntosh and Northern Spy are good varieties to use for applesauce); cut them into chunks. In a large, heavy saucepan, combine apples with 1 cup (250 mL) water. Cover and cook over medium heat for 10 to 15 minutes, until very tender. Remove from heat; stir in sugar to taste. Let cool, then package in usable quantities (we think 1-cup/250 mL portions are handy); refrigerate for up to 5 days or freeze for up to 3 months.

CHUNKY BROWN-SUGAR APPLESAUCE CAKE WITH CARAMEL SAUCE

When peaches or pears are in season, they are a great substitute for applesauce in this cake; simply peel, pit or core, and dice them before adding to the batter. The caramel sauce is a fabulous dessert sauce that's great on everything from ice cream to Christmas pudding.

Cake:

1 cup	packed brown sugar	250 mL
½ cup	softened butter	125 mL
2	eggs	2
2 tsp	vanilla	10 mL
1½ cups	cake-and-pastry flour	375 mL
2 tsp	baking powder	10 mL
1 tsp	cinnamon	5 mL
1 cup	applesauce (see sidebar)	250 mL

Topping:

½ cup	chopped walnuts	125 mL
2 tbsp	brown sugar	25 mL

Caramel Sauce:

2 cups	packed brown sugar	500 mL
3 tbsp	cornstarch	45 mL
1½ cups	boiling water	375 mL
2 tbsp	butter	25 mL
1 tsp	vanilla	5 mL
½ tsp	cinnamon	2 mL

Cake: Preheat oven to 350°F (180°C). In large bowl, cream sugar, butter, eggs and vanilla until light and fluffy. In separate bowl, sift flour, baking powder and cinnamon. Fold flour mixture into sugar mixture alternately with applesauce, until no dry spots remain. Spoon batter evenly into greased 9-inch (2.5 L) square pan.

Topping: In small bowl, combine nuts and sugar; sprinkle evenly over batter. Bake for 40 to 45 minutes or until toothpick inserted in centre of cake comes out clean. Serve warm or let cool completely in pan.

Caramel Sauce: In a large heavy saucepan, combine brown sugar and cornstarch. Cook, stirring, over medium heat, for 10 to 12 minutes, until sugar melts and mixture is golden brown; remove from heat. Carefully and at arm's length, pour in boiling water; the mixture will hiss and sputter. Return saucepan to heat, stirring to dissolve any lumps of caramelized sugar. Add butter, vanilla and cinnamon. Turn off heat; continue stirring until caramelized sugar is completely dissolved (if any lumps remain, strain sauce through a sieve). Let cool slightly. Cut cake into squares; serve with caramel sauce poured over. Any leftover sauce can be refrigerated in a covered container for up to 2 weeks.

*U*p in the Hockley Valley, northeast of Orangeville, a small group of monks founded a Cistercian Monastery in 1982. Coming from the founding abbey of Oka, the monks, a contemplative order, originally moved to Georgetown, and from there they built the current monastery. At Christmastime more than fifty thousand pounds of Christmas cake are baked and sold. Their little shop also sells Oka cheese, and at times the marvellous Trappist cheese from Manitoba made with the original Oka recipe. There are Spencer jams from Massachusetts and chocolates from Mistassini, Quebec, both Trappist monasteries.

To visit them take Highway 9 to Airport Road. Turn northward and at the 7th Line there'll be a directional marker. The shop is open from 9 a.m. to noon and from 1:30 p.m. to 5 p.m. (Monday through Saturday). The chapel is open from 6:30 a.m. to 8:30 p.m. (7 days a week).

Makes **3 cups (750 mL)**

Preparation time: **10 minutes**

Standing time: **2 days**

*D*urham, a small town located at the junction of Highway 6 and the Saugeen River, has become a centre for great grains. OntarBio, a group of organic farmers certified by the Organic Crop Improvement Association collectively stores and cleans spelt, wheat, oats, barley, rye, corn, soy, adzuki and kidney beans for province-wide distribution. Ursula Kansy-Kaupp of Sesam Mühle, a few miles north on Highway 6, grinds the grains to order and, if you arrive on a Friday, Birgit Madsen will be baking them into hearty whole grain loaves, quiches and delicious, buttery pastries.

When using organic flour, the best way to achieve accurate measurements is to weigh it. According to Ursula, the flour at the bottom of the bag becomes compacted so that a cupful of it weighs more than a cupful from the top of the bag. When a recipe calls for 1 cup (250 mL), she uses ¼ lb (125 g).

GREY COUNTY SOURDOUGH STARTER

This starter, which uses rye flour and a shot of real cultured yogurt (Saugeen Country or Perth County are good local brands to look for), lends loaves that wonderful sour aroma so typical of the best pioneer-style breads. Sourness is determined by the temperature of the room and whether any other wild yeasts are present in the atmosphere. Anita's grandmother remembers her mother simply leaving the flour-water batter to sit in the open air to begin the souring process, thus trapping airborne yeasts. This old-fashioned process is not as dependable for today's bakers, so this recipe incorporates a small amount of commercial yeast. The recipe comes from Ursula Kansy-Kaupp, owner of a natural food store north of Durham called Sesam Mühle (literally "sesame mill").

2 cups	whole rye flour	500 mL
2 cups	very hot water (130°F/54°C)	500 mL
1 tbsp	plain yogurt	15 mL
¼ tsp	active dry yeast	1 mL

In large nonmetallic bowl, whisk together flour and water. Beat in yogurt and yeast to make a smooth batter. Cover loosely with a kitchen towel; let stand at room temperature for 2 days, stirring occasionally, until the starter is bubbly. If the surface becomes dry, add a little water.

This starter is known as the "mother"; it may be covered and refrigerated for up to 1 week. Use cupfuls of it in recipes, such as Durham Spelt Seed Bread (see recipe on page 182) and Sourdough-Caraway Rye Bread (see recipe on page 18).

For every 1 cup (250 mL) of starter you use, add 1 cup (250 mL) each flour and warm water to the "mother" and let stand 1 hour at room temperature before refrigerating.

The Canadian Shield

A short day's drive from almost any major southern Ontario city, this region sweeps across the middle of northern Ontario from Algonquin Park, encompassing Manitoulin Island and the top shore of Georgian Bay—it is the Canadian Shield at its best. Up Highway 11, a.k.a. Yonge Street, you'll find dozens of summer burger stands and pickup trucks selling sweet corn or wild blueberries. Farther north good agricultural land is at a premium, so it's here that we begin to see a partial dependence on the wild. The lakes are pristine, the fish in them, although not as plentiful as they once were, are feisty and fun to catch, particularly on a fly rod. Excellent provincial campgrounds have spacious sites, spectacular locations and great interpretative programs.

Makes **6 to 8 servings**

Preparation time: **25 minutes**

Cooking time: **40 minutes**

*O*n the northeastern outskirts of Sault Ste. Marie is the largest fish hatchery in Ontario. In its raceways and tanks there are more than 1.3 million baby lake trout, brook trout and splake waiting to be placed into selected lakes from Espanola to Manitouwadge. The splake are F1 crosses—that is, they are the first generation from brook and lake trout parentage. The Visitor's Centre has aquaria and an audiovisual program to acquaint the public with the work the Ministry of Natural Resources does in replenishing the aquatic environment.

SOUP OF LAKE FISHES WITH GARLIC CREAM

Choose a variety of fresh-water fishes, such as small perch fillets, lake trout, whitefish and splake, for this hearty soup. Serve the soup topped with Garlic Cream, lots of freshly grated cheese and spicy croutons, add a green salad and you have a complete meal.

1½ lb	lake-fish fillets	750 g
3 cups	fish or chicken stock	750 mL
2	onions, finely chopped	2
2	potatoes, peeled and cut into small cubes	2
2	carrots, finely chopped	2
1	leek (white and light green parts only), cleaned and sliced	1
1 cup	dry white wine, preferably Riesling	250 mL
1	clove garlic, minced	1
1 tbsp	fresh thyme leaves	15 mL
2 cups	half-and-half cream	500 mL
	Salt and black pepper	
2 cups	shredded goat's-milk Gouda (see page 127) or Cheddar cheese	500 mL
	Garlic Cream (recipe opposite)	
	Country-Style Croutons (see recipe on page 144)	

Cut fish into large chunks, removing any small bones with tweezers. In large saucepan combine fish, stock, onions, potatoes, carrots, leek, wine, garlic and thyme. Bring to boil over medium-high heat. Reduce heat to medium-low; simmer, covered, for 30 minutes or until vegetables are tender.

In blender, process soup in batches until very smooth. Return to rinsed-out saucepan. Stir in cream and salt and pepper to taste. Heat through over medium heat; do not boil. Ladle into heated soup bowls; serve with bowls of shredded cheese, Garlic Cream and croutons alongside.

GARLIC CREAM

For best flavour, make this easy sauce a few hours before serving. Since it contains a raw egg yolk, make sure the egg you use is very fresh and the shell is undamaged. If you prefer, instead of preparing the sauce, mince 2 garlic cloves very finely and stir them into 1⅔ cups (400 mL) good-quality mayonnaise.

¼ cup	cider vinegar	50 mL
1	egg yolk	1
2	garlic cloves, chopped	2
½ tsp	dry mustard	2 mL
¼ tsp	each salt and cayenne	1 mL
1½ cups	canola or corn oil	375 mL

In a food processor or blender, combine vinegar, egg yolk, garlic, mustard, salt and cayenne. Process for 15 to 20 seconds until smooth. With machine running, gradually add oil in a thin stream until sauce is creamy and thickened. Transfer to lidded container; refrigerate for at least 4 hours or up to 3 days.

Makes 1⅔ cups (400 mL)

Preparation time: **10 minutes**

*F*rom time to time fishmongers in towns surrounding the Great Lakes sell splake. Buy it if you are lucky enough to find it. The pale pink fillets are prized for their delicate flavour, so the best preparations are the ones that don't count on heavy spices. Splake in the Great Lakes is an F5 hybrid, a cross between the original splake hybrid and lake trout. They were originally planted into the Great Lakes several decades ago. Splake grow better, larger and longer than brook trout, but they rarely reproduce naturally, so it has become, at least in these larger lakes, a "put and take" fishery. Their populations have been most successful in a number of inland lakes, away from predators like sea lamprey. At this writing no one is aquaculturing splake, but as one Ministry of Natural Resources official told us, "It's on the list."

Refrigerate leftover egg white, in covered container, for up to 2 weeks, or freeze it for up to 3 months.

Makes **8** servings

Preparation time: **25 minutes**

Cooking time: **20 to 25 minutes**

$\mathcal{S}$outh of Lake Nipissing, from Trout Creek to Corbeil, a number of artisans have created a Country Roads Studio Tour. Tours are held three times a year (Mother's Day weekend, mid-July, late October), when local craftspeople and producers open their doors in a coordinated effort to showcase their work, from herbal teas and northern gardens to a home baker and honey producer. There are watercolours and folk art, stained glass and pottery, one-of-a-kind children's clothing and kites.

To toast pine nuts, place in small heavy skillet over medium heat; cook, stirring occasionally, for 5 to 7 minutes, until golden and fragrant. Watch them carefully; they burn easily.

HARVEST PUMPKIN-APPLE SOUP

This the perfect warmer for a chilly fall day. Serve with one of our breads, add a salad and you couldn't have a better meal.

2 tbsp	butter	25 mL
2	large onions, chopped	2
4	cloves garlic, minced	4
1 tbsp	grated gingerroot	15 mL
6 cups	chicken stock	1.5 L
1	can (28 oz/796 mL) pumpkin puree (not pumpkin-pie filling)	1
4	tart apples (such as Northern Spy), peeled, cored and chopped	4
2 cups	half-and-half cream	500 mL
	Salt and black pepper	
½ cup	sour cream	125 mL
¼ cup	toasted pine nuts	50 mL

In large saucepan, melt butter over medium heat. Add onions, garlic and gingerroot; cook, stirring, for 3 to 5 minutes, until onions are soft but not brown. Stir in stock, pumpkin and apples; bring to boil over medium-high heat, stirring occasionally. Reduce heat to medium-low; cook, covered, 15 minutes, until apples are tender.

Remove from heat; let cool slightly. In blender, blend soup in batches until smooth. Return to rinsed-out saucepan. Stir in cream. Heat through over low heat, until soup is hot. Do not boil. Season with salt and pepper to taste. Ladle into heated soup bowls. Swirl a little sour cream into each portion of soup; sprinkle sour cream with pine nuts.

TARRAGON-MARINATED MUSHROOMS

For best flavour and texture, use a selection of Ontario-grown mushrooms—shiitake, cremini, portobello and button—for this easy salad. The mushrooms need little preparation; just wipe them with a damp cloth, remove any coarse stems (reserve them for making stock or soup) and slice the mushrooms thinly. Serve the salad as a side dish or spoon it onto individual lettuce-lined plates and serve as an appetizer with crusty bread.

4 cups	sliced assorted mushrooms (6 oz/175 g)	1 L
½ cup	finely chopped onion	125 mL
¼ cup	canola or corn oil	50 mL
2 tbsp	red wine vinegar	25 mL
1	clove garlic, minced	1
1 tbsp	chopped fresh tarragon or 1 tsp/5 mL dried	15 mL
1	bay leaf	1
¼ tsp	each salt and black pepper Lettuce leaves	1 mL
2 tbsp	chopped fresh parsley	25 mL

In medium saucepan, combine mushrooms, onion, oil, vinegar, garlic, tarragon, bay leaf, salt and pepper; bring to boil over high heat. Reduce heat to very low; cook, covered, for 5 minutes. Spoon contents of saucepan into nonmetallic dish; let cool. Refrigerate, covered, overnight.

To serve, discard bay leaf. With slotted spoon, spoon mushrooms into lettuce-lined serving bowl; sprinkle with parsley.

Makes **2 cups (500 mL); 4 side-salad or appetizer servings**

Preparation time: **15 minutes**

Cooking time: **6 minutes**

*I*f you trek through Ontario's northland, you'll have many opportunities to carefully harvest the forest. But what to pick? To learn more about edible wild plants, search your library for the volumes by Adam F. Szczawinski and Nancy J. Turner. Thoroughly researched, completely based on Canadian information, their books are published by the National Museum of Natural Sciences and the National Museums of Canada. Look for these titles: *Edible Garden Weeds of Canada* (1978) and *Wild Green Vegetables of Canada* (1980).

Makes **4** servings

Preparation time: **20 minutes**

Cooking time: **5 to 7 minutes**

*T*he Powassan Farmers' Market is a microcosm of what a great market should be, with a huge variety of ingredients and vendors who love to chat with their customers. Dwyla and Uwe Hartmann tease shoppers into buying their super breads by allowing them to smell the great grain aromas. They have revisited a number of ancient grains, including amaranth, quinoa, kamut and spelt. Florence White, patched umbrella in hand to shade her from the summer sun, explains her wild fruit preserves. Mountain ash (rowan berry), sumac, pincherries and elderberries are all gathered near her home in the Astorville Valley. In case you've developed an appetite, there's barbecued honey-garlic sausage served on a thick slice of homemade bread. Then, off again, to stock up on small kohlrabi (both purple and white), tomatoes, baby leeks, purple potatoes, meadow honey, fall fair prizewinning jams, just-picked salad greens and, of course, wild blueberries.

POWASSAN FARMERS' MARKET SALAD

While visiting the great little farmers' market in Powassan, we loaded up with fresh vegetables then headed back to the campsite, where Anita came up with this amazing salad. Kohlrabi is a round turnip-like vegetable with purple or green skin. Its crisp flesh adds a nice fresh bite to salads.

Don't be alarmed by the amount of oil in the mayonnaise-type dressing; this recipe makes a big batch and a little of the flavourful dressing goes a long way. Store the leftovers in a jar in the fridge for up to one week to toss with greens or your favourite coleslaw recipe.

Hazelnut Vinaigrette:

½ cup	hazelnuts (one 75 g pkg)	125 mL
2	cloves garlic	2
¼ cup	cider vinegar	50 mL
1 tbsp	dry mustard	15 mL
1 tsp	black pepper	5 mL
½ tsp	salt	2 mL
1½ cups	canola or corn oil	375 mL

Salad:

½ lb	trimmed kohlrabi (1 medium)	250 g
2	stalks celery, sliced	2
1	large tomato, chopped	1
1	small leek (white and light green parts only), cleaned and thinly sliced	1
¼ cup	chopped fresh parsley	50 mL

Hazelnut Vinaigrette: Preheat oven to 350°F (180°C). Spread hazelnuts on ungreased baking sheet; bake for 5 to 7 minutes, until skins are dark brown and nuts are fragrant. Remove nuts from oven; wrap in clean tea towel. Let cool for 5 minutes, then rub vigorously in towel to remove loose skins.

In food processor, combine nuts and garlic; process until finely chopped. Add vinegar, mustard, pepper and salt; process until well combined. With motor running, add oil in a thin, steady stream until dressing is smooth and thickened. Refrigerate in a jar until ready to serve.

Salad: Peel kohlrabi; cut into matchstick strips. In salad bowl, combine kohlrabi, celery, tomato and leek. Add parsley and enough vinaigrette (about ⅓ cup/75 mL) to coat vegetables; toss well. Season with salt and pepper to taste.

Makes **4** servings

Preparation time: **20 minutes**

Marinating time: **24 hours**

Cooking time: **6 to 10 minutes**

γancey's Meats on Highway 17 in Bruce Mines is another foodie find. It's a good news story from start to spicy finish. This is a Métis-owned business that is certainly one of the best, cleanest and most imaginative butcher shops we've seen. It is operated by Connie and Art "Yancey" Bennett, and in it you'll find only the freshest meat and fish. We bought pickerel and a small piece of smoked sturgeon. They sell all sorts of sausages and Yancey's own pastrami, corned beef and bacon. His specialty is honey-cured hickory-smoked ham. The meaty smoked pork chops look as if they belong in Waterloo County. When local hunters bag a moose or deer, Yancey will butcher, cure and smoke it to whatever specifications are provided. Once again, the advice is to take a cooler and ice packs—you may regret it otherwise.

WARM GRILLED STEAK SALAD WITH MAPLE DRESSING

Grilled steak served on a bed of cool, crisp greens is a great taste combination. Our favourite steak for this is meaty moose sirloin or economical beef flank steak.

1½ lb	boneless moose steaks, or beef flank steak in one piece	750 g
¼ cup	maple syrup	50 mL
2 tbsp	white wine vinegar	25 mL
2	cloves garlic, minced	2
1 tsp	dried thyme	5 mL
¼ tsp	each salt and black pepper	1 mL
3 cups	each washed and torn Boston lettuce and watercress (stems removed)	750 mL
¼ cup	walnut oil	50 mL
⅓ cup	coarsely chopped toasted walnuts,	75 mL
1 tbsp	snipped fresh chives or green onion tops	15 mL

Trim excess fat from steaks. If using flank steak, score steak lightly three times on both sides with sharp knife; set meat aside. In shallow nonmetallic dish large enough to hold steaks, whisk together maple syrup, vinegar, garlic, thyme, salt and pepper. Place steaks in dish, turning to coat on both sides with marinade. Refrigerate, covered, for 24 hours, turning steaks occasionally. Remove dish from fridge 30 minutes before cooking.

In large shallow salad bowl, combine Boston lettuce and watercress; refrigerate, loosely covered, until ready to serve.

Preheat barbecue to medium-high. Remove steaks from marinade, scraping garlic and herbs back into marinade. Pour marinade into small saucepan. Pat steaks dry; place on oiled barbecue grill. Grill for 2 to 4 minutes on each side, depending on thickness, for medium-rare. Transfer steaks to cutting board; let stand, loosely covered with foil, for 5 minutes.

Add walnut oil to marinade in saucepan. Bring to boil over high heat. Reduce heat to low; simmer, uncovered, for 1 minute.

Cut steaks crosswise into thin slices; arrange on top of greens. Drizzle hot marinade evenly over salad; sprinkle with walnuts and chives. Serve at once.

*T*he plants built and operated by Canada Packers helped to define small-town Ontario during the early decades of this century. Founded in 1927 with the merger of the Harris Abattoir Company, Gunns Limited and the William Davies Company, Canada Packers had processing centres from Fort William (Thunder Bay) to Windsor. In central Ontario towns such as Mount Forest, Walkerton and Harriston, Canada Packers was a cornerstone of the local economy. These rural entrepreneurs created the opportunity for Ontarians to use local ingredients, from Maple Leaf butter, Tenderflake lard and York ice cream to Maple Leaf soap, gelatine and leather, and embodied the concept of self-sufficiency in agricultural manufacturing that is once again gaining a following. "Eat locally, think globally" might best sum it up.

In 1990 Canada Packers was sold to Hillsdown Holdings P.L.C. of Great Britain. In 1991 Canada Packers was merged with Maple Leaf Mills, another Hillsdown holding, to officially become Maple Leaf Foods. The huge company remained in foreign ownership until 1995, when Wallace McCain and his family purchased it and brought ownership of Maple Leaf Foods back home to Canada.

To toast walnuts, preheat oven to 350°F (180°C). Spread walnuts on baking sheet; bake for 5 to 7 minutes, until golden and fragrant. Watch carefully; they burn easily.

Makes **4 servings**

Preparation time: **20 minutes**

Cooking time: **about 20 minutes**

$\mathcal{T}$he largest pow wow on Manitoulin Island is held in early August at Wikwemikong, Canada's only unceded Indian Reserve. The Bond Head Treaty of 1836 specified that Manitoulin and its islands were to be reserved for their native population. However, a subsequent agreement, the Manitoulin McDougall Treaty of 1862, excluded Wikwemikong because, although all other bands agreed to the signing over of their lands to the government of the day, the chiefs of this band refused to sign and hence are still bound only by the 1836 Treaty.

Perhaps it was that certainty of purpose that laid the foundation for the pride that exists in the community. This is no rough-and-ready northern town. It has style—native style. The Health Centre, you can see clearly from the air, is built in the shape of an eagle, the Medicine Lodge being its focal point. The thirteen cedar poles around the lodge symbolize the lunar year. There, traditional and modern healing are combined. The senior citizens' home is not a sterile structure, it's a log cabin. There's a cultural centre, day-care centre, band administration office and a whole town full of services.

The Wikwemikong Pow Wow, in early August, attracts dancers from all over Turtle Island (North America). The foods are consistent with other pow wows across the province. Fry bread is heaped with taco fillings and corn on the cob is dipped into butter, and there are superb wild game burgers and sausages on fresh buns.

MANITOULIN VENISON BURGERS WITH GOLDEN FRIED ONIONS

We enjoyed a version of these tasty burgers at the Wikwemikong Pow Wow on Manitoulin Island. Serve them with Sweet and Sour Mustard (see recipe on page 55) and/or Spiced Zucchini Relish (see recipe on page 82). If ground venison is unavailable, substitute lean ground beef.

Fried Onions:

1 tbsp	each butter and canola or corn oil	15 mL
1	Spanish onion, sliced and separated into rings	1
½ tsp	dried savory	2 mL

Burgers:

1 lb	ground venison	500 g
⅓ cup	dry bread crumbs	75 mL
1	egg, beaten	1
½ tsp	each salt, black pepper and dried savory	2 mL
4	multigrain buns, split	4

Fried Onions: In large heavy skillet, heat butter and oil over medium heat until butter has melted. Add onion and savory; cook, stirring occasionally, for 10 to 12 minutes, until onions are golden brown and very soft. Keep warm.

Burgers: In medium bowl, combine ground venison, bread crumbs, egg, salt, pepper and savory. Work mixture gently with your hands until well combined (do not mix too vigorously or burgers will be tough). Form mixture into four even-size patties.

Grill on oiled barbecue grill over medium-high heat for 4 to 5 minutes on each side, until no longer pink inside. Grill buns cut sides down for 1 minute until lightly toasted. Serve burgers in buns, topped with fried onions.

RICH ROSEMARY LAMB STEW

St. Joseph's Island, south of Sault Ste. Marie, is renowned for its tasty lamb. This recipe teams it with rosemary, honey and other seasonings, plus a rich brown sauce to ladle over the mashed potatoes.

Makes **4 to 6 servings**

Preparation time: **20 minutes**

Cooking time: **1¾ hours**

2 lb	lean boneless lamb	1 kg
2 tbsp	canola or corn oil	25 mL
2	large onions, sliced and separated into rings	2
2	cloves garlic, minced	2
1½ cups	beef stock	375 mL
2 tbsp	each tomato paste and liquid honey	25 mL
1 tbsp	fresh rosemary leaves	15 mL
1 tbsp	each Worcestershire sauce and red wine vinegar	15 mL
¼ tsp	each salt and black pepper Chopped fresh parsley	1 mL

Trim any excess fat from lamb; cut into 1-inch (2.5 cm) cubes. In large skillet, heat 1 tbsp (15 mL) oil over medium-high heat. Brown lamb in batches for 3 to 4 minutes, turning often, until well browned. Remove from skillet to a plate as each batch browns. Heat remaining oil in skillet. Add onions and garlic; cook, stirring, over medium heat for 3 to 5 minutes until onions are golden and softened.

Stir in stock, tomato paste, honey, rosemary, Worcestershire sauce, vinegar, salt and pepper. Bring to boil over high heat, scraping up any brown bits from bottom of skillet. Return lamb to skillet, along with any juices that have accumulated on plate. Reduce heat to low; simmer, tightly covered, for 1½ hours or until lamb is tender.

Using slotted spoon, remove lamb to serving dish; keep warm. Boil contents of skillet over high heat for 5 minutes or until sauce has reduced and thickened slightly. Spoon sauce over lamb; sprinkle with parsley.

Luxury, style, sports, fabulous food and a wine list to match . . . The Inn at Manitou, Canada's only Gold Shield member of Relais et Chateaux, has them all. Throughout the season, culinary weekends attract some of the nation's best teachers and wine educators. There is a series of winemaker's dinners where Ontario's award-winning vintners pair their vintages with the evening's menu. In the autumn there's a celebration of wild mushrooms from the woods to the table with a mycologist from Toronto leading the romp in the forest, an identification workshop and, of course, tastings.

Makes **4 servings**

Preparation time: **20 minutes**

Cooking time: **10 minutes**

*G*oin' fishin' on Manitoulin Island means your tackle box will have to have an assortment of lures that range in size from tiny trout flies to large muskie spoons. Pickerel, perch, smallmouth bass, northern pike, salmon, rainbow and lake trout and whitefish all swim in these cold northern waters. If, however, you've neither luck nor energy, head to Cold Water Fisheries in Little Current for fresh and smoked aquacultured Arctic char, rainbow trout and whitefish. Their smoked fish is well enough packaged that, if you pack it on ice, it'll easily travel many miles—if you let it get that far. We broke out a package on the homebound ferry.

To toast walnuts, preheat oven to 350°F (180°C). Spread walnuts on baking sheet; bake for 5 to 7 minutes, until golden and fragrant. Watch carefully; they burn easily.

GRILLED TROUT WITH GOAT CHEESE AND WALNUTS

Lake trout that inhabit most of Ontario's deep cold lakes weigh in at an average of 3 to 5 pounds (1.5 to 2.2 kg). This recipe uses the much smaller farmed trout, but if you have a larger lake trout, stuff it with all of the goat-cheese mixture. Measure the trout at its thickest point and grill for 10 minutes per 1 in (2.5 cm) of thickness, turning once.

½ cup	crumbled goat cheese or softened cream cheese	125 mL
⅓ cup	finely chopped toasted walnuts	75 mL
1 tbsp	fresh lemon juice	15 mL
2 tsp	horseradish	10 mL
¼ tsp	each salt and black pepper	1 mL
4	whole trout, cleaned and heads removed (10 oz/300 g each)	4

In medium bowl, combine goat cheese, walnuts, lemon juice, horseradish, salt and pepper until fairly smooth.

With sharp knife, cut 2 or 3 slashes in skin on each side of each trout. Spread goat-cheese mixture evenly inside cavity of each trout. Preheat barbecue to medium-high heat; grill trout for about 10 minutes, turning once, until flesh of trout flakes easily with a fork.

BABY POTATO AND SWEET PEPPER STIR-FRY

Use the tiniest potatoes you can find for this colourful stir-fry, or cut larger ones into quarters. Spooned over rice, it will serve four as a main course, or it will serve six as a vegetable accompaniment.

2 tbsp	softened butter	25 mL
1 tsp	tomato paste	5 mL
1 tbsp	minced fresh dill or thyme (or 1 tsp/5 mL dried)	15 mL
½ tsp	black pepper	2 mL
1 lb	tiny potatoes, scrubbed	500 g
2 tbsp	canola or corn oil	25 mL
2	cloves garlic, slivered	2
3	carrots, thinly sliced	3
½	bunch broccoli, cut into florets	½
1	each sweet red and yellow pepper, seeded and cut into strips	1
½	sweet green pepper, seeded and cut into strips	½

In small bowl, combine butter, tomato paste, dill and black pepper; set aside.

In large saucepan of boiling salted water, cook potatoes for 15 to 25 minutes (depending on size), until just tender. Drain well.

Heat wok or very large skillet over medium-high heat; add oil. When oil is hot but not smoking, add garlic; stir-fry for 10 seconds. Add carrots and broccoli; stir-fry for 2 minutes. Add peppers; stir-fry for 2 minutes or until colour of peppers intensifies. Add potatoes; stir-fry for 2 minutes, until potatoes are heated through. Stir in butter mixture, tossing gently until butter melts and coats vegetables. Serve at once.

Makes **4 to 6 servings**

Preparation time: **20 minutes**

Cooking time: **25 to 30 minutes**

*M*urray Becker's land stretches between two rivers that flow into Lake Nipissing. Plots of strawberries and raspberries lure the locals out to pick. But, for us, Murray's claim to fame is his seed potato business. The farthest field, the one high on a cliff overlooking South River, was planted in potatoes long before he took over the farm. Sacks of spuds were lugged down the embankment to be barged to logging camps. Now it's the nursery for all his antique and most special varieties, including long, golden-fleshed banana potatoes and richly hued blues. Murray ships all over the province, so you'll probably dine on his potato progeny in fine restaurants that contract local farmers to grow for them, and in inns like Langdon Hall, the fabulously elegant country-house hotel near Cambridge, which has a huge kitchen garden.

Makes **6 to 8 servings**

Preparation time: **20 minutes**

Soaking time: **1 hour or overnight**

Cooking time: **7 hours**

*W*heeler's is a gas station with a difference! The kid peeling potatoes seems somewhat disgusted when another car rolls over the bell by the pumps. Wiping his hands, out he heads. His task is to peel the mammoth bag of potatoes for the fries that go with one of the best-dressed hamburgers in the province. Skip Wheeler is a master at fast food (the kind we all crave from time to time) and the quick smile. Fairly frayed at the edges, his café is a tiny, very friendly place, and even better still, it's just down the road from the Astorville Parish Picnic. Wheeler's Gas Bar is on the corner of the Lake Nosbonsing Road and the Astorville-Corbiel Road.

ONTARIO BAKED BEANS WITH MAPLE SYRUP

Volunteers at the annual Astorville Picnic ladle out gallons of old-fashioned baked beans to go with traditional Sea Pie (a layered meat casserole). Here's our version to team with Powassan Farmers' Market Salad (see recipe on page 198).

1 lb	white pea beans (2 cups/500 mL)	500 g
12 cups	cold water	3 L
¼ lb	salt pork (or 5 slices bacon), chopped	125 g
1	large onion, chopped	1
½ cup	maple syrup	150 mL
¼ cup	each ketchup and cider vinegar	50 mL
1 tsp	each salt, black pepper and dry mustard	5 mL
¼ cup	packed brown sugar	50 mL

Pick over beans, removing any stones or grit. Rinse under cold running water; drain well. In large saucepan or Dutch oven combine beans and 6 cups (1.5 L) of water; let stand, covered, overnight. Alternatively, bring to boil over high heat. Boil for 5 minutes. Remove from heat; let stand, covered, for 1 hour. Drain well.

In same saucepan, combine beans and remaining water; bring to boil over high heat. Reduce heat to medium-low; simmer, covered, for 30 minutes. Drain well; reserving cooking liquid.

Preheat oven to 250°F (120°C). In large casserole
or bean pot, combine beans, salt pork and onion.
In glass measure, whisk together maple syrup,
ketchup, vinegar, salt, pepper and mustard until
well combined. Pour over bean mixture; stir well.
Add 1½ cups (375 mL) reserved cooking liquid
(reserve some of the remaining liquid). Bake, covered, for 5 to 6 hours, until beans are tender,
adding a little more reserved cooking liquid if
beans become too dry. Remove lid; sprinkle beans
evenly with sugar; bake, uncovered, for 30 minutes, until top is bubbly.

Makes **12 pancakes**

Preparation time: **15 minutes**

Cooking time: **about 15 minutes**

A fragrant collection of "North-ern Nectars" lines the shelves at Ann and Stefan Board's Honey and Gifts in Restoule. Their property backs onto Crown land, virgin stands of basswood and conifers that flow for thirty miles towards the French River. Two of their most special honeys are from different seasons. First is the basswood, harvested in mid-summer and infused with other flowers like clover and alfalfa. The sec-ond, a later harvest, is from purple loosestrife, wild aster and goldenrod. Ann also makes honey-sweetened jellies from the region's wild fruits. Our camp-fire-baked wild blueberry pancakes were topped with Ann's hawthorne jelly. There have been none better at any campsite we've inhabited from New-foundland to Vancouver Island.

She makes beeswax candles, honey-herbal shampoos and herb-scented creams. For the home, she's created beeswax furniture polish perfumed with rosemary, and beeswax leather paste to soften and waterproof.

Open daily (10 a.m. to 4 p.m.) May through October and at Christmas-time for a special open house.

FLUFFY BLUEBERRY PANCAKES WITH HONEY-THYME BUTTER

These fabulous pancakes can be prepared with fresh or frozen blueberries, so you can enjoy them all year round. For best flavour, however, you can't beat fresh tiny wild blueberries from the north of the province. The honey-thyme butter will keep well in the fridge for up to one week and is just as good spread on tea biscuits or your favourite muffins.

Honey-Thyme Butter:

½ cup	softened butter	125 mL
¼ cup	liquid honey	50 mL
1 tbsp	fresh thyme leaves	15 mL

Blueberry Pancakes:

1 cup	all-purpose flour	250 mL
2 tbsp	granulated sugar	25 mL
1 tsp	each baking powder and baking soda	5 mL
¼ tsp	salt	1 mL
½ cup	milk	125 mL
⅓ cup	plain yogurt	75 mL
1	egg	1
2 tbsp	melted and cooled butter	25 mL
1 cup	blueberries	250 mL
	Additional melted butter for frying	

Honey-Thyme Butter: In small bowl, stir together butter, honey and thyme until well combined. Spoon into serving dish; refrigerate, covered, until ready to serve.

Blueberry Pancakes: In medium bowl, combine flour, sugar, baking powder, baking soda and salt. In separate bowl, whisk together milk, yogurt, egg and butter until well combined. Add milk mixture to flour mixture all at once; stir until just combined (batter should still be lumpy and will be thick). Stir in blueberries.

Heat griddle or heavy skillet over medium-high heat. Brush with a little butter. Drop scant ¼ cupfuls (50 mL) of batter onto griddle, spreading with a knife to form 3-inch (8 cm) pancakes. Cook 1 to 2 minutes, until golden on underside. Turn pancakes; cook for 1 to 2 minutes until golden on second side. Keep pancakes warm while you cook the rest. Serve with Honey-Thyme Butter.

*T*he many Stewart family camping trips west to British Columbia have always included a stop at Bobbers on Highway 17 in Bruce Mines. We go out of our way to pop in for a huge sandwich, a daily special and a to-go order of the best and butteriest date squares in the region! They specialize in satisfying the appetites of northerners, so all their baked things, from muffins to slices of their freshly baked pies, are more than generous. Bobbers is a truck stop without the trucks.

Makes 4 to 6 servings

Preparation time: 20 minutes

Cooking time: 15 to 20 minutes

*D*uring syrup season, The Maple Sugar House in Sundridge, midway between Huntsville and North Bay, produces six to eight gallons of the liquid gold every weekend. Owners John, Mona and Trisha Julie boil down the maple sap from their two-hundred-acre forest near Parry Sound in a wood-fired evaporator, burning an entire cord of wood daily. In addition to the regular treats associated with sugaring-off, such as taffy-in-the-snow, The Maple Sugar House offers visitors an art gallery, a huge gift shop that sells everything from pottery to moccasins and, of course, there's maple syrup every which way—from sugar to spread to candy. At the back of the store there's a small museum collection of antique tools connected with maple-syrup production, and if you ask, John will show you an interesting video that explains the history of sugaring-off.

MAPLE-PRALINE FONDUE

For maple syrup, caramel and nut lovers, this will taste like heaven! If the accompaniments run out before the fondue, your guests will be spooning it from the pot.

Fondue:

1 cup	unblanched almonds	250 mL
½ cup	granulated sugar	125 mL
¼ cup	water	50 mL
3 tbsp	cornstarch	45 mL
2½ cups	whipping cream	625 mL
¼ cup	maple syrup	50 mL

Accompaniments:
Cubed pound cake, strawberries, dried apricots; sliced apples, pears or peaches

Preheat oven to 350°F (180°C). Spread almonds on baking sheet; bake for 5 to 7 minutes or until fragrant; set aside.

Lightly oil a baking sheet; set aside. In small, heavy saucepan combine sugar and water; cook over medium-high heat, stirring occasionally, until sugar has dissolved. Increase heat to high; bring to boil. Boil for 2 to 4 minutes or until mixture just starts to brown. Reduce heat to medium-low; cook for 2 to 3 minutes, swirling pan occasionally, until mixture is a rich caramel colour. Don't overcook or let it get too brown. Remove from heat; stir in almonds, stirring until almonds are thoroughly coated with caramel.

Pour almond praline onto oiled baking sheet and spread out slightly (mixture will not fill baking sheet). Set aside until cooled and hardened. Break praline into chunks. In food processor, process praline until coarsely ground; set aside.

In small bowl, combine cornstarch with ½ cup (125 mL) of the cream until smooth. In fondue pot, whisk together cornstarch mixture and remaining cream. Bring to boil over high heat, whisking constantly. Reduce heat to medium-low; simmer, whisking constantly, for 2 minutes or until thickened and smooth. Remove from heat; stir in praline and maple syrup. Place fondue pot over fondue burner; light burner. Serve with suggested accompaniments for dipping.

Makes **9 to 12 biscuits**

Preparation time: **20 minutes**

Cooking time: **12 to 15 minutes**

*F*or a glimpse of what pioneering life was like in this region of summer days that linger and long snowy winters, visit the Anderson Farm Museum, in downtown Lively on Highway 17. The fourteen-acre dairy farm includes a collection of original buildings and a multitude of special artifacts from the day-to-day lives of the immigrant settlers.

BLUEBERRY BUTTERMILK BISCUITS

When every small town in Ontario had its own creamery, buttermilk was the summer drink. Today, it's very difficult to find real, honest-to-goodness buttermilk, but if you do, drink it chilled as the first settlers did, or make it into these wonderful biscuits.

2½ cups	all-purpose flour	625 mL
½ cup	granulated sugar	125 mL
4 tsp	baking powder	20 mL
1 tsp	salt	5 mL
⅓ cup	shortening	75 mL
¾ cup	wild blueberries	175 mL
1¼ cups	buttermilk	300 mL

Preheat oven to 425°F (220°C). In medium bowl, stir together flour, sugar, baking powder and salt. With a pastry blender or 2 knives, cut in shortening until mixture resembles coarse crumbs. Stir in blueberries.

Stir in milk just until dry ingredients are moistened; gather up dough into loose ball. Turn out onto lightly floured surface; knead gently 5 or 6 times. Lightly pat or roll out dough to 1-inch (2.5 cm) thickness. With 2- or 3-inch (5 or 8 cm) cutter, cut into biscuits. Place on greased baking sheet. Gather up trimmings; cut out more biscuits. Bake for 12 to 15 minutes or until well risen and golden. Serve warm, split and spread with butter.

FRESH MINT ICE CREAM

When mint takes over your garden, try this fabulous ice cream. Its sparkling flavour goes beautifully with fresh Ontario summer berries.

1 cup	granulated sugar	250 mL
1 cup	water	250 mL
2 cups	packed fresh mint leaves (no stems)	500 mL
1 cup	whipping cream	250 mL
¼ cup	cider vinegar	50 mL

In small saucepan, combine sugar and water. Cook over medium heat for 2 to 3 minutes, until sugar dissolves. Bring to boil over high heat; boil for 2 minutes. Remove saucepan from heat; let cool for 10 minutes.

In food processor, combine sugar syrup and mint leaves; process until mint is finely chopped. Transfer to bowl; refrigerate, covered, until chilled.

Strain mixture through sieve, pressing on mint leaves to extract as much liquid as possible; discard mint leaves. Stir cream and vinegar into syrup (mixture may look curdled). Freeze in an ice-cream maker according to manufacturer's instructions. Alternatively, whip cream until it holds stiff peaks; fold into syrup, along with vinegar. Spoon into shallow pan; freeze until firm. Store ice cream in freezer; use within a week.

*Makes **4 servings***

*Preparation time: **20 minutes***

*Cooking time: **4 to 5 minutes***

*M*anitoulin Island has a number of dairy farms that produce milk for Farquhar's in Mindemoya. The sun shouldn't set on any summer's day without a Farquhar's ice cream cone—or, better still, a sundae—from home base in Mindemoya, in downtown Little Current or at the spanking new dairy parlour next to the Tourist Information Centre and the swing bridge. You may not have a better cone in any of your northern rambles. We didn't.

Makes **6 servings**

Preparation time: **25 minutes**

Soaking time: **2 hours**

Cooking time: **about 1 hour**

*T*he region around Lake Nipissing was the main artery into the continent for the voyageurs, rugged Frenchmen who, with their native guides, explored the continent in search of furs. They left behind an enduring Francophone presence. Just glance at a map to see the dozens of French names of villages, towns, lakes and rivers.

Foods here also speak of their early French heritage. *Cipaille*, the multi-layered dish of pastry and game, has been renamed Sea Pie and has become the mainstay, along with kettles of baked beans, of both the Bonfield and Astorville Parish Picnics. Instead of wild meat, the pastry is filled with beef, pork and boneless chicken—twenty-two pounds of meat in total for each cast-iron kettle. For more than seventy years the parishioners of Astorville and Bonfield have held these fabulous community picnics, fund-raising at its culinary best. Beatrice Bessette, the octogenarian who oversees the cooking at Astorville, explained the logistics of making Sea Pie and baked beans for a crowd of up to fifteen hundred.

For forty-eight hours, men stoke the huge outdoor brick ovens with wood till the ashes are grey and the stones inside are white-hot. Huge fifteen-inch pots of Sea Pie and beans—185 pounds to be precise, and well-seasoned with salt pork, onions, maple syrup, salt and pepper—are carefully lifted into the heat,

AROWHON'S BREAD-AND-BUTTER PUDDING WITH RUM

Helen and Eugene Kates have owned and operated Arowhon Pines, one of Algonquin Park's foremost resorts, for more than twenty-five years, and while they employ a chef and full kitchen staff, it's Helen's own recipes that are prepared in the restaurant kitchen. Helen describes this homey pudding as "unpretentious, and popular before gourmet cuisine intimidated us all into taking our friends out for dinner." At Arowhon, the dessert is prepared with bananas but we've substituted pears to give it more of an Ontario flavour. Serve the pudding warm with Vanilla Custard Sauce (see recipe on page 136) or pouring cream.

½ cup	sultana raisins, rinsed and drained	125 mL
¼ cup	dark rum	50 mL
7	½-inch (1 cm) slices good-quality day-old bread	7
⅓ cup	unsalted butter, softened	75 mL
2 cups	whole milk	500 mL
4	eggs, lightly beaten	4
1 tsp	vanilla	5 mL
¼ cup	packed brown sugar	50 mL
1 tsp	cinnamon	5 mL
	Grated rind of 1 large orange	
3	ripe pears, peeled, cored and sliced	3
1 tbsp	granulated sugar	15 mL

In small nonmetallic bowl, combine raisins and rum; set aside to soak for 2 hours.

Preheat oven to 350°F (180°C). Spread bread slices on both sides with butter. In large heavy skillet, cook bread over medium-high heat for 2 to 3 minutes on each side, until golden brown. Cut each slice into quarters; set aside one-third of the best-looking pieces for the top layer of the dessert.

Drain rum from raisins into medium bowl; whisk in milk, eggs and vanilla. Set aside.

In separate bowl, stir together brown sugar, cinnamon and orange rind.

Arrange one-third of the bread in base of buttered 11- by 7-inch (2 L) baking dish; sprinkle with half of pears. Sprinkle with half of sugar mixture and half of raisins. Repeat layers once. Dip reserved bread in egg mixture; arrange neatly on top of dessert, overlapping pieces slightly. Pour remaining egg mixture into dish, pressing down lightly on bread to make sure all bread is moistened with mixture. Sprinkle evenly with granulated sugar; bake for 40 to 45 minutes, until bubbly and starting to brown. Serve warm.

the doors are propped shut and by mid-morning steam is wafting from the ovens. Three cases of cabbages are made into coleslaw, baskets of ripe tomatoes and cucumbers are sliced, and drivers gather as many pies and cakes as they can from willing bakers. At 3:30 p.m., dinner is ready to be served! The dates are easy to remember. The Bonfield Parish Picnic is the last Sunday in July, while Astorville's is the second Sunday in August. Don't arrive too late . . . the food is too good to last!

Makes **about 7 cups (1.75 L)**

Preparation time: **15 minutes**

Cooking time: **6 to 8 minutes**

*I*n early August the Haweater Festival on Manitoulin Island is a homecoming of the first order with a street dance, horse show and craft exhibition. It celebrates the island tradition of picking hawthorn berries and making them into jam and jelly, a chore only a true islander is said to appreciate. The jelly is still made on the island at Providence Bay . . . clear, red and too well jelled for our taste—we, after all, are not Haweaters.

SPRINGTIME RHUBARB SPRITZER

When rhubarb is plentiful, whip up a batch of this refreshing concentrate. It freezes well, so you can enjoy a real taste of spring during the chilly days of fall.

10 cups	finely diced fresh rhubarb (about 2½ lb/1.2 kg trimmed)	2.5 L
4 cups	water	1 L
2½ cups	granulated sugar	625 mL
1 cup	apple cider	250 mL
	Sparkling spring water	
	Fresh mint or lemon balm sprigs	

In large saucepan, combine rhubarb and water; bring to boil over high heat. Reduce heat to medium; cook, uncovered, for 5 to 7 minutes, or until rhubarb is very soft.

Line a colander with a double thickness of cheesecloth. Strain rhubarb mixture through cheesecloth; let drip for 10 to 15 minutes, squeezing to extract as much juice as possible. Discard pulp. Pour juice into large pitcher. While juice is still warm, add sugar, stirring to dissolve. Stir in apple cider. Refrigerate, covered, until chilled.

To serve, half fill glasses with syrup. Top with sparkling water; add ice. Garnish with a sprig of mint or lemon balm.

ROSE'S PICKLED GARLIC

Our good friend Rose Murray is a regular contributor to Homemaker's Magazine, *where this recipe first appeared, and she was kind enough to share the recipe with us. Rose serves the crunchy pickled garlic cloves with pâté and good bread, and we think that's a perfect way to celebrate the Sudbury Garlic Fest!*

2 cups	garlic cloves (about 6 whole heads)	500 mL
1¼ cups	white vinegar	300 mL
¼ cup	granulated sugar	50 mL
½ tsp	each coarse salt, whole black peppercorns and mustard seeds	2 mL
1	bay leaf	1

Peel garlic cloves; cut any extra-large cloves in half lengthwise. In medium saucepan, combine vinegar, sugar, salt, peppercorns, mustard seeds and bay leaf. Bring to boil over high heat, stirring to dissolve sugar.

Add garlic; bring to boil. Simmer, uncovered, for 1 minute, stirring occasionally. Remove saucepan from heat; let cool.

Spoon garlic and liquid into 2-cup (500 mL) sterilized jar; seal tightly. Store in the refrigerator for at least 24 hours before opening. The garlic will keep for up to 2 months in the fridge.

Makes 2 cups (500 mL)

Preparation time: 30 minutes

Cooking time: 1 minute

*I*n late August, the Ukrainian community of Sudbury holds Canada's only Garlic Festival. All day long, the stinking rose is celebrated. Garlic braid weaving, a cookbook sale (the recipes have a minimum of three cloves) and bobbing for garlic are interspersed by a garlic feast, a "Geriatric Garlic Gallop" and a perogi-eating contest.

This is an elemental region, wild and fully untamed in parts, with white-water rivers pounding through the ancient shield rimming Lake Superior—the largest, deepest and coldest of the Great Lakes—before rising towards James Bay. On its eastern extremities is the wide, fertile growing region near New Liskeard. There you'll see ripening fields of canola, potatoes by the hectare, wheat and corn. Holstein cattle graze in pastures supplying a vigorous dairy industry. Bracketing it in the west is Thunder Bay with as unique a set of foodways as anywhere in the province. Families migrated from Finland to an area that was reminiscent of their homeland. Other Scandinavian countries are also well represented, and there is a large population of Italians.

The ultimate realities in this region, more than anywhere else in the province, are winter and wilderness. The folk who live here know how to play in the cold. Snowmobiling, alpine and cross-country skiing (Big Thunder and the World Nordic Games), and ice fishing all give way in summer to fabulous fishing, canoe-tripping and kayaking of the first order. There are farmers' markets, great ethnic restaurants and warm, warm hospitality.

FINNISH SALTED FISH

Eva Hakala came to Canada from Finland in 1951, and in her younger days she worked as number-two cook in a bush camp near Thunder Bay, good cooking credentials if ever we heard them! Eva now runs a cottage industry preparing Finnish specialties for Thunder Bay area delicatessens. She serves this delectable Finnish version of gravlax thinly sliced on rye bread with chopped green onions and fresh dill. Any leftovers will keep in the fridge for up to 24 hours. Eva says that sockeye salmon is the best fish to choose if you can get it, but the recipe also works well with good-quality whitefish.

2	salmon fillets with skin (¾ lb/375 g each)	2
¼ cup	coarse salt	50 mL
2 tbsp	packed brown sugar	25 mL
1 cup	coarsely chopped fresh dill	250 mL
	Fresh dill sprigs for garnish	

With tweezers, remove any small bones from salmon. Place fillets side by side and skin-side down in 13- by 9-inch (3 L) glass dish.

In small bowl, combine salt and sugar; sprinkle evenly over salmon. Sprinkle salmon with dill. Place a piece of plastic wrap directly over salmon to cover it completely. Place a slightly smaller dish inside the one containing salmon; place large food can in smaller dish to weigh it down. Refrigerate for 24 hours.

When ready to serve, remove salmon from dish. Scrape off dill; pat salmon dry with paper towels. Starting at the thicker (head) end, slice salmon very thinly diagonally across the grain of the fish, detaching each slice from the skin. Arrange on a platter; garnish with fresh dill sprigs. Serve with rye bread.

Makes **8 to 10 appetizer servings**

Preparation time: **20 minutes**

Marinating time: **24 hours**

*T*he first thing many Finns who return home for a visit to Thunder Bay order is a salt fish (*suola kala*) sandwich. Marinated in salt and sugar and dill, it's always best on rye bread with dill and chopped onion. Although it is usually made with salmon, (the redder the better), many cooks also use lake or rainbow trout.

Makes **6** appetizer servings

Preparation time: **20 minutes**

Cooking time: **7 to 10 minutes**

*I*vanhoe Lake Provincial Park was once a centre for the fur trade. The Hudson's Bay Company had a post on the lake to which Ojibwa Indians paddled in canoes laden with furs. Thereafter the railway pushed through, opening the region to logging. The park itself is 1,548 hectares of forest, lakes and sand beaches. The intensive interpretative program features an Edible Wilds Weekend and Canoefest, always held on Civic Holiday weekend in August. The Visitor's Centre is transformed into a Hudson's Bay Post, there are Ojibwa games, and campers are encouraged to harvest as many berries as possible. For days the staff help in storing and sorting wild foods. Raspberry leaves are dried for tea, the local Ministry of Natural Resources may contribute some bear meat, local hunters donate moose, which is made into pemmican, and wild rice is sent down from the park near Fort Frances for the "World's Wildest Rice Pudding." Fireweed flowers decorate the foraged salads. About three hundred people attend, and the campground is full. As the name implies, canoe skills are taught, and Sunday morning's voyageur breakfast entails paddling to an island and cooking bannock over the fire. The highlight is a paddle-making workshop.

CRISPY FRIED FIDDLEHEADS WITH HONEY-MUSTARD DIP

You can use fresh or frozen fiddleheads for this recipe. If using frozen, skip the cleaning stage, and don't cook them before frying; simply thaw them, then pat dry on paper towels.

Honey-Mustard Dip:

½ cup	sour cream	125 mL
2 tbsp	snipped fresh chives	25 mL
1 tbsp	honey mustard (see page 55)	15 mL
¼ tsp	each salt and black pepper	1 mL

Fried Fiddleheads:

½ lb	fiddleheads	250 g
¼ cup	all-purpose flour	50 mL
¾ tsp	each salt and black pepper	4 mL
1	egg	1
1 tbsp	water	15 mL
¾ cup	dry bread crumbs	175 mL
	Canola or corn oil for deep frying	

Honey-Mustard Dip: In small bowl, stir together sour cream, chives, mustard, salt and pepper until well combined. Refrigerate, covered, until ready to serve.

Fried Fiddleheads: In sink full of cold water, swish fiddleheads around to remove any dirt and brown papery bits. With sharp knife, trim off ends and any discoloured parts. Drain well.

Plunge fiddleheads into large pot of boiling, salted water. Bring back to boil; boil for 2 minutes. Drain well; refresh under cold running water. Drain again. Spread fiddleheads out on a clean tea towel; pat dry. Set aside.

In medium bowl, stir together flour and ¼ tsp (1 mL) each salt and pepper. In separate bowl, beat together egg and water. In third bowl, combine bread crumbs and remaining salt and pepper. Toss fiddleheads in flour mixture until evenly coated. Place a few at a time in egg mixture, turning with a fork until evenly coated. Transfer fiddleheads to bread crumbs; turn with a fork to coat well. As fiddleheads are coated, arrange in single layer on platter. (Recipe can be prepared ahead to this point; refrigerate, uncovered, up to 2 hours.)

Preheat oven to 300°F (150°C). In large pot, heat 2 inches (5 cm) of oil over high heat until candy thermometer registers 375°F (190°C), or use deep-fat fryer following manufacturer's instructions. When oil is hot, deep-fry fiddleheads in batches for 1 to 2 minutes, until golden and crisp. As each batch cooks, remove with slotted spoon and place on paper-towel-lined platter; keep warm in oven. Once all fiddleheads are cooked, serve at once with Honey-Mustard Dip.

*D*own the back roads and rural byways of the province, it's easy to spot the honey hives sitting like little wooden castles beside a meadow or in a yellow field of flowering canola. Roadside signs announce the sale of this year's crop of honey, and in farmers' markets vendors sell combs, golden liquid and creamed honey. The variety is astounding. But little wonder—there are 8,500 beekeepers in the province at last count and they harvest 9 million pounds from more than 100,000 busy hives.

*T*o use honey in preserving, it must first be a delicately flavoured vintage. No buckwheat here! Make a light syrup by stirring 1 to 1½ cups (250 to 375 mL) honey into 4 cups (1 L) boiling water, or for a medium syrup add 2 cups (500 mL) honey to 4 cups (1 L) boiling water. Proceed as your recipe directs, packing raw, prepared ripe fruit into jars, covering with appropriate syrup (light for sweet fruits, medium for tart) and processing in a boiling water bath for the required length of time. These syrups are also ideal for freezing fruit. Or if you'd like, simply drizzle honey, to taste, over fresh sliced fruit. Because honey prevents darkening, the addition of ascorbic acid is not necessary.

*T*o substitute honey for granulated sugar, use ⅔ cup (150 mL) honey for 1 cup (250 mL) sugar. Reduce oven heat by 25°F (15°C).

Makes **16 pieces**

Preparation time: **20 minutes**

Cooking time: **20 to 25 minutes**

$\mathcal{T}$he Highway Book Shop near Cobalt on Highway 11 (still an extension of Yonge Street) is one of the most eccentric and wonderful bookstores in the province. Inside, the shelves bend and droop under the weight of antiquarian and new books. The smell of printer's ink is pervasive, because in addition to selling books the owners also publish them. Dr. and Mrs. Douglas Pollard are the people who make literary Canada worth living in. They have faith in their authors and their subject matter. As long as it pertains to the north, it is important. One of the most recent books to go into reprint is the *Wanapatei Canoe Trippers' Cookbook*. Written by dedicated paddler Carol Hodgins, it guides readers through the rigours of a canoe trip in the wilds. This delightful book includes recipes for Hungarian Goulash (for the first day only), instructions for bread that are as simple as "bake in a greased pan"—simply because there are no ovens—and a section on how to pack your *wanigan* (food box).

BANNOCK WITH SMOKED FISH AND APPLE CIDER MAYONNAISE

Bannock turns up in many guises at native gatherings around the province, and no native cookbook is complete without a recipe for the light biscuits. One of our favourite collections of Cree recipes, Traditional Indian Recipes *(Highway Book Shop, Cobalt), for instance, includes recipes for bannock with pike eggs and bannock with currants. Here, we've teamed our version of bannock with a mild-flavoured mayonnaise and the wonderful smoked fish from the north of the province. Serve the fish-topped bannock as a nibble with drinks or as a sit-down appetizer for six or eight people. Bannock may also be torn into pieces and served warm in place of dinner rolls, or spread with butter and maple syrup and served at breakfast. The recipe for Apple Cider Mayonnaise makes more than you'll need for this dish, but it will keep in the fridge for up to 3 days and is delicious on sandwiches, burgers and with salads.*

Bannock:

2 cups	all-purpose flour	500 mL
2 tsp	baking powder	10 mL
¾ tsp	salt	4 mL
⅔ cup	buttermilk	150 mL
1 tbsp	each canola or corn oil and cold water	15 mL
½ lb	smoked trout or smoked freshwater herring	250 g
	Chive blossoms or snipped fresh chives for garnish	

Apple Cider Mayonnaise:

2	egg yolks	2
¼ cup	cider vinegar	50 mL
1 tsp	dry mustard	5 mL
½ tsp	salt	2 mL
¼ tsp	black pepper	1 mL
1¼ cups	canola or corn oil	300 mL

Bannock: Preheat oven to 400°F (200°C). In medium bowl, stir together flour, baking powder and salt. In large bowl, stir together buttermilk, oil and water. Gradually add flour mixture to buttermilk mixture, stirring until a soft dough forms, kneading gently as dough becomes stiffer.

When dough no longer sticks to your fingers, turn it out onto lightly floured surface. Pat out to 1-inch (2.5 cm) thick round; place on oiled baking sheet. Bake for 20 to 25 minutes until lightly browned. Let cool 10 minutes on wire rack.

Split the bannock horizontally; cut each half into 8 wedges. Top each wedge of bannock with a piece of smoked fish and a dollop of Apple Cider Mayonnaise. Serve at once, garnished with chive blossoms.

Apple Cider Mayonnaise: In food processor or blender, combine egg yolks, vinegar, mustard, salt and pepper. Process for a few seconds until smooth. With motor running, add oil in thin steady stream; process until mayonnaise is thickened and smooth. Pour into clean, dry jar; seal tightly. Refrigerate for up to 3 days.

Before you cast a fishing line into any of Ontario's streams, rivers or lakes, you must have an Outdoors Card. It may be obtained from most sporting goods stores or at local outfitters or fishing lodges. For a summary of this year's regulations, seasons and fees, contact the Ministry of Natural Resources Information Centre in Toronto.

Use very fresh, uncracked eggs, and refrigerate the mayonnaise immediately after making. If you prefer, use commercial mayonnaise. Refrigerate leftover egg whites, in covered container, for up to 2 weeks, or freeze them for up to 3 months.

Makes **6 servings**

Preparation time: **20 minutes**

Cooking time: **10 to 15 minutes**

*F*ood, its harvesting and its preparation have long been high on the list of priorities for northern peoples. Missinaibi House, a lodge forty miles west of Kapuskasing, mirrors that reality. Denyse Korpela is the cook, and Owen, her husband, is the guide. The place is secluded from the highway, and the view from the dining room is over a duck pond. The lakes are rich with northern pike, pickerel and perch; the forests yield up bear, rabbit, partridge and moose. Denyse's mom was a cook and her father was a butcher, so when a guest bags a 1,400-pound moose in the backwoods, it's Denyse who counsels him/her on how to deal with it. In the restaurant, she serves wild boar and venison. But for her family she'd just as soon sauté a bear (spring bears are best for steak, she says, because they're lean and haven't exercised for a few months) or a fat little beaver. She smokes pike over hickory or apple wood and keeps it for canoe tripping. In the springtime there are fiddleheads; in the early summer, she forages for dandelion greens for salads. Wild strawberries grow in her yard, and raspberries, which she uses in desserts and flavoured oils, line the ditches When she has extra time and lots of toothpicks, she'll dip wild blueberries into melted chocolate to sprinkle onto ice cream. Autumn brings mushrooms, and then the short season is over and the snow begins to fly. But by that time, the freezer is full of good wild game and enough fish to last till the following year.

MISSINAIBI DANDELION SALAD

In the spring Denyse Korpela of Mississauga House prepares this salad. "We have three acres of dandelions," she explains, "so we might as well use them!" Pick dandelion leaves before the plants flower or they will taste bitter. Later on in the season, substitute watercress or spinach for the dandelion leaves.

3	medium potatoes, scrubbed (about 1 lb/500 g)	3
6 cups	washed and dried young dandelion leaves	1.5 L
4	slices bacon, chopped	4
1	small red onion, chopped	1
½ cup	mixed coarsely chopped fresh herbs, such as marjoram, parsley, chives and basil	125 mL
½ tsp	black pepper	2 mL
¼ cup	cider vinegar	50 mL

Cut potatoes into ½-inch (1 cm) cubes. In large saucepan, combine potatoes and enough salted water to cover them; bring to boil over high heat. Reduce heat to medium-low; cook, covered, for 5 to 10 minutes, until just tender. Drain well; return saucepan to low heat to dry potatoes slightly. Remove from heat; set aside.

Place dandelion leaves in large salad bowl; refrigerate, loosely covered, until ready to serve.

In small skillet, cook bacon over medium-high heat for 3 to 5 minutes until crisp. With slotted spoon, remove bacon from skillet, reserving drippings in skillet; drain bacon on paper towels.

Just before serving, add potatoes, bacon, onion, herbs and pepper to dandelion leaves; toss gently. Add vinegar to bacon drippings remaining in skillet; bring to boil over high heat. Drizzle vinegar mixture over salad; toss well. Serve at once.

Makes **6 to 8 servings**

Preparation time: **15 minutes**

Cooking time: **about 3 hours**

*I*t's not surprising that the restaurant at
The Unicorn Inn is consistently listed as
among the finest in the area. David
Nobel, chef-owner of The Unicorn Inn,
prepares his guests' meals from his small
kitchen with the professional attention
he has devoted to his craft for more than
a decade. The inn is located in South
Gillies, about thirty-five minutes west
of Thunder Bay. The meals are created
using the best ingredients Nobel can
buy. All summer long he contracts growers to produce leeks, shallots, lettuces
and herbs. Edible flowers are strewn on
the salads, which he splashes with simple
vinaigrettes. There's asparagus in the
springtime and berries in the summer.
Peaches have to be "imported" from
southern Ontario, as does the wine.

David's trademark is his baking.
Hard wheat flour finds its way into
loaves of many descriptions. After a day
on the slopes or groomed back-country
trails that are all minutes from the inn,
there could hardly be a better meal than
a steaming bowl of David's pumpkin
soup and his inn-baked peasant bread
with garlic-herbed butter.

VENISON POT ROAST WITH MUSHROOMS

*When Janice Morrison's husband, Bill, comes home
from a hunting trip, this is one of the family's
favourite ways to prepare a venison roast. Janice
serves the roast with creamed horseradish and scalloped potatoes and says that the recipe works just as
well with a 3-pound (1.5 kg) moose or beef roast.*

2 tbsp	canola or corn oil	25 mL
3 lb	boneless venison roast	1.5 kg
1	large onion, cut into wedges	1
1 cup	chopped celery leaves	250 mL
4	cloves garlic, thinly sliced	4
1 cup	each beef stock and tomato juice	250 mL
1 tsp	dried thyme	5 mL
½ tsp	each salt and black pepper	2 mL
1	bay leaf	1
½ lb	mushrooms	250 g
2 tbsp	each cornstarch and cold water	25 mL

Preheat oven to 325°F (160°C). In large Dutch
oven, flameproof casserole or roasting pan with
tight-fitting lid, heat oil over medium-high heat.
Add roast; cook for 3 to 5 minutes, turning often,
until browned on all sides. Remove roast from
pan; pour off all but 1 tbsp (15 mL) fat from pan.

Add onion, celery leaves and garlic to fat remaining in pan; cook, stirring, over medium heat for
3 to 5 minutes, until onion is softened. Add beef
stock, tomato juice, thyme, salt, pepper and bay
leaf; bring to boil over high heat. Return roast to
pan, turning to coat with juices; cover tightly.
Bake in oven for 2½ hours. Add mushrooms to
pan; cook, covered, 30 minutes or until meat is
very tender and mushrooms are soft.

Remove roast to heated cutting board; cover loosely with foil and keep warm. Place pan over high heat; bring cooking juices to boil. In small bowl, combine cornstarch and water until smooth. Add cornstarch mixture to pan; reduce heat to medium. Simmer, stirring constantly, until juices are slightly thickened and smooth. Season with salt and pepper to taste; discard bay leaf. Slice roast; serve with gravy.

A host of cottage breweries and micro-breweries have sprung up over the past few years. The difference? A micro-brewery produces less than 75,000 hL (hectolitres) per year, and a cottage brewery is licensed to produce less than 25,000 hL.

Makes **8 servings**

Preparation time: **25 minutes**

Cooking time: **about 2¾ hours**

*A*rthur Black, former Thunder Bay resident and host of CBC's *Basic Black*, says: "One word summons up Thunder Bay for me—and you won't find it in either official language. The word is *Hoito*. It refers to a literally underground restaurant located in the bowels of Finlandia Hall in the (but of course) Finnish section of town. The Hoito's not fancy, either, but the food is good, and there's lots of it. The quintessential Sunday morning cultural dining experience in Thunder Bay involves lassoing a raft of weekend newspapers, calling up half a dozen friends and heading down to the Hoito, there to commandeer a table and eat and yak and read and smoke for as long as you like. Nobody will roust you, your coffee cup will never be empty, and if you can spend more than fifteen bucks—I'll pay for your dessert!"

ROAST LOIN OF WILD BOAR WITH RICE-APPLE STUFFING

Denyse Korpela, who shared this recipe with us, specializes in cooking wild meats, such as bear and beaver, at Missinaibi House, the lodge she runs with her husband, Owen, in Mattice. According to Denyse, the very best wild meat to be found in Northern Ontario is lynx. "It's delicious roasted," she says. Denyse also roasts wild boar, even though the boar isn't, in fact, wild but is farmed nearby. Boar is very similar to pork, though the flavour is more gamey. If you can't find wild boar, substitute pork in this recipe.

2 tbsp	butter	25 mL
2	carrots, grated	2
2	apples or pears, peeled, cored and chopped	2 mL
1	medium onion, chopped	1
2	cloves garlic, minced	2
⅓ cup	brown rice, cooked	75 mL
¼ cup	chopped fresh parsley	50 mL
2 tbsp	fresh lemon juice	25 mL
2 tsp	ground marjoram	10 mL
½ tsp	salt	2 mL
¼ tsp	hot pepper flakes	1 mL
5 lb	centre-cut boneless wild boar loin roast	2.2 kg
1 cup	red wine	250 mL
1 cup	whipping cream	250 mL
	Black pepper	

In large skillet, heat butter over medium heat. Add carrots, apples, onion and garlic; cook, stirring, for 3 to 5 minutes, until onion is softened but not brown. Remove from heat; stir in rice, parsley, lemon juice, 1 tsp (5 mL) marjoram, the salt and hot pepper flakes. Let cool completely.

Preheat oven to 325°F (160°C). Untie roast; open out on work surface. Mound rice mixture onto one half of roast; re-form roast to enclose stuffing. Tie securely with string. Pat roast dry with paper towels; place on greased rack in shallow roasting pan. In small bowl, whisk together ½ cup (125 mL) wine and remaining marjoram; pour over roast. Cook in oven for 2¼ to 2½ hours or until meat thermometer inserted into roast registers 160°F (70°C). Remove roast to cutting board; cover loosely with foil. Let stand for 15 minutes before carving.

Meanwhile, pour excess fat from roasting pan; add cream and remaining wine to drippings remaining in pan. Place roasting pan over medium-high heat; boil for 3 to 5 minutes until cream mixture has reduced and thickened slightly, stirring to scrape up any brown bits from bottom of pan. Season with salt and pepper to taste. Cut roast into slices; serve with gravy.

*I*n 1918, a group of Finnish labourers who were living in the then brand-new building at 314 Bay Street hired a cook. The legendary Hoito Restaurant was born. The menu is huge, and there's a blackboard listing still more daily specials. Most people know Hoito for its gargantuan Finnish pancakes. A little thicker than crepes, they fill the eleven-inch plates right to the edge and are topped with whipped cream and strawberry sauce. Lake trout and salmon are added to the milky fish *mojakka,* or soup; there are *nakki,* or Finnish weiners, light in colour and flavour; and *lenkki,* a sausage that is grilled and served with mashed potatoes and vegetables. Every day they make their supply of *viili,* or clotted milk, which is served in small bowls with salt fish (cured salmon) sandwiches. The rice pudding is freshly cooked with butter, sugar and salt to either serve as dessert or be stuffed into another specialty, *piirakka. Piirakka* begins with sour rye dough that is rolled thin before being filled with the pudding. It's baked until the crust is crisp then dipped in melted butter. When it is served, it's topped with a helping of egg salad.

Go early, stay late and enjoy your feast of Finnish culture!

Makes **4 servings**

Preparation time: **30 minutes**

Cooking time: **about 1½ hours**

ROAST DUCK WITH BAKED APPLES AND CRANBERRY SAUCE

Roast duck is very underrated these days, which we think is a great shame. It's easy to prepare, and if you invest in a pair of sturdy kitchen shears, it's even easier to serve. Cut duck into quarters as described below; arrange the duck quarters on separate dinner plates, together with cranberry-stuffed baked apples, and you're ready to impress your dinner guests.

1	4-lb (2 kg) duck	1
¼ tsp	each salt and black pepper	1 mL
½ cup	fresh parsley sprigs	125 mL
6	sprigs fresh marjoram	6
2	cloves garlic	2
1	small onion	1
2	Golden Delicious apples	2
¼ cup	water	50 mL
4 tsp	melted butter	20 mL
3 cups	cranberries	750 mL
½ cup	granulated sugar	125 mL
½ cup	red wine, such as Maréchal Foch	125 mL
	Fresh marjoram sprigs for garnish	

Preheat oven to 400°F (200°C). Pat duck dry with paper towels; sprinkle with salt and pepper. Place parsley, marjoram, garlic and onion in duck cavity; place duck on rack in shallow roasting pan. With needle or sharp skewer, prick duck skin all over. Roast for 1½ hours, pricking skin again after 30 minutes, until meat thermometer registers 185°F (85°C) and juices run clear when thickest part of thigh is pierced with a skewer. Remove from oven; cover loosely with foil. Let stand 10 minutes.

Fifteen minutes before the end of cooking time, cut apples in half; scoop out cores with melon baller. Arrange apple halves cut-sides up in shallow baking dish; pour water into dish. Drizzle 1 tsp (5 mL) butter over each apple half; bake, uncovered, for 15 minutes until apples are tender. Keep warm.

Meanwhile, in medium saucepan, combine cranberries, sugar and wine. Bring to boil over high heat. Reduce heat to medium; simmer, uncovered, for 2 to 3 minutes, stirring occasionally, until cranberries pop and mixture thickens. Keep warm.

When ready to serve, place duck breast-side down on cutting board with cavity towards you. With kitchen shears, cut along each side of backbone; remove backbone. Open up duck, discarding flavourings inside cavity. Cut duck in half along breast bone. Turn duck halves skin-side up; cut each in half crosswise. Divide duck among four dinner plates; garnish with marjoram sprigs. Spoon a little cranberry sauce into hollow in each apple; place apples on dinner plates. Pass remaining cranberry sauce separately.

Makes **4** servings

Preparation time: **20 minutes**

Cooking time: **15 to 20 minutes**

*I*n Thornloe, Ault Foods has a small Cheddar plant. It's a treat in this region to be able to buy fresh curds and old Cheddar.

MOOSE MEATBALLS STUFFED WITH CHEESE

These easy meatballs make a great family supper. Moose meat is very lean, with a rich flavour that's almost indistinguishable from beef. Venison would also work well. Substitute lean ground beef if you don't have any generous hunting friends.

1 lb	ground moose meat, venison or lean ground beef	500 g
1 tsp	dried thyme	5 mL
½ tsp	each salt and black pepper	2 mL
2 oz	Swiss or Gouda cheese	50 g
1 tbsp	canola or corn oil	15 mL
1 cup	red wine	250 mL
½ cup	whipping cream	125 mL
2 tbsp	chopped fresh parsley	25 mL

In medium bowl, combine moose meat, thyme, salt and pepper; mix lightly but thoroughly until well combined (do not overmix or meatballs will be tough). Cut cheese into 20 ½-inch (1 cm) cubes.

Form meat mixture into 20 even-size meatballs. Press a cube of cheese into centre of each one, re-forming the meatball to enclose cheese completely.

In large nonstick skillet, heat oil over medium heat. Add meatballs; reduce heat to medium-low. Cook for 12 to 15 minutes, turning meatballs carefully, until browned on the outside and no longer pink inside (cheese will ooze slightly).

With slotted spoon, remove meatballs from skillet; keep warm. Drain off all fat from skillet. Add wine to skillet; bring to boil over high heat. Boil for 3 to 4 minutes, scraping up any brown bits from bottom of skillet, until liquid is reduced to about ½ cup (125 mL). Add cream; boil until heated through. Serve meatballs over rice or mashed potatoes, with sauce drizzled over top. Garnish with parsley.

THUNDER BAY BAKED PICKEREL WITH SPRING VEGETABLES

In 1994, Tim Matthews, chef-instructor in the culinary management department of Confederation College in Thunder Bay, wrote a fund-raising cookbook called A Taste of Thunder Bay. *The book sold out and raised $11,000 for the United Way. This is one of our favourite recipes from Tim's book. If you can't find pickerel, substitute any local fish fillets.*

1 lb	asparagus, trimmed and cut diagonally into 1-inch (2.5 cm) pieces	500 g
¾ lb	red potatoes, thinly sliced (about 3 potatoes)	375 g
¾ lb	carrots, thinly sliced diagonally (about 3 carrots)	375 g
1	small onion, thinly sliced into rings	1
2 tbsp	canola or corn oil	25 mL
1 tbsp	fresh thyme leaves (or ¾ tsp/4 mL dried)	15 mL
½ tsp	each salt and black pepper	2 mL
4	6-oz (175 g) pickerel fillets	4
1	clove garlic, minced	1
1 tbsp	fresh lemon juice	15 mL
¼ tsp	paprika	1 mL
	Fresh thyme sprigs for garnish	

Makes **4 servings**

Preparation time: **25 minutes**

Cooking time: **about 40 minutes**

Preheat oven to 400°F (200°C). In oiled 13- by 9-inch (3 L) baking dish, combine asparagus, potatoes, carrots, onion, 1 tbsp (15 mL) oil, half the thyme and ¼ tsp (1 mL) each salt and pepper; toss well. Spread vegetables evenly in dish; cover with foil. Bake for 30 minutes, until potatoes and carrots are tender.

Pat fish fillets dry on paper towels; arrange in single layer on top of vegetables, tucking thin tail ends under. In small bowl, combine remaining oil, thyme, salt and pepper, the garlic, lemon juice and paprika. Drizzle oil mixture evenly over fish. Bake, uncovered, for 8 to 10 minutes, until fish flakes easily with a fork. Serve garnished with fresh thyme.

Lake Superior is a major source of lake trout, but it also has a substantial chinook salmon population. However, the numbers have been declining in recent years. Pink salmon were introduced into the lake as early as 1955, with chinook being released shortly thereafter. It wasn't until the 1970s that the chinook finally took hold. Because there's no commercial fishery allocation, it's not possible to buy salmon, and there's no officially recognized season for salmon fishing. But in early June and late August, there's always a flurry of angling for the big fish. Lures and downriggers are the method of choice. Wawa, a beautifully groomed mining town on the shore of Lake Superior, holds an annual salmon derby in mid-August at spawning time. Although the prizes are generous, the profits help with the raising and releasing of thousands of salmon fry into the Michipicoten River.

Makes **4 servings**

Preparation time: **15 minutes**

Cooking time: **8 to 10 minutes**

*T*he firewood is neatly stacked behind the shop on a back street in Timmins. Tamara and Ed Dabrowski have been in Canada for eight years but have only been in the smoked meat business for three. Dabrowski's Smoked Meats in Timmins uses the best meat they can buy to make ham kielbasa or, "smokies" (the favourite with area hunters because it carries so well), "luck" ham (a raw smoked carpaccio-like beef), homemade sauerkraut and perfect perogies filled with meat or cheese.

The Golden Crust Bakery, just down Wilson Street from Dabrowski's, has a special treat for local customers. Every Thursday, Friday and Saturday they bake beans in their bread ovens to sell with their fluffy loaves. It's a perfect dinner to take with you when you're heading into the back country or down the road to Ivanhoe Lake Provincial Park.

Pan-Fried Wild Northern Greens

Each summer Ivanhoe Lake Provincial Park near Foleyet hosts an Edible Wilds Weekend and Canoefest to introduce park visitors to the delights of foraging for wild plants. This recipe comes from the park's fascinating recipe booklet produced for the event. The booklet suggests using a mixture of clover, dandelion leaves, fireweed shoots, chickweed and mountain sorrel; it also suggests arming yourself with a good field guide to ensure that you pick only edible plants! We find the recipe also works well with tender spinach leaves with any tough stems removed. Incidentally, according to Tricia Gardner, the natural-heritage education leader at Ivanhoe Lake Provincial Park, we have the Hudson's Bay Company to thank for the dandelions that adorn our lawns in the summertime. The company originally imported dandelions from Britain to use for making wine!

2 tbsp	butter	25 mL
1	medium onion, chopped	1
10 cups	fresh young greens, washed and dried	2.5 L
1 tbsp	fresh lemon juice	15 mL
	Salt and black pepper	

In large skillet, melt butter over medium heat. Add onion; cook, stirring, for 5 minutes or until onion is golden. Add greens; stir to coat with onion-butter mixture. Cook, covered, for 3 to 5 minutes, just until leaves have wilted. Sprinkle with lemon juice and salt and pepper to taste. Serve at once.

WILD RICE AND MUSHROOM CASSEROLE

For best flavour, use wild mushrooms if possible in this easy casserole (picking only those you can clearly identify as being safe to eat); otherwise substitute button, shiitake or portobello mushrooms.

¼ cup	wild rice, rinsed and drained	50 mL
1 tbsp	canola or corn oil	15 mL
1	onion, chopped	1
1	clove garlic, minced	1
½ cup	long-grain rice	125 mL
2 cups	sliced mushrooms (about 6 oz/175 g)	500 mL
1 cup	chicken stock	250 mL
½ cup	apple cider	125 mL
½ tsp	dried thyme	2 mL
1	bay leaf	1
¼ tsp	each salt and black pepper	1 mL

In large saucepan of boiling water, cook wild rice for 30 minutes. Drain well; set aside.

Preheat oven to 375°F (190°C). In 4-cup (1 L) flameproof casserole, heat oil over medium-high heat; add onion and garlic. Cook, stirring, for 2 to 3 minutes. Add long-grain rice; cook, stirring, for 2 minutes or until rice is translucent. Stir in wild rice, mushrooms, chicken stock, apple cider, thyme, bay leaf, salt and pepper; bring to boil. Bake, covered, for 30 minutes or until rice is tender and liquid absorbed. Discard bay leaf.

Makes **4 servings**

Preparation time: **20 minutes**

Cooking time: **1 hour, 5 minutes**

*O*ne of the most precious wild foods in the north is wild rice (*Zizania aquatica*), which in reality is a tall, water-bound grass. Most of Ontario's crop flourishes near the Lake of the Woods and is still harvested in the original fashion by the Ojibwa. Beginning in mid-August, canoes float delicately between the stands of grass, and long poles are used to draw the seed heads over the canoe so that the "rice" can be beaten off. Grains that fall wide of the canoe reseed the lake bottom for the following year.

Makes **about 80 cookies**

Preparation time: **25 minutes**

Cooking time: **about 12 minutes**

*L*abrador Tea (*Ledum palustre L.*) is also known as swamp tea or Hudson's Bay tea. The long, curled, leathery leaves are fuzzy underneath. The tea is used by the first peoples from coast to coast. It is best when young leaves are picked in the springtime, dried completely and stored in an airtight container. They can also be brewed when fresh. Toss a handful of leaves into about 4 cups (1 L) boiling water. Simmer, without boiling, for no longer than 5 minutes.

Raspberry Tea (sp. *Rubus*) may be made with the fresh or fully dried leaves of wild raspberry, blackberry or thimbleberry plants. Pour boiling water over a large handful of cleaned leaves and twigs. Allow it to steep, as you would regular tea, for 5 to 10 minutes. Fresh or dried berries may also be added for colour and flavour.

Fireweed Tea (*Epilobium angustifolium L.*) comes from one of the most beautiful and prolific plants growing in the north. After a fire burns a forest, the ensuing meadow is quickly filled with the tall, hot pink spires. This hardy flower covers over clear cuts and lines many a logging road. Pick the younger leaves, before the plant flowers, brewing it as you would Raspberry Tea, by steeping it in boiling water. Fireweed was also known to the voyageurs, who cooked it as a vegetable and named it "*l'herbe frette.*"

FINNISH SPICE COOKIES

Nancy Niva, owner of the Scandinavian House Restaurant in Thunder Bay, was born in Canada to a Swedish father and a Finnish mother. Finnish was Nancy's first language as a child, and her mother, who, says Nancy, was a wonderful cook, prepared Finnish specialties, such as these spicy cookies. When Nancy shared the original recipe with us, the ingredients were listed as "one pound of butter (not quite), 2 cups of sugar (not quite)" and so on! We hope our revised version does justice to Nancy's mother's original. In Finland the cookies are flavoured with a traditional Finnish spice called maustepippuria, *which roughly translates as "spicy pepper." If you have a Scandinavian grocery store nearby, you might be able to find the real McCoy; if so, use 2 tsp (10 mL) in place of the black pepper and cardamom.*

⅓ cup	corn syrup	75 mL
2 tsp	cinnamon	10 mL
1 tsp	each black pepper, cardamom, ground cloves and ginger	5 mL
4½ cups	all-purpose flour	1.125 L
2 tsp	baking soda	10 mL
1¾ cups	granulated sugar	425 mL
1¾ cups	butter, softened	425 mL
⅓ cup	table cream	75 mL

In small saucepan, combine corn syrup, cinnamon, pepper, cardamom, cloves and ginger; bring to boil over high heat, stirring occasionally. Remove from heat. Pour syrup mixture into large bowl; let cool to lukewarm.

In medium bowl, stir together flour and baking soda. In separate bowl, cream together sugar and butter until fluffy.

Beat sugar mixture into cooled syrup mixture
until well combined. Beat in cream. Gradually
beat in flour mixture until well combined and a
soft dough forms. Divide dough in half. Gather
dough into two balls; wrap in plastic wrap. Chill
in refrigerator for at least 30 minutes.

Preheat oven to 325°F (160°C). On lightly
floured surface, gently roll out dough to ¼-inch
(5 mm) thickness. Cut out cookies with 2½-inch
(6 cm) cookie cutter; arrange a little apart on
baking sheets. Bake for 10 to 12 minutes, until
golden brown; let cool slightly on baking sheets.
Remove from baking sheets; let cool completely
on wire racks.

Makes **12 tarts**

Preparation time: **20 minutes**

Standing time: **20 minutes**

Cooking time: **12 to 15 minutes**

*T*he scent of cardamom wafts from the toasted *pulla* or coffee bread at the Kivela Bakery. Customers drive for miles to buy this special Finnish-style bread in Michael and Hazel Settala's bakery café. Try the sourdough rye bread, especially if you happen to be lucky enough to have some salted fish (*suola kala*), which every Finnish household in the city seems to relish. And if you're heading into the wilderness for a camping expedition and need a dry bread that'll carry well, buy a round of his "hard tack" or brittle bread—Michael's the only baker in the city carrying on this tradition.

CAROLYN'S BEAUTIFUL BUTTER TARTS

The fiercest of debates rage over butter tarts. There's the "don't even think of putting nuts in" faction, and the "ugh, raisins?" brigade, to name but two. Carolyn Gall, our recipe tester, has come up with the perfect compromise: a gooey buttery filling with sultanas (which you can leave out if you prefer) enclosed in a rich, nutty pastry. Use a food processor to chop the nuts very finely.

1 cup	boiling water	250 mL
½ cup	sultana raisins	125 mL
	Pastry for 9-inch (23 cm) single-crust pie (see recipe on page 112)	
¼ cup	very finely chopped pecans or walnuts	50 mL
½ cup	each packed brown sugar and corn syrup	125 mL
1	egg, lightly beaten	1
1 tsp	vanilla	5 mL
¼ tsp	salt	1 mL
¼ cup	butter, softened	50 mL

Preheat oven to 425°F (220°C). In small bowl, combine boiling water and sultanas; set aside for 20 minutes.

On lightly floured surface or floured clean tea towel, roll out pastry to ⅛-inch (3 mm) thickness, scattering evenly with 1 tbsp (15 mL) nuts as you roll. As each spoonful of nuts is incorporated into pastry, scatter more nuts over pastry until you use them all up. With 4-inch (10 cm) cutter or drinking glass, cut out 12 rounds. Fit rounds gently into 12-cup muffin pan; set aside.

In medium bowl, whisk together sugar, corn syrup, egg, vanilla and salt; whisk in butter until small pieces of butter are evenly distributed throughout filling. Drain sultanas; divide evenly among tart shells. Fill each tart two-thirds full with sugar mixture. Bake for 12 to 15 minutes, until pastry is golden and filling is bubbly. Let cool in pan on wire rack for 15 minutes. Remove tarts from pan; let cool completely on wire rack.

*I*f you've been in search of a recipe for *syyskeitto* (Finnish autumn vegetable stew) or perhaps an authentic version of *sykksyn uuniomenat* (baked apples), look no further. Readers of *Canadan Uutiset* have them all and share them generously. Since 1915, the Finnish newspaper of Thunder Bay has been publishing weekly. Its subscription base now reaches from Florida to Singapore. The ideals are simple—to preserve Finnish language and culture as part of and within the community of Canada.

Makes **25 bars**

Preparation time: **25 minutes**

Rising time: **1½ to 2 hours**

Cooking time: **about 35 minutes**

*I*n 1923 the Scandinavian Home Society was founded to provide a little cultural centre for the new immigrants to the region centred on Port Arthur and Fort William, now Thunder Bay. Today membership has been extended to all those interested in the ethnic background of these communities. "The Scand" has a little, inexpensive restaurant open for breakfast and lunch (7 a.m. to 4 p.m.), and everything is honest and homemade. Breakfast always has bacon and eggs; every two weeks there's baked beef hash, and there will always be thin Swedish or Finnish pancakes with berries and whipped cream. At noon, or earlier if you're lucky, *mojjaka*, a Finnish beef soup, may be served with sour rye bread and rice pudding topped with strawberries. Or there may be a spice-laden meat loaf with mashed potatoes—the good kind with lumps in them. Manager Nancy Niva turns bushels of beets into pickles to go with beef sausage.

EVA'S BLUEBERRY DESSERT BARS

These traditional bars, called in Finland mustikka piirakka, *are a favourite in the Finnish bakeries in Thunder Bay. Eva Hakala of Thunder Bay, who shared the recipe with us, says that if there's any dough left over she uses it to make cinnamon buns. Serve the moist bars as a dessert with ice cream or whipped cream.*

Dough:

½ cup	warm water (105°F/41°C)	125 mL
¾ cup	granulated sugar	175 mL
1	pkg (8 g) dry active yeast	1
6 to 7 cups	all-purpose flour	1.5 to 1.75 L
2 cups	warm whole milk (105°F/41°C)	500 mL
2	eggs, lightly beaten	2
1 tsp	salt	5 mL
¾ cup	butter, softened	175 mL

Filling:

4 cups	blueberries	1 L
¾ cup	granulated sugar	175 mL
2 tsp	fresh lemon juice	10 mL
1 tsp	cinnamon	5 mL
Pinch	salt	Pinch
2 tbsp	each cornstarch and water	25 mL

Dough: In large bowl, whisk together water and ¼ cup (50 mL) sugar until sugar dissolves. Sprinkle yeast over top; set aside in warm place for 15 minutes until puffy. Stir in 3 cups (750 mL) flour, the warm milk, eggs, salt and remaining sugar; beat well. Stir in butter and enough of the remaining flour to make a soft dough, using your hands when dough becomes too stiff to stir. Turn out onto work surface; knead for 10 to 12 minutes, working in additional flour to keep dough from sticking. Form dough into ball; place in lightly oiled bowl, turning dough to coat with oil. Cover loosely with plastic wrap; let rise in warm, draft-free place for 1½ to 2 hours or until doubled in size.

Filling: In large saucepan, combine blueberries, sugar, lemon juice, cinnamon and salt. In small bowl, combine cornstarch and water until smooth; stir into blueberry mixture. Bring to boil over medium-high heat, stirring constantly. Reduce heat to medium-low; simmer, stirring constantly, for 3 to 5 minutes, until mixture is thickened and bubbly. Remove from heat; let cool slightly.

Preheat oven to 350°F (180°C). Punch dough down. On lightly floured surface, roll out two-thirds of dough to ⅓-inch (8 mm) thickness; line base and sides of a 15- by 10-inch (38 by 25 cm) rimmed baking sheet with dough, trimming off excess.

Spread blueberry mixture evenly over dough. Roll out remaining dough; cut into ½-inch (1 cm) wide strips. Arrange strips of dough over blueberry mixture in a lattice fashion, sealing edges well. Bake for 30 minutes, until golden brown. Let cool slightly on baking sheet; cut into bars. Serve warm.

Makes **6 servings**

Preparation time: **15 minutes**

Cooking time: **40 to 45 minutes**

*B*unchberries (*Cornus canadensis L.*) are among the wild foods gathered by campers and staff at Ivanhoe Lake Provincial Park for their Edible Wild Food Fest. Found primarily in damp, coniferous woodlands, the small white flower is a member of the dogwood family. Its scarlet berries sit atop a whorl of deep green leaves. Cook the berries and press them through a sieve or food mill to remove the seeds. The cooked pulp can be used in savoury or sweet sauces, with meats or as a dessert topping.

NORTHERN BLUEBERRY CRISP

Wild blueberries have very intense flavour but are very difficult to cultivate, and often the bears get to them first! According to Foodland Ontario, ninety-five percent of Ontario's wild blueberry crop comes from naturally occurring stands. The cultivated, or highbush, blueberries are more readily available, and both varieties work well in this easy crisp.

4 cups	blueberries	1 L
2 tbsp	granulated sugar	25 mL
1 cup	all-purpose flour	250 mL
½ cup	packed brown sugar	125 mL
1 tsp	cinnamon	5 mL
½ cup	cold butter, cubed	125 mL
½ cup	chopped walnuts	125 mL

Preheat oven to 350°F (180°C). Pick over blueberries; rinse lightly under cold running water. Drain. In 8-inch (2 L) square baking dish, combine blueberries and granulated sugar; toss gently.

In medium bowl, combine flour, brown sugar and cinnamon. With pastry blender or two knives, cut in butter until mixture is well combined and crumbly; stir in walnuts.

Sprinkle nut mixture evenly over blueberries. Bake for 40 to 45 minutes, until blueberries are tender and topping is golden brown. Serve warm with whipped cream or Crème Fraîche (see recipe on page 108).

CREAMY WILD RICE PUDDING WITH MAPLE GLAZE

This is one of the most comforting desserts we know. It may take a little while to cook, but it needs no real attention and uses ingredients you probably have in your cupboard already. Make sure you use a short-grain rice such as Italian-style or arborio for this dessert; regular long-grain rice doesn't contain sufficient starch to thicken the milk.

Makes **4 to 6 servings**

Preparation time: **10 minutes**

Cooking time: **2¾ hours**

¼ cup	wild rice	50 mL
2 cups	water	500 mL
⅓ cup	short-grain rice	75 mL
3 cups	whole milk	750 mL
¼ cup	granulated sugar	50 mL
1 tbsp	butter, cut into small pieces	15 mL
¼ tsp	grated nutmeg	1 mL
Pinch	salt	Pinch
3 tbsp	maple sugar	45 mL

Place wild rice in sieve; rinse and drain well. In small saucepan, bring water to boil over high heat; stir in wild rice. Reduce heat to medium-low; cook covered for 40 minutes; drain well. (This can be done ahead.)

Preheat oven to 300°F (150°C). Place short-grain rice in sieve; rinse and drain well. In 8-cup (2 L) baking dish, combine wild and short-grain rice, milk, granulated sugar, butter, nutmeg and salt. Bake, uncovered, for 2 hours, stirring every 30 minutes, until rice is tender and pudding is creamy.

Remove from oven; stir. Sprinkle top evenly with maple sugar. Place under hot broiler for 2 to 3 minutes, until maple sugar caramelizes and is golden brown. Let stand for 10 minutes before serving.

Makes **5 half-pint (250 mL) jars**

Preparation time: **20 minutes**

Cooking time: **about 20 minutes**

Processing time: **15 minutes**

*L*ow-bush cranberries and serviceberries, and dwarf raspberries—Ontario's
north is far more than blueberries.
The longer the hours of sunlight, the
more berries seem to flourish in the
wilderness.

Low-bush cranberries (*Vaccinium
vitis-idaea L.*) have many names: par-
tridgeberries, lingonberries, rock, alpine,
mountain or European cranberries, and
finally foxberry. They are bright red and
tart with lots of acidity. They may be
made into a full-flavoured jam or a tart
sauce for your Thanksgiving goose.

Serviceberries (sp. *Amelanchier*) are,
in reality, the treasured Saskatoon berry
from the prairies and the Indian Pear
from Nova Scotia. Aficionados say there
is no better berry pie *in the world*! The
rub is that there are many different varieties of the berry, and some are indeed
more luscious than others. So, taste
away, and when you find a glorious
bush, make yourself a deep-dish pie.

The dwarf raspberry is another
plant that has spread around the northern hemisphere. The plants are shrubby
and bog-loving, and the berries are
called bakeapples by Newfoundlanders.
In Scandinavia, they're called cloudber-
ries. One single red-orange berry grows
atop the shiny, raspberry-like leaves.
Picking them is very arduous, so be fru-
gal and simply garnish your dessert with
them, or eat them as a snack while
you're hiking.

SIOUX LOOKOUT CRANBERRY KETCHUP

*Ida Isleifson of Sioux Lookout prepares this tangy
relish with the pulp left over from making highbush
cranberry jelly. Some people say highbush cranberries
are an acquired taste. They are much more tart than
regular cranberries, and even fans like Ida admit
they are somewhat odoriferous when they're cooking
(like smelly feet, she says). We've adapted Ida's recipe
so it can be made with regular cranberries. To speed
up preparation, we use a food processor to chop the
cranberries and onion.*

6 cups	chopped cranberries (about 1½ lb/750 g)	1.5 L
3 cups	packed brown sugar	750 mL
⅔ cup	white vinegar	150 mL
1	medium onion, finely chopped	1
½ tsp	cinnamon	2 mL
¼ tsp	ground cloves	1 mL

In large stainless steel or enamel saucepan, combine cranberries, sugar, vinegar, onion, cinnamon
and cloves. Bring to boil over medium-high heat,
stirring constantly. Reduce heat to medium-low;
simmer, uncovered and stirring often, for 15 to
20 minutes, until mixture has thickened slightly.

Immediately ladle into 5 hot, sterilized ½-pint
(250 mL) jars, leaving ¼ in (5 mm) headspace.
Wipe jar rims to remove any excess ketchup; seal
with two-piece lids, tightening screw bands until
just fingertip tight. Process in hot-water bath for
15 minutes. Remove jars from canner; let cool for
24 hours. Check jar seals (sealed lids curve downwards). Remove screw bands; label jars. Store
ketchup in cool, dark place.

Farmers' Markets

ONTARIO'S FARMERS' MARKETS ARE THE MOST VITAL IN ALL OF CANADA.
They are also an integral part of the province's agricultural history. Twenty-six
of the hundred and twenty-five that exist today were in operation before
1900. The oldest is Toronto's huge St. Lawrence Market (1803), followed by
one in Belleville (1816), and Ottawa's beautiful By Ward Market (1830).
From Sarnia in the southwest to Rainy River and Kapuskasing in the north,
they dot Ontario's landscape. The vendors are entrepreneurs of the first order,
while the customers provide the best test market for any new product you
can imagine. In the colourful and bustling markets, you can sense the agricultural heartbeat of the province. The seasons roll by.

Spring brings the freshwater smelt, first-run maple syrup, smoked sausages,
pork chops and cheeses of every description. Ontario is the province of
Cheddar cheese, and it's at the markets that you'll find the very finest. When
the snow finally melts and the forests warm, there'll be bunches of wild leeks
and baskets of fiddleheads; intricately painted Ukrainian Easter eggs;
kochkase (cooked cheese) and slices of sweet shoo-fly pie. Fresh fruits and
vegetables, many not available elsewhere, pile the stands. Baskets of black
walnuts, organic herbs, heritage tomatoes, peppers by the heaping bushel . . .
until it's time once again for pumpkins, squash and Thanksgiving, the most
special time of the year for our farmers. On our thickly sliced homemade
bread, we now can taste apple butter made in the old-fashioned way and
freshly pressed cider sometimes sweetened with late-harvest pears. There will
be pheasant and quail and free-range turkey all in time for Christmas. Fruit-
cakes are removed from their brandy-soaked cheesecloth shrouds; thousands
of dozens of cookies and squares are baked, and customers line up for special
seasonal breads, filled with fruit and dripping with icing.

ALGOMA FARMERS' MARKET
Sault Ste. Marie
Summer – Roberta Bondar Park
Winter – Wellington Square Mall
Wednesday & Saturday
8 A.M. to 1 P.M. — May/June
7 A.M. to 1 P.M. — July/October

ALMONTE FARMERS' MARKET
Elizabeth Kelly Public Library
Parking Lot
June to October
Saturday
9 A.M. to 12 NOON

ARGYLE FARMERS' MARKET
Port Loring beside Wilson Lake
July to August
Wednesday
9 A.M. to 1 P.M.

ARNPRIOR FARMERS' MARKET
John Street North
Mid May to Early October
Saturday
8 A.M. to 12 NOON

BARRIE FARMERS' MARKET
City Hall
Saturday
Summer — 8 A.M. to 1 P.M.
Winter — 8 A.M. to 12:30 P.M.

BELLEVILLE FARMERS' MARKET
Adjacent to City Hall
All Year
Tuesday, Thursday & Saturday
8 A.M. to 6 P.M.

BRACEBRIDGE FARMERS' MARKET
Jubilee Park
Mid May to Mid October
Saturday
8:30 A.M. to 12 NOON

BRAMPTON FARMERS' MARKET
Main Street
June to October
Saturday
7 A.M. to 1 P.M.

BRANTFORD FARMERS' MARKET
City Parking Garage
All Year
Thursday
9 A.M. to 5 P.M.
Friday
9 A.M. to 6 P.M.
Saturday
6 A.M. to 2 P.M.

BRIGHTON FARMERS' MARKET
Main Street Bank of Commerce
parking lot
May to October
Saturday
8 A.M. to 12 NOON

BROCKVILLE FARMERS' MARKET
Market Street
Early May to End of October
Tuesday, Thursday & Saturday
7 A.M. to 1 P.M.

BURLINGTON DOWNTOWN FARMERS' MARKET
City Hall
June to October
Saturday
8 A.M. to 2 P.M.

BURLINGTON MALL FARMERS' MARKET
Burlington Mall Parking Lot
Early May to End of November
Wednesday & Friday
8 A.M. to 5 P.M.

CALEDONIA FARMERS' MARKET
172 Argyle Street North
June to October
Saturday
7 A.M. to 1 P.M.

CAMBRIDGE FARMERS' MARKET
Corner of Ainslie and Dickson
Streets
All Year
Saturday
5:30 A.M. to 1 P.M.
Wednesday
6 A.M. to 1 P.M.

CAMPBELLFORD FARMERS' MARKET
Town Hall
May to October
Saturday
8 A.M. to 12 NOON

CARLETON PLACE FARMERS' MARKET
Post Office
May to October
Saturday
8 A.M. to 12 NOON

CARP FARMERS' MARKET
Carp Agricultural Fairgrounds
May to October
Saturday
8 A.M. to 1 P.M.

CENTRE MALL FARMERS' MARKET
Centre Mall Parking Lot, Hamilton
All Year
Friday & Saturday
8 A.M. to 5:30 P.M.
Wednesday
8 A.M. to 5:30 P.M. (May to November)

CLOVERBELT COUNTRY FARMERS' MARKET
Fairgrounds, Dryden
Mid July to End of September
Saturday
9 A.M. to 12 NOON

CLOVER VALLEY FARMERS' MARKET
Fort Frances
May to October
Saturday
8 A.M. to 2 P.M.

COBDEN FARMERS' MARKET
Memorial Hall, Main Street
May to October
Saturday
8 A.M. to 11 A.M.

COBOURG FARMERS' MARKET
Market Building
May to October
Saturday
7 A.M. to 12 NOON
July and August
Tuesday
5 P.M. to 8 P.M.

COCHRANE FARMERS' MARKET
Cochrane Agricultural Society
Fairgrounds
Mid July to End of September
Saturday
10 A.M. to 12 NOON

COMBERMERE FARMERS' MARKET
Highway #62 in Combermere
July to September
Saturday
7:30 A.M. to 10 A.M.

CORNWALL DOWNTOWN FARMERS' MARKET
Municipal Parking Lot
May to October
Saturday
7 A.M. to 1 P.M.
Wednesday
12 NOON to 5 P.M.

CRYSLER PARK FARMERS' MARKET
Upper Canada Playhouse,
Morrisburg
July to Early October
Saturday
8 A.M. to 12 NOON

DORSET OUTDOOR FARMERS' MARKET
Nordic Inn Restaurant/Resort
Late June to Early September
Saturday
10 A.M. to 2 P.M.

DRAYTON FARMERS' MARKET
Drayton Fairgrounds
Mid June to Mid October
Saturday
8 A.M. to 12 NOON

DUNDAS FARMERS' MARKET
Intersection of King and Sydenham
Streets
All Year
Thursday
9 A.M. to 6 P.M.

DUNNVILLE FARMERS' MARKET
Market Street
May to November
Tuesday and Saturday
7 A.M. to 12 NOON

ESSEX FARMERS' MARKET
Town of Essex parking lot
June to October
Saturday
8 A.M. to 2 P.M.

ETOBICOKE FARMERS' MARKET
Etobicoke City Hall
Mid July to Early October
Saturday
8 A.M. to 2 P.M.

FLESHERTON AND DISTRICT FARMERS' MARKET
Arena parking lot
May to Thanksgiving
Saturday
8 A.M. to 1 P.M.

GANANOQUE FARMERS' MARKET
Knights of Columbus Building
May to October
Saturday
7 A.M. to 12 NOON

GEORGETOWN FARMERS' MARKET
Main Street South
Mid June to Mid October
Saturday
7 A.M. to 1 P.M.

GODERICH FARMERS' MARKET
Court House Square
June to End of October
Saturday
8 A.M. to 1 P.M.

GORE BAY FARMERS' MARKET
Gore Bay Arena, Manitoulin Island
Mid May to Mid October
Friday
9 A.M. to 1 P.M.

GRAVENHURST FARMERS' MARKET
Lion's Pavilion, Sagamo Park
May to October
Wednesday
9:30 A.M. to 2:30 P.M.

GUELPH FARMERS' MARKET
Gordon Street and Waterloo
Avenue
All Year
Saturday
7 A.M. to 12 NOON
July to October
Thursday
11 A.M. to 6 P.M.

HAGERSVILLE FARMERS' MARKET
At the four corners in centre of
town
All Year
Wednesday
7 A.M. to 1 P.M.

HAMILTON FARMERS' MARKET
Jackson Square Shopping Mall
All Year
Tuesday and Thursday
7 A.M. to 6 P.M.
Friday
9 A.M. to 6 P.M.
Saturday
6 A.M. to 6 P.M.

HIGHLAND FARMERS' MARKET
Tourist Information Grounds,
South River
Mid June to September
Saturday
8:30 A.M. to 2 P.M.

HUNTSVILLE FARMERS' MARKET
Canadian Tire Store Parking Lot
Late May to Mid October
Thursday
9 A.M. to 2 P.M.

KAKABEKA FARMERS' MARKET
Kakabeka Falls
May to October
Saturday & Sunday
9 A.M. to 4 P.M.

KAPUSKASING FARMERS' MARKET
Kapuskasing
Mid July to September
Saturday
8 A.M. to 12 NOON

KEADY FARMERS' MARKET
Tara
All Year
Tuesday
8 A.M. to 12 NOON

KEMPTVILLE AND AREA FARMERS' MARKET
Town Hall Parking Lot
May to October
Saturday
8 A.M. to 12 NOON
July to End of season
Thursday
3 P.M. to 6 P.M.

KINGSTON PUBLIC MARKET
City Hall
All Year
Tuesday, Thursday, Saturday and Sunday
6 A.M. to 6 P.M.

KITCHENER FARMERS' MARKET
Market Square
All Year
Saturday
6 A.M. to 2 P.M.

LINDSAY FARMERS' MARKET
Lindsay Exhibition Grounds
May to October
Saturday
7 A.M. to 1 P.M.

LIONS'S HEAD AND AREA FARMERS' MARKET
Arena Parking Lot
Mid June to Mid September
Saturday
8 A.M. to 12 NOON

LITTLE CURRENT FARMERS' MARKET
Little Current, Manitoulin Island
Mid June to Mid October
Saturday
9 A.M. to 12 NOON

LONDON COVENT GARDEN MARKET
130 King Street
All Year
Monday to Saturday
8 A.M. to 6 P.M.

MAGNETAWAN FARMERS' MARKET
Magnetawan Community Centre
Mid June to September
Saturday
10 A.M. to 1 P.M.

MEADOWVALE FARMERS' MARKET
3051 Battleford Road, Mississauga
May to End of October
Saturday
8 A.M. to 1 P.M.

MEAFORD FARMERS' MARKET
Town Hall
June to September
Saturday
8 A.M. to 1 P.M.

METCALFE FARMERS' MARKET
Metcalfe Agricultural Society Fairgrounds
Mid May to Early October
Saturday
8 A.M. to 12 NOON

MILTON FARMERS' MARKET
Main Street
May to October
Saturday
7 A.M. to 12:30 P.M.

MISSISSAUGA CENTRAL LIONS FARMERS' MARKET
Square One Shopping Mall
Late June to Late October
Friday
8 A.M. to 8 P.M.
Sunday
10 A.M. to 5 P.M.

MONKTON FARMERS' MARKET
Across from arena, beside the firehall
July to September
Friday
4 P.M. to 8 P.M.

NAPANEE FARMERS' MARKET
Town Hall
All Year
Tuesday, Wednesday, Friday and Saturday
7 A.M. to 6 P.M.

NIAGARA FALLS FARMERS' MARKET
Park Street
All Year
Saturday
6 A.M. to 1 P.M.

NIAGARA FALLS SYLVIA PLACE MARKET
Main and Ferry Street
All Year
Saturday
6 A.M. to 1 P.M.

NORTH GOWER FARMERS' MARKET
5 km west of North Gower village on Regional Road 6
late June to September
Saturday
8 A.M. to 1 P.M.

ORANGEVILLE FARMERS' MARKET
Municipal Parking Lot
May to Mid October
Saturday
8 A.M. to 2 P.M.

ORILLIA FARMERS' MARKET
Opera House Parking Lot
All Year
Saturday
7 A.M. to 1 P.M.

OSHAWA CENTRE FARMERS' MARKET
Oshawa Centre Mall
May to October
Friday
8 A.M. to 6 P.M.

OSHAWA DOWNTOWN FARMERS' MARKET
Simcoe St. North
End of May to End of October
Saturday
8 A.M. to 2 P.M.

OTTAWA BY WARD MARKET
By Ward Market Square
All Year
7 days/week
May to October
6 A.M. to 6 P.M.
November to April
9:30 A.M. to 5:30 P.M.

OTTAWA ORGANIC FARMERS' MARKET
Kingsway United Church,
630 Island Park Drive
June to September
Saturday
10 A.M. to 2 P.M.
Wednesday
4 P.M. to 7 P.M.

OTTAWA PARKDALE MARKET
Parkdale Avenue at Wellington
7 days/week
April to December 24
7 A.M. to 6 P.M.

OWEN SOUND AND DISTRICT FARMERS' MARKET
Beside City Hall
All Year
Saturday
7 A.M. to 12 NOON

PARIS FARMERS' MARKET
Paris Fairgrounds Market building
May to October
Saturday
7 A.M. to 1 P.M.

PEMBROKE FARMERS' MARKET
Market Square
June to October
Thursday
2 P.M. to 6 P.M.

PENETANGUISHENE FARMERS' MARKET
Village Square Mall
June to October
Saturday
8 A.M. to 1 P.M.

PERTH FARMERS' MARKET
Across from the Town Hall
May to Thanksgiving
Saturday
8 A.M. to 1:30 P.M.

PETERBOROUGH FARMERS' MARKET
Morrow Park Exhibition Grounds
All Year
Saturday
7 A.M. to 1 P.M.

PETROLIA AND DISTRICT FARMERS' MARKET
Fletcher Street
April to October
Saturday
7 A.M. to 1 P.M.

PORT COLBORNE FARMERS' MARKET
Market Square
All Year
Friday
6 A.M. to 12 NOON

PORT HOPE FARMERS' MARKET
Behind Town Hall
May to October
Saturday
8 A.M. to 12 NOON

PORT PERRY FARMERS' MARKET
Port Perry Agricultural Fairgrounds
June to October
Saturday
8 A.M. to 1 P.M.

POWASSAN FARMERS' MARKET
Powassan Agricultural Society
Fairgrounds
May to Mid October
Saturday
9 A.M. to 1 P.M.

PRESCOTT FARMERS' MARKET
Town Square
May to October
Tuesday, Thursday & Saturday
7 A.M. to 1 P.M.

PROVIDENCE BAY FARMERS' MARKET
Providence Bay Arena
Mid June to Mid October
Saturday
9 A.M. to 12 NOON

RAINY RIVER FARMERS' MARKET
CN Train Station
Mid May to Mid October
Saturday
9 A.M. to 1 P.M.

RENFREW FARMERS' MARKET
Railway Street beside the town
library
Early June to Late October
Saturday
7 A.M. to 12 NOON

RIVERSIDE FARMERS' MARKET
Riverside Place
June to October
Saturday
8 A.M. to 12 NOON

ST. CATHARINES FARMERS' MARKET
Market Square
All Year
Tuesday, Thursday & Saturday
5:30 A.M. to 6 P.M.

ST. JACOBS FARMERS' MARKET
King Street — 2 km south of
St. Jacobs
All Year
Tuesday
8 A.M. to 3 P.M.
Thursday
7 A.M. to 4 P.M.
Saturday
7 A.M. to 3 P.M.

ST. LAWRENCE FARMERS' MARKET
Front Street East, Toronto
All Year
Saturday
5 A.M. to 5 P.M.

ST. MARYS FARMERS' MARKET
Jones Street parking lot
Mid June to October
Saturday
8 A.M. to 12 NOON

ST. THOMAS HORTON STREET FARMERS' MARKET
Manitoba Street
All Year
Saturday
7 A.M. to 12 NOON

SARNIA FARMERS' MARKET
Ontario and Proctor streets
All Year
Wednesday & Saturday
5 A.M. to 3 P.M.

SCHOMBERG FARMERS' MARKET
Schomberg Community and
Agricultural Arena
June to October
Saturday
8 A.M. to 1 P.M.

SEAWAY VALLEY GROWERS FARMERS' MARKET
Cornwall
Mid July to End of October
Wednesday & Saturday
7 A.M. to 12 NOON

SEYMOUR AUTO MALL FARMERS' MARKET
North Bay
Mid May to End of October
Thursday & Friday
9 A.M. to 5 P.M.

SHERWAY GARDENS FARMERS' MARKET
Sherway Gardens Shopping
Centre, Toronto
May to October
Friday
8 A.M. to 4 P.M.

SIMCOE FARMERS' MARKET
Home Craft Building, Fairgrounds
All Year
Thursday
10 A.M. to 5 P.M.

SMITHS FALLS FARMERS' MARKET
Main Street West, by the Falls
Parking Lot
Mid May to Mid October
Saturday
8 A.M. to 12 NOON

SPANISH AND AREA FARMERS' MARKET
Spanish
May to September
Saturday
9 A.M. to 2 P.M.

STEELES WEST MARKET
2375 Steeles Avenue West, Toronto
April to November
Saturday & Sunday
7 A.M. to 6 P.M.

STRATFORD FARMERS' MARKET
Stratford Agricultural Fairgrounds
All Year
Saturday
7 A.M. to 12 NOON

STRATHROY FARMERS' MARKET
Town Hall
June to End of October
Saturday
7:30 A.M. to 12 NOON

STREETSVILLE FARMERS' MARKET
Vic Johnson Arena
Mid May to End of October
Saturday
8 A.M. to 1 P.M.

SUDBURY FESTIVAL FARMERS' MARKET
City carpark
Mid May to Late October
Saturday & Sunday
7 A.M. to 5 P.M.

THE VILLAGE MARKET
Thornhill
All Year
Saturday
9 A.M. to 1 P.M.

THUNDER BAY FARMERS' MARKET
Wilson Street
May 20 to October 28
Wednesday & Saturday
7:30 A.M. to 11:30 A.M.
FW Gardens Curling Club
July 11 to September 8
Tuesday & Friday
7:30 A.M. to 11:30 A.M.
Intercity Shopping Centre
July 13 to September 7
Thursday
5:30 A.M. to 9 P.M.
Sept 13 to October 25
Wednesday
1 P.M. to 4 P.M.

Northwood Park Plaza
May 20 to June 24
August 12 to October 23
Saturday
1 P.M. to 4 P.M.
Victoriaville
May 11 to July 7 (Spring)
Thursday & Friday
8 A.M. to 2:30 P.M.
Sept 12 to December 22
Tuesday & Friday
8 A.M. to 2:30 P.M.
Christmas Market — December
15, 19, 21, 22

TILLSONBURG FARMERS' MARKET
Bridge and Bidwell streets
July to September
Tuesday
2 P.M. to 5 P.M.
April to November
Saturday
8 A.M. to 12 NOON

TIMMINS COUNTRY MARKET
Mountjoy Arena
June to Early October
Saturday
8 A.M. to 12 NOON

TIVERTON FARMERS' MARKET
Tiverton Community Centre
Early May to Late September
Saturday
8 A.M. to 12 NOON

TORONTO ORGANIC MARKET
Mirvish Village, Toronto
(May to October)
Cello's Restaurant, Toronto
(October to May)
All Year
Saturday
8 A.M. to 2 P.M.

TOTTENHAM FARMERS' MARKET
The Old Mill
May to October
Sunday
10 A.M. to 3 P.M.

TRENTON FARMERS' MARKET
Riverside Parking Lot
April to November
Tuesday, Thursday & Saturday
6 A.M. to 2 P.M.

WALKERTON AND DISTRICT FARMERS' MARKET
Walkerton Agricultural Fairgrounds
May to December
Friday
1:30 to 6 P.M.

WALLACEBURG FARMERS' MARKET
McNaughton Avenue Plaza
July to October
Saturday
8 A.M. to 2 P.M.

WATERFORD FARMERS' MARKET
Alice Street
All Year
Friday
10 A.M. to 4 P.M.

WATERLOO FARMERS' MARKET
Weber Street North, just outside
Waterloo city limits
All Year
Saturday
6 A.M. to 2 P.M.
Wednesday
8 A.M. to 2 P.M.

WELLAND FARMERS' MARKET
Young and Division streets
All Year
Wednesday & Saturday
6 A.M. to 12 NOON

WESTON FARMERS' MARKET
John Street parking lot
June to End of October
Saturday
7 A.M. to 2 P.M.

WINDSOR FARMERS' MARKET
City Hall
All Year
Tuesday & Thursday
7 A.M. to 4 P.M.
Friday
7 A.M. to 8 P.M.
Saturday
5 A.M. to 4 P.M.

WOODSTOCK FARMERS' MARKET
Woodstock Agricultural
Fairgrounds
All Year
Saturday
7 A.M. to 12 NOON

YORK FARMERS' MARKET
7509 Yonge Street, Thornhill
All Year
Friday
12 NOON to 9 P.M.
Saturday
7 A.M. to 4 P.M.

Selected Exhibitions, Tours and Festivals

To find out more about some of the exhibitions, tours and festivals listed in this book contact:

ALL RABBITS INC., Tel: 905 372 2669.

ALLISTON POTATO FESTIVAL, Tel: 705 435 9708.

APPLE BUTTER AND CHEESE FESTIVAL, Box 298, Wellesley, Ontario
    N0B 2T0, Tel: 519 656 2400; 519 656 2078.

APPLE ROUTE GUIDE, Northumberland County Tourism, Tel: 905 372 0141;
    Fax: 905 372 3046.

ASTORVILLE AND BONFIELD PARISH PICNICS, Tel: 800 387 0516;
    705 474 6634.

BALA CRANBERRY FESTIVAL, Tel: 705 762 5663.

BRIGHTON APPLEFEST, Tel: 613 475 2775.

BRITISH EMPIRE CHEESE SHOW, Tel: 613 969 0628; Fax 613 969 9516.

BRUCE COUNTY, EXPLORE THE COUNTRY TOUR, Tel: 800 268 3838.

BRUCE'S MILL CONSERVATION AREA, Tel: 416 661 6600.

COLLEGE ROYAL SOCIETY OFFICE, Tel: 519-824-4120 ext. 8366 or on their
    website at: http://www.uoguelph.ca.

CORNUCOPIA (Ottawa), Tel: 613 237 2206.

COUNTRY ROADS STUDIO TOUR, Tel: 800 387 0516; 705 474 6634.

DURHAM HERB FAIR, Tel: 800 268 3838.

ELORA RESEARCH STATION, Tel: 519 846 5521.

FEDERATED WOMEN'S INSTITUTES OF ONTARIO, Guelph Agricultural Centre,
    Box 1030, Guelph, Ontario, Tel: 519 836 3078.

FESTIVAL CARAVAN, Tel: 416 977 0486.

FLAT CREEK FARMS INC, R.R. 1, Mitchell, Ontario N0K 1N0.

GARLIC FESTIVAL (Sudbury), Tel: 705 673 7404.

GREAT GANARASKA COUNTRYSIDE ADVENTURE, Tel: 905 983 9339.

HARROW FALL FAIR, Tel: 519 839 5546.

HAWEATER FESTIVAL (Manitoulin Island), Tel: The Manitoulin Tourism
    Association, 705 368 3021.

HILLSIDE FESTIVAL, Tel: 519 763 6396.

HILTON WHOLE GRAIN MILLERS, R.R.#2, Staffa, Ontario N0K 1Y0
Tel/Fax: 519 345 2582.

HIRAM WALKER CANADIAN CLUB DISTILLERY, tour supervisor,
Tel: 519 254 5171.

INTERNATIONAL PLOWING MATCH, Tel: 519 632 8600.

KERNAL PEANUTS, factory tours, Tel: 519 426 9222; Fax: 519 426 9229.

KNIVES AND FORKS, Tel: 416 532 3997; Fax: 416 532 6605.

KORTRIGHT CENTRE FOR CONSERVATION, Tel: 416 832 2289; 416 661 6600.

LANG PIONEER VILLAGE, 470 Water Street, Peterborough, Ontario
K9H 3M3, Tel: 705 295 6694.

LEAMINGTON MENNONITE SALE AND AUCTION, Tel: 519 326 2721
(or the Leamington Chamber of Commerce, Tel: 519 326 2721).

LIQUOR CONTROL BOARD OF ONTARIO, Tel: 1 800 ONT LCBO, for
toll-free information on current listings in stores across the province,
locations and hours of operation, advice on public winery and distillery
tours, and duty-free regulations for those travelling outside the country.

LITTLE STREAM BAKERY, Tel: 613 278 2504.

MAITLAND VALLEY CONSERVATION AUTHORITY, Tel: 519 335 3557;
Fax: 519 335 3516.

MENNONITE CENTRAL COMMITTEE, Kitchener, Tel: 519 745 8458.

MINISTRY OF NATURAL RESOURCES INFORMATION CENTRE (to obtain an
Outdoors Card), Macdonald Block, Room M1-73, 900 Bay Street,
Toronto, Ontario M7A 2C1, Tel: 416 314 1177.

NIAGARA'S CUVÉE, c/o Grey Gables School, Tel: 905 685 4577 or The Wine
Council of Ontario, Tel: 905 684 8070.

NORTH OF SUPERIOR TOURISM ON-LINE. Log on to
http://www.nosta@lakeheadu.ca.

ONTARIO ASSOCIATION OF AGRICULTURAL SOCIETIES, Box 220, Blackstock,
Ontario L0B 1B0.

ONTARIO FARM AND COUNTRY ACCOMMODATIONS, Box BR, R.R.2, Alma,
Ontario N0B 1A0. (Include a self-addressed stamped #10 envelope—
it'll take two stamps.)

ONTARIO PLOWMEN'S ASSOCIATION, Tel: 519 767 2928; Fax: 519 767 2101.

ONTARIO PORK CONGRESS, Tel: 519 625 8811, or Tourism Stratford at
800-561-SWAN or 519-271-5140.

ONTARIO TRAVEL, for all your questions, Tel: 800 668 2746 (English) or 800 268 3736 (French); Teletypewriter-TTU/Telecommunication Device for the Deaf: TTD 416 314 6557 or call collect; from Toronto calling area, Tel: 416 314 0944 (English) or 416 314 0956 (French).

OTTAWA FOOD AND WINE SHOW, Tel: 613 567 6408.

OUTDOOR FARM SHOW, Tel: 800 563 5441.

OWEN SOUND FOOD EXHIBITION, Tel: 800 268 3838.

PELEE TREASURES, to order whitefish caviar, Tel: 800 233 9912.

PERTH COUNTY AGRI-TOURS/TOURISM STRATFORD, Tel: 800-561-SWAN or 519-271-5140.

REDPATH SUGAR MUSEUM, Tel: 416 366 3561.

RIDGETOWN COLLEGE OF AGRICULTURAL TECHNOLOGY, Tel: 519 674 1630 or 1 800 981 5492.

ROYAL AGRICULTURAL WINTER FAIR, Tel: 416 393 6400; Fax: 416 393 6488.

SCANDINAVIAN HOME SOCIETY (Thunder Bay), Tel: 807 345 7442.

TORONTO VEGETARIAN ASSOCIATION, Tel: 416 533 3897.

VISION NIAGARA, Box 1391, Fonthill, Ontario L0S 1E0.

WATERLOO TOWN AND COUNTRY FARM TOUR, Waterloo County OMAFRA, Tel: 519 884 5390.

WAWA SALMON DERBY, Box 1068, Wawa, Ontario P0S 1K0.

WIKWEMIKONG POW WOW, Tel: 705 368 3021.

WINE REGIONS OF ONTARIO, 35 Maywood Avenue, St. Catharines, Ontario L2R 1C5.

WOODLAND CULTURAL CENTRE, Brantford, Tel: 519 759 2650.

WORLD PUMPKIN CONFEDERATION WEIGH-OFF AND PUMPKINFEST (Port Elgin), Tel: the Pumpkinfest Committee, 1 800 387 3456.

ZURICH BEAN FESTIVAL, Tel: 519 236 4974.

Recipe Index

A

Appetizers:
    Bannock with Smoked Fish and Apple Cider
        Mayonnaise, 222
    Buttery Baked Garlic Potato Wedges, 59
    Crispy Fried Fiddleheads with Honey-Mustard
        Dip, 220
    Finnish Salted Fish, 219
    Mini Baked Potatoes with Whitefish Caviar and
        Crème Fraîche, 2
    Roasted Garlic with Herbed Goat Cheese, 116
    Smoked Trout Paté with Toasted Walnuts, 168
Apple-Glazed Huron County Rutabaga, 14
Arowhon's Bread-and-Butter Pudding with Rum, 214
Autumn Greens with Maple Apples and Spiced
    Pine Nuts, 170
Autumn Pears Poached in Late-Harvest Riesling
    with Vanilla Custard Sauce, 136

B

Baby Potato and Sweet Pepper Stir-Fry, 205
Baked Pine River Cheese and Pasta, 176
Bannock with Smoked Fish and Apple Cider
    Mayonnaise, 222
Beans:
    Lamb Shanks Braised with Huron County
        White Beans, 8
    Ontario Baked Beans with Maple Syrup, 206
Beef:
    Chinese-Style Beef with Cherry Tomatoes, 172
    Hearty Steak, Mushroom and Sausage Pie with
        Dark Ale, 90
    Warm Grilled Steak Salad with Maple Dressing,
        200
    Whisky-Braised Beef with Celery, 62
Blueberry and Goat Cheese Phyllo Parcels, 76
Blueberry Buttermilk Biscuits, 212
Blueberry Coffeecake, 24
Braided Portuguese Sweet Bread, 70
Breads and Buns:
    Bannock with Smoked Fish and Apple Cider
        Mayonnaise, 222
    Braided Portuguese Sweet Bread, 70
    Cheddar Beer Bread with Onions and Sesame
        Seeds, 180

Cheddar Buns with Cider, 157
    Corn Bread Studded with Crisp Bacon, 16
    Curve Lake Fried Indian Bread, 134
    Durham Spelt Seed Bread, 182
    Grey County Sourdough Starter, 192
    Pumpkin-Apricot Bread, 181
    Relief Sale Cream Buns, 74
    Sourdough-Caraway Rye Bread, 18
    Zwieback, 72
Bruce County Beef Soup with Barley and Winter
    Root Vegetables, 167
Buckwheat Crepes with Maple Poached-Apple
    Filling, 80
Butter Lettuce with Light Yogurt-Dill Dressing,
    169
Buttery Baked Garlic Potato Wedges, 59

C

Cakes:
    Blueberry Coffeecake, 24
    Chunky Brown-Sugar Applesauce Cake with
        Caramel Sauce, 190
    Peach Shortcake with Cassis, 52
    Sour-Cream Hazelnut Coffeecake, 159
    Upside-Down Hazelnut-Apricot Cake, 44
Candy:
    Scottish-Style Fudge, 164
Caribbean Rice and Peas, 101
Carolyn's Beautiful Butter Tarts, 238
Carrot and Zucchini Ribbon Salad, 146
Cheddar Beer Bread with Onions and Sesame
    Seeds, 180
Cheddar Buns with Cider, 157
Cheese:
    Baked Pine River Cheese and Pasta, 176
    Blueberry and Goat Cheese Phyllo Parcels, 76
    Goat Cheese and Spinach Torte, 152
    Grilled Trout with Goat Cheese and Walnuts,
        204
    Moose Meatballs Stuffed with Cheese, 232
    Roasted Asparagus Soup with Goat Cheese, 28
    Roasted Garlic with Herbed Goat Cheese, 116
    Spaghetti Squash Smothered in Cheese Sauce,
        42
    The Great Ontario Cheese Fondue, 127

Chilled Cucumber Soup, 61
Chilled Spiced Peach Soup, 26
Chilled Strawberry Soup with Pepper Cream, 118
Chinese-Style Beef with Cherry Tomatoes, 172
Chunky Brown-Sugar Applesauce Cake with
  Caramel Sauce, 190
Cider-Roasted Pork with Braised Fennel, 124
Cookies:
  Finnish Spice Cookies, 236
  Ontario Nut Lace Cookies with Black Currant
    Sabayon and Summer Berries, 186
  Pine-Nut Biscotti, 102
  Staffa Toasted Oatmeal Crisps, 69
Corn Bread Studded with Crisp Bacon, 16
Country-Style Croutons, 144
Creamy Wild Rice Pudding with Maple Glaze, 243
Crepes and Pancakes:
  Buckwheat Crepes with Maple Poached-Apple
    Filling, 80
  Fluffy Blueberry Pancakes with Honey-Thyme
    Butter, 208
  Hanukkah Potato Pancakes, 99
Crispy Cornmeal-Coated Pickerel Fillets, 126
Crispy Fried Fiddleheads with Honey-Mustard
  Dip, 220
Crispy Roasted Parsnips with Basil, 98
Curve Lake Fried Indian Bread, 134

D
Desserts:
  Arowhon's Bread-and-Butter Pudding with
    Rum, 214
  Autumn Pears Poached in Late-Harvest Riesling
    with Vanilla Custard Sauce, 136
  Blueberry and Goat Cheese Phyllo Parcels, 76
  Buckwheat Crepes with Maple Poached-Apple
    Filling, 80
  Chilled Spiced Peach Soup, 26
  Chunky Brown-Sugar Applesauce Cake with
    Caramel Sauce, 190
  Dim-Sum Custard Tarts, 106
  Eva's Blueberry Dessert Bars, 240
  Eagle Lake Rhubarb Squares, 132
  Fresh Mint Ice Cream, 213
  Fruit Platz, 22
  Good Neighbours' Apple and Elderberry Pie,
    138
  Josephine Varty's Butterscotch Pie, 188

June Johnston's Yummy Cranberry Squares, 184
Lanark County Maple Mousse with Cranberry
  Coulis, 160
Maple-Pecan Pie with Maple-Whisky Cream,
  110
Maple-Praline Fondue, 210
Niagara Nut and Maple Squares, 48
Northern Blueberry Crisp, 242
Ontario Berry Clafoutis, 78
Ontario Nut Lace Cookies with Black Currant
  Sabayon and Summer Berries, 186
Peach and Raspberry Hazelnut Crumble, 50
Peach Shortcake with Cassis, 52
Pear and Candied Ginger Tart with Almond
  Crust, 46
Pear and Cranberry Deep-Dish Pie, 112
Pumpkin-Caramel Ice Cream, 162
Relief Sale Cream Buns, 74
Rosemary-Scented Berry Compote, 108
Sour-Cherry Cobbler, 54
Upside-Down Hazelnut-Apricot Cake, 44
Dim-Sum Custard Tarts, 106
Drinks:
  Iroquois Strawberry Drink, 84
  Lang Pioneer Village Hay-Time Switchell, 140
  Springtime Rhubarb Spritzer, 216
Durham Spelt Seed Bread, 182

E
Eagle Lake Rhubarb Squares, 132
Easy Dried Tomatoes, 142
Essex County Field Tomato Soup, 3
Eva's Blueberry Dessert Bars, 240

F
Faheem's Foolproof Basmati Rice, 100
Finnish Salted Fish, 219
Finnish Spice Cookies, 236
Fish:
  Bannock with Smoked Fish and Apple Cider
    Mayonnaise, 222
  Crispy Cornmeal-Coated Pickerel Fillets, 126
  Finnish Salted Fish, 219
  Flash-Grilled Lake Huron Whitefish, 175
  Grilled Trout with Goat Cheese and Walnuts, 204
  Italian Salt-Cod Salad, 88
  Maple-Marinated Georgian Bay Salmon with
    Cranberry Salsa, 174

Mini Baked Potatoes with Whitefish Caviar and Crème Fraîche, 2
Shorthill's Trout Baked with Riesling, Red Onion and Thyme, 40
Smoked Trout Pate with Toasted Walnuts, 168
Soup of Lake Fishes with Garlic Cream, 194
Steamed Ginger-Lemon Pickerel, 150
Thunder Bay Baked Pickerel with Spring Vegetables, 233
Flash-Grilled Lake Huron Whitefish, 175
Fluffy Blueberry Pancakes with Honey-Thyme Butter, 208
Fondues:
    Maple-Praline Fondue, 210
    The Great Ontario Cheese Fondue, 127
Fresh Asparagus with Strawberry Vinaigrette, 154
Fresh Corn and Roasted Red Pepper Salsa, 119
Fresh Mint Ice Cream, 213
Fruit Platz, 22

G
Game:
    Manitoulin Venison Burgers with Golden Fried Onions, 202
    Moose Meatballs Stuffed with Cheese, 232
    Roast Loin of Wild Boar with Rice-Apple Stuffing, 228
    Roast Pheasant with Spiced Sour Cherry Sauce, 38
    Venison Pot Roast with Mushrooms, 226
    Warm Grilled Steak Salad with Maple Dressing, 200
Garlic Cream, 195
Glazed Sweet Potatoes with Bacon and Rosemary, 155
Goat Cheese and Spinach Torte, 152
Good Neighbours' Apple and Elderberry Pie, 138
Grandma Brown's Salad Dressing, 5
Grey County Sourdough Starter, 192
Grilled Trout with Goat Cheese and Walnuts, 204

H
Hanukkah Potato Pancakes, 99
Harvest Pumpkin-Apple Soup, 196
Hearty Steak, Mushroom and Sausage Pie with Dark Ale, 90
Hellishly Hot Cherry Pepper Jelly, 165

Honey:
    Crispy Fried Fiddleheads with Honey-Mustard Dip, 220
    Fluffy Blueberry Pancakes with Honey-Thyme Butter, 208
    Honey-Date Muffins, 104
    Roasted Beets on Spring Greens with Honey Vinaigrette, 128
Honey-Date Muffins, 104
Hot and Spicy Garlic Rabbit, 122
Hot-Pepper Sherry, 86

I
Ice Creams:
    Fresh Mint Ice Cream, 213
    Pumpkin-Caramel Ice Cream, 162
Iroquois Strawberry Drink, 84
Italian Salt-Cod Salad, 88

J
Josephine Varty's Butterscotch Pie, 188
Jump-Fried Chicken with Summer Vegetables and Simcoe Peanuts, 34
June Johnston's Yummy Cranberry Squares, 184

L
Lamb:
    Lamb Kebabs with Fresh Peach Mint Sauce, 36
    Lamb Shanks Braised with Huron County White Beans, 8
    Mustard-Glazed Ontario Leg of Lamb, 147
    Rich Rosemary Lamb Stew, 203
Lamb Kebabs with Fresh Peach Mint Sauce, 36
Lamb Shanks Braised with Huron County White Beans, 8
Lanark County Maple Mousse with Cranberry Coulis, 160
Lang Pioneer Village Hay-Time Switchell, 140
Leamington-Style Cabbage Soup, 4

M
Manitoulin Venison Burgers with Golden Fried Onions, 202
Maple-Glazed Acorn Squash, 130
Maple-Marinated Georgian Bay Salmon with Cranberry Salsa, 174
Maple-Pecan Pie with Maple-Whisky Cream, 110
Maple-Praline Fondue, 210

Maple Syrup:
  Autumn Greens with Maple Apples and Spiced
    Pine Nuts, 170
  Buckwheat Crepes with Maple Poached-Apple
    Filling, 80
  Creamy Wild Rice Pudding with Maple Glaze,
    243
  Lanark County Maple Mousse with Cranberry
    Coulis, 160
  Maple-Glazed Acorn Squash, 130
  Maple-Marinated Georgian Bay Salmon with
    Cranberry Salsa, 174
  Maple-Pecan Pie with Maple-Whisky Cream,
    110
  Maple-Praline Fondue, 210
  Niagara Nut and Maple Squares, 48
  Ontario Baked Beans with Maple Syrup, 206
  Warm Grilled Steak Salad with Maple Dressing,
    200
  Wellington County Smoked Pork Chops with
    Maple Glaze, 68
Marilyn's Make-Ahead Mash, 178
Marinated Summer Vegetables with Mint, 32
Mini Baked Potatoes with Whitefish Caviar and
  Crème Fraîche, 2
Missinaibi Dandelion Salad, 224
Moose Meatballs Stuffed with Cheese, 232
Muffins and Biscuits:
  Blueberry Buttermilk Biscuits, 212
  Honey-Date Muffins, 104
  Peach Shortcake with Cassis, 52
  Prince Edward County Black-Cherry Muffins,
    131
  Rhubarb-Crisp Muffins, 20
  Wild Elderberry Muffins, 158
Mustard-Glazed Ontario Leg of Lamb, 147

N
Niagara Nut and Maple Squares, 48
Niagara Wine-Berry Sauce, 49
Northern Blueberry Crisp, 242

O
Old-Fashioned Black Currant Preserves, 17
Old-Fashioned Creamed Corn with Whisky, 15
Ontario Baked Beans with Maple Syrup, 206
Ontario Berry Clafoutis, 78

Ontario Nut Lace Cookies with Black Currant
  Sabayon and Summer Berries, 186
Ontario-Style Onion Soup, 145

P
Pan-Fried Wild Northern Greens, 234
Pasta:
  Baked Pine River Cheese and Pasta, 176
  Pasta Tossed with Heat-Wave Bruschetta
    Topping, 7
Pasta Tossed with Heat-Wave Bruschetta Topping, 7
Peach and Raspberry Hazelnut Crumble, 50
Peach Shortcake with Cassis, 52
Pear and Candied Ginger Tart with Almond Crust,
  46
Pear and Cranberry Deep-Dish Pie, 112
Pies and Tarts:
  Carolyn's Beautiful Butter Tarts, 238
  Dim-Sum Custard Tarts, 106
  Goat Cheese and Spinach Torte, 152
  Good Neighbours' Apple and Elderberry Pie,
    138
  Hearty Steak, Mushroom and Sausage Pie with
    Dark Ale, 90
  Josephine Varty's Butterscotch Pie, 188
  Maple-Pecan Pie with Maple-Whisky Cream,
    110
  Pear and Candied Ginger Tart with Almond
    Crust, 46
  Pear and Cranberry Deep-Dish Pie, 112
Pine-Nut Biscotti, 102
Pork:
  Cider-Roasted Pork with Braised Fennel, 124
  Shedden Rhubarb Festival Pork Chops, 10
  Spareribs with Caraway Sauerkraut and
    Dumplings, 64
  Tenderloin of Pork with Cabbage and Mustard
    Sauce, 148
  Wellington County Smoked Pork Chops with
    Maple Glaze, 68
Potato-Cheddar Varennyky, 96
Poultry:
  Jump-Fried Chicken with Summer Vegetables
    and Simcoe Peanuts, 34
  Roast Capon with Shiitake Mushroom and
    Wild Rice Stuffing, 120
  Roast Chicken Breast with Fresh Basil and
    Summer Peach Sauce, 12

Roast Duck with Baked Apples and Cranberry Sauce, 230

Szechuan-Style Chicken and Eggplant, 94

Tandoori Chicken Kebabs, 92

Powassan Farmers' Market Salad, 198

Preserves, Pickles and Relishes:

Hellishly Hot Cherry Pepper Jelly, 165

Hot-Pepper Sherry, 86

Old-Fashioned Black Currant Preserves, 17

Prizewinning Rosemary Apple Cider Jelly, 114

Rose's Pickled Garlic, 217

Sioux Lookout Cranberry Ketchup, 244

Spiced Plum-Raisin Chutney, 56

Spiced Zucchini Relish, 82

Sun-Dried Tomato Pesto, 141

Sweet and Sour Mustard, 55

Prince Edward County Black-Cherry Muffins, 131

Prizewinning Rosemary Apple Cider Jelly, 114

Pumpkin-Apricot Bread, 181

Pumpkin-Caramel Ice Cream, 162

R

Rabbit:

Hot and Spicy Garlic Rabbit, 122

Rainbow-Pepper Salad, 33

Relief Sale Cream Buns, 74

Rhubarb-Crisp Muffins, 20

Rice:

Caribbean Rice and Peas, 101

Creamy Wild Rice Pudding with Maple Glaze, 243

Faheem's Foolproof Basmati Rice, 100

Roast Capon with Shiitake Mushroom and Wild Rice Stuffing, 120

Roast Loin of Wild Boar with Rice-Apple Stuffing, 228

Wild Rice and Mushroom Casserole, 235

Rich Rosemary Lamb Stew, 203

Roast Capon with Shiitake Mushroom and Wild Rice Stuffing, 120

Roast Chicken Breast with Fresh Basil and Summer Peach Sauce, 12

Roast Duck with Baked Apples and Cranberry Sauce, 230

Roast Loin of Wild Boar with Rice-Apple Stuffing, 228

Roast Pheasant with Spiced Sour Cherry Sauce, 38

Roasted Asparagus Soup with Goat Cheese, 28

Roasted Beets on Spring Greens with Honey Vinaigrette, 128

Roasted Garlic with Herbed Goat Cheese, 116

Roasted Ontario Summer Ratatouille with Fresh Herbs, 129

Rose's Pickled Garlic, 217

Rosemary-Scented Berry Compote, 108

S

Salad Dressings:

Apple Cider Mayonnaise, and Bannock with Smoked Fish, 222

Grandma Brown's Salad Dressing, 5

Honey Vinaigrette, with Roasted Beets on Spring Greens, 128

Light Yogurt-Dill Dressing, with Butter Lettuce, 169

Maple Dressing, with Warm Grilled Steak Salad, 200

Strawberry Vinaigrette, with Fresh Asparagus, 154

Salads:

Autumn Greens with Maple Apples and Spiced Pine Nuts, 170

Butter Lettuce with Light Yogurt-Dill Dressing, 169

Carrot and Zucchini Ribbon Salad, 146

Italian Salt-Cod Salad, 88

Missinaibi Dandelion Salad, 224

Powassan Farmers' Market Salad, 198

Rainbow-Pepper Salad, 33

Roasted Beets on Spring Greens with Honey Vinaigrette, 128

Simply the Best Tomato Salad, 6

Tarragon-Marinated Mushrooms, 197

The Best-Ever Greek Salad, 87

Warm Grilled Steak Salad with Maple Dressing, 200

Waterloo County Hot Spinach Salad, 60

Sauces:

Black Currant Sabayon, with Ontario Nut Lace Cookies and Summer Berries, 186

Caramel Sauce, with Chunky Brown-Sugar Applesauce Cake, 190

Cranberry Coulis, with Lanark County Maple Mousse, 160

Cranberry Salsa, with Maple-Marinated Georgian Bay Salmon, 174

Fresh Peach Mint Sauce, with Lamb Kebabs, 36
Garlic Cream, 195
Maple-Whisky Cream, with Maple-Pecan Pie, 110
Mustard Sauce, and Tenderloin of Pork with Cabbage, 148
Niagara Wine-Berry Sauce, 49
Summer Peach Sauce, with Roast Chicken Breast and Fresh Basil, 12
Sun-Dried Tomato Pesto, 141
Sweet and Sour Mustard, 55
Vanilla Custard Sauce, with Autumn Poached Pears in Late-Harvest Riesling, 136
Scottish-Style Fudge, 164
Shedden Rhubarb Festival Pork Chops, 10
Shorthill's Trout Baked with Riesling, Red Onion and Thyme, 40
Simply the Best Tomato Salad, 6
Sioux Lookout Cranberry Ketchup, 244
Smoked Trout Paté with Toasted Walnuts, 168
Soups:
    Bruce County Beef Soup with Barley and Winter Root Vegetables, 167
    Chilled Cucumber Soup, 61
    Chilled Spiced Peach Soup, 26
    Chilled Strawberry Soup with Pepper Cream, 118
    Essex County Field Tomato Soup, 3
    Harvest Pumpkin-Apple Soup, 196
    Leamington-Style Cabbage Soup, 4
    Ontario-Style Onion Soup, 145
    Roasted Asparagus Soup with Goat Cheese, 28
    Soup of Lake Fishes with Garlic Cream, 194
    Southbrook Farms' Gazpacho, 86
    Springtime Soup, 144
    Three Sisters Soup, 58
    Velvety Butternut Squash Soup, 30
Soup of Lake Fishes with Garlic Cream, 194
Sour-Cherry Cobbler, 54
Sour-Cream Hazelnut Coffeecake, 159
Sourdough-Caraway Rye Bread, 18
Southbrook Farms' Gazpacho, 86
Spaghetti Squash Smothered in Cheese Sauce, 42
Spareribs with Caraway Sauerkraut and Dumplings, 64
Spiced Plum-Raisin Chutney, 56
Spiced Zucchini Relish, 82
Springtime Rhubarb Spritzer, 216

Springtime Soup, 144
Squares and Bars:
    Eagle Lake Rhubarb Squares, 132
    Eva's Blueberry Dessert Bars, 240
    Fruit Platz, 22
    June Johnston's Yummy Cranberry Squares, 184
    Niagara Nut and Maple Squares, 48
Staffa Toasted Oatmeal Crisps, 69
Steamed Ginger-Lemon Pickerel, 150
Sun-Dried Tomato Pesto, 141
Sweet and Sour Mustard, 55
Szechuan-Style Chicken and Eggplant, 94

T
Tandoori Chicken Kebabs, 92
Tarragon-Marinated Mushrooms, 197
Tenderloin of Pork with Cabbage and Mustard Sauce, 148
The Best-Ever Greek Salad, 87
The Great Ontario Cheese Fondue, 127
Three Sisters Soup, 58
Thunder Bay Baked Pickerel with Spring Vegetables, 233

U
Upside-Down Hazelnut-Apricot Cake, 44

V
Vegetable Side Dishes:
    Apple-Glazed Huron County Rutabaga, 14
    Baby Potato and Sweet Pepper Stir-Fry, 205
    Buttery Baked Garlic Potato Wedges, 59
    Crispy Fried Fiddleheads with Honey-Mustard Dip, 220
    Crispy Roasted Parsnips with Basil, 98
    Easy Dried Tomatoes, 142
    Fresh Asparagus with Strawberry Vinaigrette, 154
    Fresh Corn and Roasted Red Pepper Salsa, 119
    Glazed Sweet Potatoes with Bacon and Rosemary, 155
    Hanukkah Potato Pancakes, 99
    Maple-Glazed Acorn Squash, 130
    Marilyn's Make-Ahead Mash, 178
    Marinated Summer Vegetables with Mint, 32
    Mini Baked Potatoes with Whitefish Caviar and Crème Fraîche, 2
    Old-Fashioned Creamed Corn with Whisky, 15